The Cambridge Introduction to
Tragedy

Tragedy is the art form created to confront the most difficult experiences
we face: death, loss, injustice, thwarted passion, despair. From ancient
Greek theatre up to the most recent plays, playwrights have found, in
tragic drama, a means to seek explanation for disaster. But tragedy is
also a word we continually encounter in the media, to denote an event
which is simply devastating in its emotional power. This introduction
explores the relationship between tragic experience and tragic
representation. After giving an overview of the tragic theatre canon –
including chapters on the Greeks, Shakespeare, Ibsen and Chekhov,
American tragedy and post-colonial drama – it also looks at the
contribution which philosophers have brought to this subject, before
ranging across other art forms and areas of debate. The book is unique
in its chronological range, and brings a wide spectrum of examples,
from both literature and life, into the discussion of this emotional and
frequently controversial subject.

JENNIFER WALLACE is Fellow, Lecturer and Director of Studies in
English at Peterhouse, University of Cambridge.

Cambridge Introductions to Literature

This series is designed to introduce students to key topics and authors. Accessible and lively, these introductions will also appeal to readers who want to broaden their understanding of the books and authors they enjoy.

- Ideal for students, teachers, and lecturers
- Concise, yet packed with essential information
- Key suggestions for further reading

Titles in this series:

Eric Bulson *The Cambridge Introduction to James Joyce*

John Xiros Cooper *The Cambridge Introduction to T. S. Eliot*

Kirk Curnutt *The Cambridge Introduction to F. Scott Fitzgerald*

Janette Dillon *The Cambridge Introduction to Early English Theatre*

Janette Dillon *The Cambridge Introduction to Shakespeare's Tragedies*

Jane Goldman *The Cambridge Introduction to Virginia Woolf*

Kevin J. Hayes *The Cambridge Introduction to Herman Melville*

David Holdeman *The Cambridge Introduction to W. B. Yeats*

M. Jimmie Killingsworth *The Cambridge Introduction to Walt Whitman*

Pericles Lewis *The Cambridge Introduction to Modernism*

Ronan McDonald *The Cambridge Introduction to Samuel Beckett*

Wendy Martin *The Cambridge Introduction to Emily Dickinson*

Peter Messent *The Cambridge Introduction to Mark Twain*

David Morley *The Cambridge Introduction to Creative Writing*

Ira Nadel *The Cambridge Introduction to Ezra Pound*

Leland S. Person *The Cambridge Introduction to Nathaniel Hawthorne*

John Peters *The Cambridge Introduction to Joseph Conrad*

Sarah Robbins *The Cambridge Introduction to Harriet Beecher Stowe*

Martin Scofield *The Cambridge Introduction to the American Short Story*

Emma Smith *The Cambridge Introduction to Shakespeare*

Peter Thomson *The Cambridge Introduction to English Theatre, 1660–1900*

Janet Todd *The Cambridge Introduction to Jane Austen*

Jennifer Wallace *The Cambridge Introduction to Tragedy*

The Cambridge Introduction to
Tragedy

JENNIFER WALLACE

CAMBRIDGE UNIVERSITY PRESS
Cambridge, New York, Melbourne, Madrid, Cape Town, Singapore, São Paulo

Cambridge University Press
The Edinburgh Building, Cambridge CB2 8RU, UK

Published in the United States of America by Cambridge University Press, New York

www.cambridge.org
Information on this title: www.cambridge.org/9780521671491

First published 2007

Printed in the United Kingdom at the University Press, Cambridge

A catalogue record for this publication is available from the British Library

Library of Congress Cataloguing in Publication data
Wallace, Jennifer.
The Cambridge introduction to tragedy / Jennifer Wallace.
    p.   cm. – (Cambridge introductions to literature)
Includes bibliographical references and index.
ISBN-13: 978 0 521 85539 6 (hardback)
ISBN-10: 0 521 85539 X (hardback)
ISBN-13: 978 0 521 67149 1 (pbk.)
ISBN-10: 0 521 67149 3 (pbk.)
1. Tragedy.   2. European drama (Tragedy) – History and criticism.   I. Title.   II. Series.
PN1892.W28   2007
809.9'162 – dc22   2006039239

ISBN   978-0-521-85539-6 hardback
ISBN   978-0-521-67149-1 paperback

Contents

Illustrations

Acknowledgements

This book could not have been completed in its present form without the fantastic picture research of photo editor and friend, Sunita Sharma-Gibson. I am extremely grateful to her for her help and to the following photographers who generously gave me their images for nothing or for greatly reduced permission fees: Robert Wallis, Geraint Lewis, Philip Mynott, and Corbis on behalf of Kevin Carter. Various friends and colleagues read portions of this book and I have benefited hugely from their comments and expertise: Mark Berry, Jean Chothia, Jacobia Dahm, Martin Golding, Peter Howarth, Ben Quash, and Robert Wallis. But more than anyone, my students continue to challenge and inspire me. Invidious to name individuals, their questions and reactions to these tragic texts and issues over the last twelve years have shaped incalculably the ideas in this book.

Chapter 1

Approaching the subject

Tragedy is the art form created to confront the most difficult experiences we face: death, loss, injustice, thwarted passion, despair. From ancient Greek theatre up to the most recent plays, playwrights have found, in tragic drama, a means to seek explanation for disaster. Questions about the causes of suffering, which are raised in each culture, are posed powerfully in tragedy. Indeed, the rules and conventions of tragic drama arguably make the dramatisation of those questions possible. Tragedy, we might say, attempts to stage what might otherwise, by virtue of its extreme, harrowing nature, be considered unstageable. Tragedians have traditionally used the pattern and order of aesthetic form in order to test whether such order exists in the world they represent or whether surplus, inexplicable suffering somehow eludes them. So the theatre (literally 'the place for watching things') allows us to bear witness to the worst and most exemplary moments of sorrow and desperation that face us as human beings. This activity is something which we are prepared to pay money for, something that we traditionally admire, for the aesthetic and moral good which tragic representation can afford us.

But tragedy is also a word we continually encounter in the media. Just this week, as I write this paragraph, a five-year-old child has died in Cornwall in a 'beach tragedy', an investigation into the 'tragic police shooting' of an innocent Brazilian man in London has been made public, two 'tragic planes crashes' in Greece and Venezuela have been reported, and the world is witness to the private anguish of families forced from their homes in the Gaza Strip. These are individual tragedies, but meanwhile wars, genocide and natural disasters kill thousands of people every year, on a scale which is almost unimaginable to those not involved. While the 'beach tragedy' of Abbie Livingstone-Nurse has grabbed tabloid headlines, for instance, the fatal bombing of forty people in Baghdad this week barely merits a mention. And this is not even to begin to describe the forgotten millions who are wiped out yearly by disease, starvation and the effects of poverty. Yet these events too are described as 'tragedies', if and when reports are published.

1

How can we reconcile these different senses of the term, 'tragedy'? The common use of the term suggests that it is the event (the death, the loss) which is tragic. But the dramatic sense of the term suggests that it is the attempt to give the event aesthetic form on stage which lies at the heart of tragedy. Moreover, the common use of the term suggests that there are few rules – other than the media's responsibility to protect public sensibilities from the horrific and shocking – and that a tragic event is simply devastating in its emotional power. The dramatic sense of the term, on the other hand, suggests that there are generic expectations which give a pattern to the representation on stage and make it bearable.

So a book on tragedy, first and foremost, raises the issue of the relationship between literature and life. This is a matter which has long been debated among writers on the subject. Arguing for a narrowly aesthetic definition, W. B. Yeats differentiated between the profound tragedy of a Greek or Shakespearean hero and merely 'some blunderer [who] has driven his car on to the wrong side of the road'.[1] Following this tradition, George Steiner argued that tragedy, or, in other words, the concept of 're-enact[ing] private anguish on a public stage' is narrowly ancient Greek and that, 'till the moment of their decline, the tragic forms are Hellenic'.[2] More recently Timothy Reiss has reiterated this distinction between tragedy and the tragic, quoting the French philosopher Henri Gouhier in his support: 'Tragedy belongs to literature and to theatre, the tragic belongs to life'. Tragedy, Reiss goes on to argue, is 'a kind of discourse, intended for stage performance', which is designed to mitigate the potential 'absence of significance' found in everyday life.[3] In other words, each period of history has been faced with new experiences which might challenge understanding, but the sense of bewilderment is contained by the staging of tragic drama. Tragedy, therefore, must not be confused with experience.

Countering this aesthetic definition, the Marxist critics Raymond Williams and Terry Eagleton charge those who are prepared to divorce the term 'tragedy' from its normal, everyday usage with being elitist and indifferent to ordinary suffering. In order to deny the fact that the demise of ordinary people might be termed tragic, critics like Steiner make a distinction between what they consider 'universal principles' of tragedy (that is, models based on classical tragedy) and the 'merely accidental'. But Williams shows that events which are dismissed as 'merely accidental' actually arise from widespread conditions of social injustice and exploitation. 'The events which are not seen as tragic are deep in the pattern of our own culture: war, famine, work, traffic, politics', Williams writes. 'To see no ethical content or human agency in such events, or to say that we cannot connect them with general meanings . . . is to admit a strange and particular bankruptcy.'[4] Eagleton, meanwhile, points out that the 'lunatic' distinction between aesthetic tragedy and merely terrible events in life is based on the false assumption that 'real life is shapeless and art alone is orderly'. This so-called orderliness allows the tragedies on stage to end in a positive manner, since, as Eagleton comments sarcastically, 'only in art can the value released by destruction be revealed'.[5]

At the heart of the debate is the question of whether the definition of tragedy ultimately depends upon its content or its form. Is it enough, in other words, to say simply that tragedies are sad, that they deal with misery and despair and fear? Or should we rather seek structural features which seem to recur in the plots of tragedies and which therefore might appear to be essential to the genre? According to Reiss, for example, tragedy is a formal, aesthetic structure, a 'machine' for making sense of things. 'Our emotions are not to be confused with that machine', he maintains. But Williams, writing in 1966, rejected the coldly academic approach to the subject represented most recently by Reiss, and argued instead that tragedy is defined by its effect on people, by the normal, commonplace but still unbearable emotions of grief and devastation. 'In the case of ordinary death and suffering, when we see mourning and lament, when we see men and women breaking under their actual loss, it is at least not self-evident to say that we are not in the presence of tragedy', he maintains (p. 47). Williams' interpretation of tragedy implies that there is not a narrow canon of tragic drama, utterly separated from our experience of tragic events in everyday life. Instead his analysis of tragic drama or novels is informed by his understanding of the structures of political, social life and how we are shaped by them; our response to aesthetic tragedy shares important correspondences with our response to particular crises – political, ethical, social – which occur in history.

There are certain features which seem to recur in different tragedies. Many plays work up towards a particular crisis and explore the subsequent feeling of irreversibility. Many tragic plays dramatise loss, whether that be the loss of life or simply the loss of hope. Most plays include some element of conflict, chiefly between one individual and the world, fate or the gods. But not all plays, which are universally regarded as tragedies, contain these features. And none of these plot features means anything if they do not stir emotion. To be mechanistic or rigidly prescriptive about it is to deny the power of tragedy and to fail to explain its recurring hold over the cultural imagination.

Although the definition of tragedy must take account of both form and content – and some tragedies derive their power precisely for their failure to meet these generic expectations – I believe that ultimately the source of tragedy lies in its capacity to elicit the audience's response. Indeed this is why tragedy has traditionally been contemplated in the theatre, since this is the place where

1. Tractor displaying the victims of civil war in a breakaway region of Moldova, former USSR, 1992. © Robert Wallis

licensed witness takes place and is positively demanded. Even the response to real tragedies often is managed in ways which shares correspondences with tragic theatre. During the civil war in the former Soviet republic of Moldova, following the break-up of the Soviet Union, one local man confronted the savage slaughter of his family in a way that the ancient Greeks in their theatre in Athens would have recognised. Loading the bodies onto his farm trailer, he drove around the village to parade the corpses to its inhabitants. 'Look', he was saying, 'this is what was done to my family. This is the tragic result of this civil war.' His trailer became an improvised *ekkyklema*, the ancient stage machinery which allowed the bodies of the tragic heroes to be displayed to the audience. 'Do not seek to justify or explain their killing', the man was saying, 'but bear witness to this atrocity'.[6]

According to the Spanish mystic philosopher Miguel de Unamuno, in *The Tragic Sense of Life*, written in the early twentieth century, the tragic sense arises in the opposition between experience and understanding. 'For living is one thing and knowing is another', he writes. 'As we shall see, perhaps there is such an opposition between the two that we may say that everything vital is anti-rational, not merely irrational, and that everything rational is anti-vital. And this is the basis of the tragic sense of life.'[7] Characters in tragedy are driven by the quest to reconcile this opposition, a reconciliation which the tragic form, by its structural order, seems to make possible, and then they are buffeted by the relentless realisation of the impossibility of this reconciliation. King Lear, for example, tries to understand rationally the nature of love or the notion of sovereignty or, indeed, the 'cause' of his suffering. But his quest is thwarted by the cruelty of events and the indifference of the elements to his questions, and by the end he can only barely survive, without rational understanding: 'I fear I am not in my perfect mind' (IV.vii.64). No wonder that the poet John Keats referred to 'the fierce dispute / Betwixt damnation and impassioned clay' in 'On Sitting Down to Read *King Lear* Once Again', since 'dispute' between passion and damnation, or between meaningful understanding and meaningless annihilation, lies at the heart of the play's business. But, despite the title of Keats' famous poem, the play was created to be *watched*, not read. Indeed the play's insistence on knowledge and perception, from the king's declamatory first line '*Know* that we have divided in three our kingdom' (I.i.35–6 (my italics)) to the physical gouging of Gloucester's eyes on stage, ensures that Unamuno's 'opposition' remains at the forefront of the audience's consciousness, demanding that they bear witness both to the quest and its futility. Spectators have repeatedly testified to the unwatchability of *King Lear*, from Charles Lamb's 'to see an old man tottering about the stage . . . has nothing in it but what is painful and disgusting', to A. C. Bradley's 'the mere physical horror of [the blinding of Gloster] would in the theatre be a sensation so violent as to overpower the purely tragic emotions . . . *King Lear* is too huge for the stage.'[8] However, the act of witnessing a play like *King Lear* – and acknowledging the difficulty of witnessing it – is, for Unamuno, also part of the tragic process, along with Lear's experience. 'The remedy', he writes of the tragic sense, 'is to consider our mortal destiny without flinching, to fasten our gaze upon the gaze of the Sphinx, for it is thus that the malevolence of its spell is discharmed'.[9]

If tragedy is deemed to be a matter of response, rather than purely aesthetic structure, then it immediately has implications for ethics. What is the purpose of stirring our emotions? We may feel sympathy for the hero's pain or shock at the cruelties inflicted on stage – Aristotle's pity or fear – but these feelings must have a function if the experience of tragedy is to offer anything other than a cheap thrill. Eagleton makes a passionate case for the politics of compassion. Tragedy, according to him, plays a crucial role in revealing 'our frailty and vulnerability, in which any authentic politics must be anchored'.[10] The recognition that we all share the capacity to suffer, that suffering offers a 'communality of meaning', constitutes the first step in formulating resistance to oppression and forcing political change. Tragedy can awaken this recognition. But of course this ethical claim for tragedy is complicated by the fact that we are distanced from events or from what is represented on stage, as much as we are connected. Witnessing tragedy engages the onlooker's emotional participation but also his independent curiosity. 'I find the joy of life in its cruel and powerful struggles', wrote the Swedish playwright Strindberg, with scientific detachment, 'and my enjoyment comes from getting to know something'.[11]

These questions about the appropriate response to suffering and the ethics of tragedy are perhaps more relevant than ever now, when we are bombarded with pictures of horror from areas around the world devastated by war and when the virtual image is hard to distinguish from the real. In the television age, as Guy Debord wrote, we live in a 'society of spectacle'.[12] We have closer access to atrocity than ever before, in that images of war and famine can be beamed across the world almost immediately, and yet we are removed from the horror of these experiences because they are mediated by cameras. We can flick channels or turn them off. So insidious has become the influence of the moving image upon our imaginations that many people reportedly compared the destruction of the World Trade Center on September 11th with a horror movie. The planes swooped in towards the twin towers and the buildings collapsed again and again as the film clip was repeated endlessly on television. The additional fact that it was not possible to see the horror inside the planes or the buildings also gave the event a strange quality as spectacle. It was 'catastrophe observed from a safe distance. Watching death on a large scale, but seeing no one die', as Ian McEwan's character Henry Perowne reflects in the novel *Saturday*.

Given the surplus of images today and the ubiquity of televised or photographed horror, is it any longer possible to be shocked? Does tragedy have a place? And is the sense of shock an ethical necessity anyway? According to Susan Sontag, our diminishing capacity to be shocked is not based upon a surfeit of images nor the fact that our sensibilities are jaded, but rather it is produced by our sense of powerlessness. 'People don't become inured to what they are shown . . . because of the *quantity* of images dumped on them. It is passivity that dulls feeling.'[13] We have been shown images of war or famine so many times before and nothing we do seems to change that situation. Playwrights and photographers have perennially responded to what is popularly known as 'compassion fatigue' by outdoing each other in the graphic violence of their representations; Sontag regards shock as only useful if it can galvanise us into action. Writing primarily about war photography but clearly with implications for the witnessing of tragedy more generally, she echoes Eagleton's conclusions about the communality of suffering. 'It seems a good in itself to acknowledge, to have enlarged, one's sense of how much suffering caused by human wickedness there is in the world we share with others.'[14] But that 'enlarged sense' must be driven by understanding, rather than simply by emotion or compassion. Sontag describes the goal of 'standing back from the aggressiveness of the world' and thus being freed 'for observation and elective attention'. But how do we gain that 'elective attention'? Indeed the question of how to make something significant or uniquely impressive upon our sensibilities is both a demand and a source of uncertainty for writers and journalists alike today.

The origins of tragic drama lie in Greece. So what can we learn from ancient Greek tragedy? What relevance does it have to the questions about emotion, ethics and shock which I have been discussing so far? How does the experience of watching mythological characters in a comfortable theatre amount to anything other than a diversion from twenty-first-century war and social injustice? On the one hand, Greek tragedy is specifically about its own time and place and arguably celebrates the values of Athenian culture. Indeed some critics focus upon the historical context of tragedy and maintain that Greek tragedy can only be approached as a fifth-century BC cultural phenomenon. They stress the mythological, religious and political concerns of the plays, which ultimately owe their origins to Homer and to religious and civic practice. Richard Seaford, for example, maintains that tragedy 'deploys the restoration of ritual normality to express the historical contradiction between household and polis' and thus the tragic plays are of interest as anthropological curiosities, for what they reveal about the development of the Athenian fifth-century 'polis'.[15] But on the other hand, critics like Jean-Pierre Vernant, who famously observed that Greek tragedy 'does not reflect reality but calls it into question', are interested in how the plays of Aeschylus, Sophocles and Euripides depart from their immediate context.[16] In questioning its own culture, Greek tragedy paradoxically raises some of the pressing concerns which continue to concern the later tradition of tragedy: community, spectatorship, metaphysical belief, causation.

Greek tragedy is clearly central to the tragic tradition, and the fact that it has been staged and restaged over the centuries reflects its continuing capacity to speak to us. The American tour of *The Trojan Women*, using the pacifist Gilbert Murray's translation, during World War I; Deborah Warner's production of *Electra* in Derry in 1992, just after the outbreak of sectarian violence in Northern Ireland; two productions of *Hecuba* in the winter of 2004–5 in London, while the 'insurgents' continued to blow up Iraqi police recruits in great numbers (plus a few American soldiers): these theatre productions are just a few examples of Greek tragedy offering 'modern agnostics exactly the disturbing combination of open-ended metaphysics, aesthetic beauty and hard-core suffering' which chimes with their contemporary experience.[17]

But 'tragedy' is not exclusive to the Greeks, and, despite Steiner's warning, it is not dead. Rather than seeing 'tragedy' as basically 'retrospective', I prefer to see it as a natural human response to particular historical circumstances or conditions.[18] In this respect, Vernant's comment about the historical moment which gave rise to Greek tragedy is equally applicable to other historical periods and cultures: 'The tragic turning point occurs when a gap develops at the heart of the social experience. It is wide enough for the oppositions between legal and political thought on the one hand and the mythical and heroic traditions on the other to stand out quite clearly. Yet it is narrow enough for the conflict in values still to be a painful one.'[19] Tragic drama seems to be produced often in periods when beliefs are changing, when there is a shift in values, when politics seem unstable. These revolutions create the conditions in which what Felicity Rosslyn calls 'a social reorganisation' is 'profound enough to shake the individual into heightened self-consciousness and draw all his old relations into question'.[20]

Tragedy has been a topic to which philosophers have returned again and again over the centuries. Certainly Aristotle, Hegel, Schopenhauer, Kierkegaard, Nietzsche, Freud and Camus, among others, have found themselves drawn to the problems of injustice, madness, trauma and despair which tragic drama dwells upon because they believe that these issues raise even more general questions about the limits of human thinking. Their writing is important because the theoretical discussion about tragedy, in which these philosophers engage, replicates the activity of tragic drama itself. Their attempt to explain tragedies mirrors the effort of playwrights to pattern suffering into narrative on stage. It is also instructive to read these philosophers' works and then to begin to see the broad conceptual questions potentially lying behind individual tragedies. But ultimately the emotional punch which tragedy packs derives from our inability to understand the worst events we experience and from our unwilling recognition of the cruel justice or injustice of the world. Particular examples of loss or destruction or maliciousness resist any well-meaning attempt at consolation or rationalisation; of course, this is why philosophers have been drawn to these examples, precisely to ponder what intellectual enquiry is unable to intellectualise.[21]

So this is a book about the specific moments in tragic dramas when audiences are confronted with these critical questions and emotions. It is a book, too, about tragedies before it is about tragedy. Peter Szondi in his *Essay on the Tragic* observed that 'the concept of the tragic disastrously rises out of the concrete situation of philosophical problems into the heights of abstraction' and that it needs to 'sink down into the most concrete element of tragedies if it is to be saved'.[22] In other words, the staging of tragic drama should be essential to thinking about the metaphysics of tragedy. The issues which witnessing a performance raises – issues of the audience's embodiment and shared experience of pain and pity, of its ambiguous sense of detachment, of the actors' presence in time – prevent the study of tragedy from becoming over-abstract and removed from emotional difficulty. With this in mind, I deal in this book first with the 'concrete' tragedies before considering tragic theory, for this chronology replicates the watching experience, in which we are first moved by particular tragic dramas and only later begin to reflect upon our response. At the end of the two main sections on 'tragic drama' and on 'tragic theory', I have focused upon some case studies. These draw out thematically those specific moments in performance in which theories might come into conflict with practice and when the question of perspective might alter one's interpretation of the issue.

To write a textbook on tragedy is a contradictory process, since textbooks are, by nature, pedagogical and unambiguous while I believe that tragedy – both as theatrical form and aesthetic concept – is quite the opposite. There is, admittedly, a tradition of associating tragedy with didacticism. The observation which the chorus in Aeschylus' *Oresteia* utters, that we 'learn through suffering', has been taken out of context as a wise commentary on the function of tragedy. Meanwhile the comic, satirical portrayal of tragic playwrights in Aristophanes' *The Frogs*, which finishes with the hope that the ghost of Aeschylus can save Athens, is sometimes misleadingly interpreted as an argument for the general therapeutic purpose of ancient tragedy.[23] I want to make it clear that tragedy, as a form, has traditionally searched for meaning or explanation, but whether it has found them is – and has been over the centuries – a matter for debate.

In tracing what is, in effect, a history of Western drama, this book considers why theatre matters, how it can help to make sense of terrible events, how it shapes sorrowful experience. But it is right that comparisons should be made between theatre and other efforts to make sense of suffering: other artistic representations, such as sculpture and painting; eyewitness accounts and photographic images of war and atrocity; memorials and ritual; theological and psychoanalytic debate. While the primary focus of this book is upon tragic drama, therefore, it also ranges out in the final section to begin to engage with other tragic art forms, with theological and psychoanalytic discussions and with the element of tragedy in daily life.

Chapter 2

Tragic drama

2.1 The Greeks

Competition

Tragic drama was accorded a special function in fifth-century Athenian civic life. It was performed at the City Dionysia festival each March, over a series of about three or four days, and attended by all the citizens of Athens.[1] The burden for producing the plays fell upon the *choregos*, a wealthy private citizen, appointed by the city annually, whose public duty it was to fund and train a chorus of young, male citizens for the performance. Before the performances, the city engaged in a series of processions, sacrifices and public ceremonies, all designed, as Simon Goldhill has argued, to 'use the state festival to glorify the state'.[2] Integral to the celebration of the city (the 'polis' in Greek) was the performance of tragedy itself. This took the form of a competition between three playwrights, who each wrote three tragedies and a satyr play, to be staged in a single day. At the beginning of the festival, the ten judges were chosen by lot, from a list of names drawn from the ten tribes of the citizen body. While the judges' verdict was final, it might be influenced by the noisy approval or disapproval of the general audience. Appealing to the crowd was consequently hugely important and, before each day's performances, the playwright would mount a platform with his chorus to display himself to the people. Socrates, for example, recalls in the *Symposium* seeing the playwright Agathon stepping onto 'the platform with your troupe – how you sent a straight glance at that vast assembly to show that you meant to do yourself credit with your production'.[3]

It is important to understand the original context of Greek tragedy in social political life and in dramatic competition, because democracy and individual prowess are central concerns of the tragedies themselves. Competition lay at the heart of Athenian culture. It featured in the democratic assembly, since citizens needed to win over their audience to their point of view through scintillating rhetoric. Competition of course also played a crucial part in the athletic games

10

which took place in Greece regularly. At the early games at Olympia, Delphi, Nemea and other places, competitions in music and poetry were included as well as the more conventional sporting events like running and wrestling. They were all considered acts of performance, designed to display the talents of the performer and garner the admiration of the crowd.[4]

The Greek language reflects the intimate connection between physical competition, acting and internalised tragic experience. The Greek word *agonia* initially meant gymnastic exercise or wrestling while the *agōn* was the place where the wrestling contest took place. The verb *agōnizesthai* meant to contend for a prize in the games and then later 'to contend for a prize on stage', or to 'act'. But later these same words develop a more abstract or internalised meaning, so that *agōn* meant more metaphorically a 'struggle' or a 'battle', while *agonia* developed our modern sense of 'agony' or 'anguish'.

It was through *agōn* – competition, acting, agony – that the Greeks developed a sense of who they were. By testing themselves against certain standards, be they the gods, mythical heroes or each other, they could learn the limits of their capabilities and, supposedly, the boundaries of the democratic, human condition. It was important to excel as far as was humanly possible, but to succeed too far was to rival the gods and to be guilty of *hubris* or arrogance. The gods ensured that nobody crossed the boundary of what was appropriate for a mortal to accomplish unpunished. The heroes from myth – half god and half human – offered a model to inspire endeavour. The poet Pindar, who composed poems to celebrate the victors at the athletic games at Olympia or Delphi, used to compare the athletes with mythical figures in order to convey a sense of their supreme talents. But he always included a warning about the dangers of excessive pride, reminding his subjects of their limits and mortality. The sentiment is tragic. 'Creatures of a day!', he wrote, 'What is someone? What is no one? [*ti de tis? Ti de outis?*] Man: a shadow's dream.'[5]

Pindar's pithy 'what is someone? What is no one?' reflects the alarmingly thin boundary between success and failure in Greek culture, or between excelling honourably and rivalling the gods dishonourably. It is an equivocal distinction which tragedy explored and the city judged. The chorus in Sophocles' *Antigone* describes man's dilemma in this situation:

> Man the master, ingenious past all measure
> past all dreams, the skills within his grasp –
>   he forges on, now to destruction
>   now again to greatness. When he weaves in
>   the laws of the land, and the justice of the gods

that binds his oaths together
　　　　　he and his city rise high [*'hypsipolis'*] –
　　　　　but the city casts out [*'apolis'*]
that man who weds himself to inhumanity
thanks to reckless daring.

　　　　　　　　　(*Antigone*, 406–15; Fagles translation)

Just as in Pindar's poem ('someone' (*tis*), 'no one' (*outis*)), a simple prefix in this chorus marks all the difference between ecstasy and agony. When man is excelling but remaining just within the boundaries of human acceptability, he is said to be '*hypsi* -polis', high in the city, the top guy, the winner. But if he transgresses the boundary and is guilty of *hubris* ('reckless daring'), he quickly becomes '*a* -polis', without a city, nobody.

The difficulty in tragedy is that the boundaries are frequently unknown, inscrutable for mere mortals or distorted by intervening events and passions. The nature of Antigone's virtue, for example, has been a matter for debate, both for critics over the centuries and within the play itself. According to Antigone, and Romantic critics like A. W. Schlegel, there is nothing more virtuous than being prepared to die for the principle of burying one's brother.[6] 'What greater glory could I win [*kleos*] than to give my own brother decent burial?', Antigone tells the ruler Creon after she is arrested. 'These citizens here would all agree, they would praise me too if their lips weren't locked in fear' (561–5). But in fact the chorus accuses Antigone of going 'too far, the last limits of daring – smashing against the high throne of Justice' (943–4) and thus transgressing the boundary of appropriate female behaviour by publicly disobeying the laws of the city. Antigone's tragedy, as her sister Ismene predicted at the beginning, is caused by a disregard for the guidance of good judgement and an over-reliance upon her own self-will. As all the repeated references to Antigone's independence and her lack of *sōphron* (prudence or moderation) or *phronon* (sensible thinking) suggest, this could be interpreted as a classic case of *hubris*.

If Antigone's virtue is possibly compromised by her excessive desire to win glory, Sophocles' Electra's has allowed her perspective to be completely dis-torted by passion and circumstances. Indeed, the perversion of Electra can best be appreciated when it is contrasted with that of Antigone. For while Antigone imagines being honoured for the arguably pious act of burying her brother, Electra thinks she will win accolades for the cold murder of her own mother. 'Do you not see what glory you will win / Both for yourself and me by doing this?', she says to her sister Chrysothemis. 'For all will cry, Argive or foreigner, / When they behold us: "See! there are the sisters / Who saved their father's house from desolation; / Who, when their enemies were firmly set / In power, avenged a murder, risking all. / Love and respect and honour are their

2. Electra, in abject grief, contemplates corpse at the beginning/end of the play. Cambridge Greek Play, 2001, directed by Jane Montgomery. © Philip Mynott

due'" (973–81; Kitto translation). And while Antigone's breach of moderation takes the form of action, Electra's 'reckless daring' is simply to mourn without modesty or restraint. 'Yours is a grief beyond the common measure' (140), the chorus says to her, with a certain degree of implied criticism, and a little later, Electra responds: 'In what I suffer, is there moderation?' (236). In the event, Electra remains on stage while her brother, Orestes, commits the murder of their mother Clytemnestra and later of their uncle Aegisthus. In keeping with the passivity and internalisation of her character, Electra experiences the murder of Clytemnestra vicariously, shouting encouragement to Orestes off stage. The play ends before the arrival of the Furies and so without the obvious signs of any punishment for Electra and Orestes.[7]

The gods

Sophocles' version of Electra is arguably less conclusive and more disturbing than the versions by Aeschylus (*The Libation Bearers*) and Euripides (*Electra*) because no gods appear. There is no judgement made of Electra's and Orestes' behaviour. The gods in Greek tragedy are problematic and unpredictable, sometimes all-too-present and punitive but at other times disturbingly absent. While fifth-century Athens still adhered to the traditional worship of the Olympian gods, with vast wealth being poured into the building of Athene's temple, the Parthenon, on the acropolis and sacrificial ritual permeating public life, religious scepticism and secular philosophical enquiry was growing. The group of philosophers known as the Sophists were challenging orthodox beliefs, throwing everything open to question and logical analysis in the new climate of the fledgling democracy. 'Concerning the gods', one Sophist, Protagoras wrote, 'I am unable to discover whether they exist or not, or what they are like in form; for there are many hindrances to knowledge, the obscurity of the subject and the brevity of human life.'[8] Although the plays were performed at the festival of the god Dionysus and the events were preceded by a sacrifice to the god, the tragedies reflect some of these contemporary doubts over the relationship between the mortals and the gods.

Aeschylus depicts the gods in conflict, striving to assert their particular powers and priorities. Now we will see 'war god against war god' (461) says Orestes at one point in the *Libation Bearers*, highlighting the fact that in the *Oresteia* there is no one divine order or absolute truth. Apollo demands one act of revenge; the Furies demand another. Zeus, who is forever invoked but never seen, supposedly holds the scales of justice. And Athene attempts to arbitrate but appears to couch her decision in the language of one side of the debate, by now hopelessly corrupted and uncertain. So the cosmic order appears to rest upon compromise between wilful, subjective gods, rather than upon eternal divine laws. It is for this reason that Nietzsche vividly described Aeschylus in *The Birth of Tragedy* placing 'the Olympian world on his scales of justice'. Of course, gods prevail in Aeschylus. There is no doubting the might of Zeus at the end of *Prometheus Bound*, when Prometheus is hurled down to Tarturus, but the source of that might is contingent upon the historical moment, open to negotiation and, if Prometheus' prophecy about Zeus' future demise is true, ultimately limited in the long term.[9]

In Sophocles' plays, the gods consistently demarcate and guard what is lawful or unlawful for mortals unequivocally, but those laws and distinctions are often hard to identify. So Philoctetes is bitten by a snake sent by the gods because he inadvertently crossed a sacred boundary. So, also, Oedipus is punished for his great violation of their laws when he murders his father and marries his mother, but the riddling oracles of the gods made it almost impossible for him to know the heinous nature of his actions at the time of committing them.

Antigone appeals to the laws of the gods, known in Greek as *nomos*, to justify her violation of the laws of Creon. To bury one's brother, she argues, is of higher value than to obey the laws of the city, because the gods are eternal and part of the nature of things while the city is dependent upon social, written contracts:

> It wasn't Zeus, not in the least,
> who made this proclamation – not to me.
> Nor did that Justice, dwelling with the gods
> beneath the earth, ordain such laws for men [*nomous*].
> Nor did I think your edict had such force
> that you a mere mortal, could override the gods,
> the great unwritten, unshakable traditions [*agrapta nomima*].
>
> (499–505; Fagles translation)

The clarity of *nomos*, however, is compromised by circumstances and by the competing demands of city life. Ismene, after all, does not think it more important to obey the laws of the unseen gods than to comply with Creon's very tangible decree. And the chorus also keeps a low profile and does not resist the city.

In the case of *Oedipus* and *Antigone*, the gods punish the transgression of their laws. At the beginning of *Oedipus*, the city of Thebes is suffering from plague. It emerges, when Creon returns from consulting the oracle at Delphi, that the plague has arisen as a direct result of the murder of Laius. In other words, the city of Thebes is being punished because it is sheltering the murderer of the previous king and thus harbouring a polluted figure. Similarly, when Creon continues to refuse to bury Polyneices in *Antigone*, the gods register their disapproval by causing the birds to vomit up the body they have pecked onto the city's altars. In these cases, the physical state of pollution – what the Greeks called *miasma* – indicates a breach in nature and a violation of the laws of the gods. There is a strange comfort in the justice of this. While mortals might themselves suffer in the process, the gods ensure that there is consistency in the order of the world. Every transgression of what is sacred will result in *miasma* and punishment. So certain is this that when the chorus in *Oedipus* ponders the alternative, it suffers a complete disorientation:

> Those who seek dishonourable advantage
> And lay violent hands on holy things
> And do not shun impiety –
> Who among these will secure himself from the wrath of God?
> If deeds like these are honoured,
> Why should I join in the sacred dance?
>
> (889–984; Kitto translation)

'Why should I join in the sacred dance?' (*Choreuein* in Greek) could also be translated as 'why should I be a member of the chorus'. The chorus contemplates a scenario in which an act of *hubris* is not punished and where the gods do not preside over a consistent and coherent system of divine justice. In that hypothetical situation, members of the chorus suggest, they could not continue as a chorus, they would lose their very identity and become nothing, nobody.

This is precisely the scenario which Euripides' plays present repeatedly. While the gods appear as characters on stage and play important roles in the plots, their status is treated with a large degree of scepticism. Sometimes protagonists on stage actually voice their doubts about the existence or worth of the gods, partly because of the injustice which they witness all around them. Orestes, in Euripides' version of the play, driven mad by the Furies after murdering his mother, confesses to Menelaus that 'we are the slaves of the gods, whoever the gods may be' (418; my translation). Most strikingly in the *Bacchae*, the plot of which revolves around the recognition of the god Dionysus, the king Pentheus refuses to acknowledge his divinity. Dionysus is therefore determined to 'show to him and all the Thebans that I am a god' (48; Morwood translation), but he does this paradoxically by 'chang[ing] to this mortal form and transform[ing] [his] appearance to human shape' (53–4). In creating his revenge to punish Pentheus for his impiety, Dionysus in fact inverts or perverts conventional religious practice to the extent that he undermines his own case for divinity. The natural Bacchic ritual out on Cithaeron, in which an animal is sacrificed by women to the god, is converted into an unnatural family slaughter as Agave is blinded with madness by the god and tears apart her own son Pentheus. Dionysus makes the tearing apart of Pentheus, or ritual '*sparagmos*', easy for Agave, who would not otherwise have had the strength. According to the messenger's report she 'tore out his shoulder – not through her own strength: it was the god who made her handiwork easy' (1127–8; Morwood translation). At the end of the *Bacchae*, Dionysus punishes those he believes to have neglected his worship and imposes a new, strict dispensation, even if it seems to be based more upon his unpredictable whim than upon objective justice. Cadmus tells Dionysus that he 'came down on us with too heavy a punishment' (1346; Morwood translation), appropriating the language normally reserved for the hubristic mortal. The gods have immortal physical strength but mortal moral weakness, a disastrous combination when they have the power to impose apparently arbitrary laws.

Euripides' *Trojan Women* depicts an even bleaker world. There, the gods abandon the mortals just after the beginning of the play. Poseidon and Athene meet at the start, to discuss the Greeks' desecration of their altars in Troy, and then they leave, to pursue the Greeks back to their homeland in vengeance. While some recent productions have kept Athene and Poseidon on stage for the rest of the play's action, it is important that the women of Troy have been deserted by everyone: their men, their friends, their good fortune, their gods. Through most of the play, the queen Hecuba retains some faith in the old, steadfast values. She believes that her youngest son will grow up to avenge his father, only to witness the Greeks' merciless killing of him. She trusts that justice will prevail when she demands punishment for Helen for her role in starting the war, only to find that Menelaus, Helen's husband, is the judge and will soon be bowled over by her beauty all over again. And at the end, she discovers that even the gods are no longer listening to her prayers. Calling on Apollo and the altars of her city and the dead in Hades, she breaks off for a moment: 'O you gods! – And yet why do I call upon the gods? They did not hear me in the past when I called to them' (1280–1). But nevertheless, as she is dragged off to slavery, she keeps asking the same question, beating the ground and demanding a divine answer that never comes: 'Do you see? Do you hear?'. The atrocities at Troy carry even worse implications than those in *The Bacchae*, because there are supposedly no witnesses. Any amount of brutality can be unleashed upon the women because the gods are no longer present or interested in guarding moderation and order. Euripides testifies to the terrifying emptiness of a godless universe. Highlighting this nihilistic vision, Hecuba's cries are littered with negatives: 'without a tomb', 'without a friend', 'without knowledge', 'without fame'. In Sophocles' plays, then, the gods remain inscrutable but return with a grimly and appropriately punitive response. In Euripides, they do not even offer the comfort of witnessing mortal suffering.

Shame

As well as through the gods, the Greeks also derived a sense of success or excess from the reaction of other people to their actions. The measure of how far they had kept within the boundaries of acceptable behaviour or had exceeded them was to be located in the well-developed sense of shame. The simple dichotomies of what E. R. Dodds has termed the Greek 'shame-culture' can be seen in Homer's *Iliad*.[10] There, the success of a warrior, his honour, is measured in tangible rewards, such as slave girls, tripods, all the war booty known as *geras*. Thus, when these physical objects are removed, he is publicly shamed. Achilles, for example, rightly interprets Agamemnon's seizure of his slave girl, Chriseis, at the beginning of the epic as an act of dishonour. The rest of the epic follows the impact of this dishonour, Achilles refusing to fight and finally allowing Patroclus to fight in his place with tragic consequences. At one point,

Achilles questions the heroic code, refusing to fight even when he is offered tripods and slave girls, the traditional signs of respect. But when he re-enters the battlefield in Book XXI, equipped with the glorious armour forged by the god Hephaistus, the code is re-established.

The notion of being exemplary still depended to a degree on public approval or disapproval in fifth-century Athens. So fearful were the Athenians of a possible return to the political tyrannies of the sixth century when they were establishing the new, experimental democracy, that they set up the practice of 'ostracism', or banishment from Athens for anybody who garnered the popular vote. In other words, anybody who appeared to be too powerful or successful or hubristic could be exiled from the city if enough people voted against him. The ostracised man became like the tragic hero. 'The only things held against the ostracised man were the very superior qualities which had raised him above the common herd, and his exaggerated good luck which might call down the wrath of the gods upon the town', comments Jean-Pierre Vernant.[11]

The tragic hero who most fits Vernant's description of the ostracised man is Oedipus. On the one hand, Oedipus' fate is unique. It is extremely rare for somebody to murder his father and to sleep with his mother. But on the other hand, Oedipus' story is really about the insignificance of man in the cosmic scheme of things and the limitation of his knowledge. Oedipus' tale is, in other words, also the story of Everyman and this is the source of its power. The play addresses the question of the ordinariness or extraordinariness of Oedipus. The priest appeals to him at the beginning, carefully stressing that he 'cannot equal the gods . . . but we do rate you first of men' (39, 41; Fagles translation). And Oedipus, in reply, describes the ambivalent role of the king, who is both an individual and representative of the collective: 'Your pain strikes each of you alone . . . but my spirit grieves for the city, for myself and all of you' (74–6). Indeed, Oedipus has reached the position of king through his own talents and it is the irony of the play that his 'superior qualities' which are so admired can paradoxically bring about his demise. Through solving the riddle of the sphinx by his intelligence Oedipus was able to marry the queen, his mother; through his clever power of logic he is able to untangle the riddle of his origins and realise his tragedy. Thus the play perfectly brings together the agency and passivity of Oedipus. At each stage of the narrative, he is active in the plot, an autonomous individual, deciding to murder Laius, deciding to sleep with Jocasta. So he actively transgresses and must later feel shame. But retrospectively, when the story is considered as a whole, it is apparent that the gods and his fate have shaped his life. He has been, as he says, the victim of his cruel *daimon*. According to Jean-Pierre Vernant, 'the logic of tragedy consists in "operating on both planes"', that of human agency and that of divine agency, or what he calls *ethos* and *daimon*. These two determining forces are held in tension but inseparable, necessarily testing the limits of individual responsibility and power. For only by contemplating the double cause for any action can the ambivalent place of man in his world be properly questioned. 'In his purely human dimensions the agent is not the sufficient cause and reason for his actions: on the contrary, it is his action, recoiling upon him as the gods have, in their sovereignty, ordered, that reveals him to himself, showing him the true nature of what he is and what he does', writes Vernant.[12]

By the time Sophocles came to produce *Oedipus at Colonus*, about twenty years later, his treatment of Oedipus was quite different. In this play, the blame for Oedipus' fate rests entirely with the gods. He stresses that he acted in ignorance, without malice or deliberate intention. But the fact still remains that Oedipus is now polluted and his state of taboo is unequivocal. It is a fame which goes before him. When he arrives at the grove of Colonus, just outside Athens, led by his daughter Antigone, he discovers that the chorus has already heard about him. His is a story that can be shared communally, that has grown bigger than he is. In the exchange that ensues, when the chorus gives sanctuary to Oedipus in return for his tale of suffering – 'give in' (*sterzon*) the chorus says and 'obey' (*peithou*) – we witness the beginnings of tragedy, where suffering is transformed painfully but beneficially into narrative. Oedipus' shame becomes a source of awe and wisdom for the whole community. And thus whichever land becomes his final resting place when he dies will be blessed. He has transgressed the boundaries of human experience so far that he has paradoxically touched upon divine wisdom. 'Don't reject me as you look into the horror of my face, these sockets raked and blind', he says to the chorus. 'I come as someone sacred, someone filled with piety and power [*hierōs eusebēs*], bearing a great gift for all your people' (310–14; Fagles translation). To confirm this, the messenger describes Oedipus' death almost as a religious experience: it is *thaumastos* or marvellous. And he speculates on the standard criteria by which his story could be measured: 'Consider my story madness if you will [*mē dokō phronōn legein*]. I don't want your belief, not if you think I'm mad' (1892–3). Oedipus' shame is now transfigured into an awesome phenomenon shared communally and thus it reshapes the old standard measurement of possibility, of 'sense' or the Greek *phronon*.

In Oedipus' case, the gods and the polis confirm his simultaneous shame and worth. For Ajax, the issue is far more complex. The shamefulness of his act of slaughter before the play's opening is interpreted very differently by the gods, by Ajax and by his fellow Greeks. According to the gods, Ajax is blameworthy because he has scorned their aid and is guilty of *hubris*. 'Any fool can win with God beside him; I intend to win glory and honour on my own account' (767–9; Watling translation), he is reported to have said. So Athene fills Ajax with a self-destructive fury and the tragic events follow. But Ajax, whose Homeric sense of honour has been offended because the *geras* in the form of Achilles' armour has not been awarded to him, is unrepentant about his attitude to the gods and is mortified that he has failed to kill the Greek chiefs and slaughtered sheep instead. The Greeks, meanwhile, whose notions of honour have progressed since the Homeric code, are outraged that Ajax could even have contemplated murdering his fellow warriors. The response to shame in each case is to laugh scornfully (*gelōs*) but for different reasons. So Athene invites Odysseus to laugh (*gelan*) at mad Ajax; Ajax imagines all the Greek laughing at 'his brave handiwork among these innocent dumb beasts' (366); the chorus describes Menelaus coming to 'laugh at our suffering' after Ajax's suicide.

Thus, in contrast to *Oedipus*, the play dramatises a radical incoherence of response and of values. There is no perfect match of divine and mortal responsibility and no unanimity of affect. The suffering of Ajax provokes pity and disgust confusingly in equal measure; laughter and tragedy are intimately connected. When Ajax's body is discovered, pierced by a sword, it is an object arguably of repugnance as much as of reverence. Tecmessa wraps him in her mantle so that, unusually for Greek tragedy, the dead body of the hero may not be seen. And it requires Odysseus' cunning rhetoric to win round the various factions and facilitate the burial of the corpse. For Odysseus is as at home with the bewildering condition of the play's modernity as Ajax was at odds with it. In the arguably fickle new climate of the play, where, as Odysseus says, the 'change from friend to foe' is 'common', Ajax's steadfast adherence to outmoded Homeric values has alienated him from all his surroundings. This is a play in which, like in *Hamlet*, 'time is out of joint' and appropriately its hero's sanity – the moment when he has actually been released from his god-given madness or *nosos* – is continually open to doubt. Only when Odysseus begins to speak of Ajax's worth and recalls his heroic service in the war can some form of community consensus be recovered. Finally it seems as if we are back to the end of *Antigone* or *Oedipus at Colonus*, when a city can gather in respect at the death and burial of a hero. But, even here, *Ajax* sounds a flawed note. When Teucer rejects Odysseus' offer to be present at Ajax's burial, for 'fear of offending the dead', he continues the fractious lack of unity with which the play opened.

The word which Euripides' Medea uses to describe her potential shame is the same one which occurs throughout *Ajax*: '*gelōs*'. Medea is afraid that if she meekly accepts the orders of Jason and goes into exile with her children, she will be the laughing stock or *gelōs* of every city she enters. Her shame will haunt her. But unlike Ajax, Medea's is only a hypothetical shame, one imagined by her in

3. Medea with her murdered child in her arms. *Medea* directed by Deborah Warner at the Queen's Theatre, London, 2001. © Geraint Lewis

the future. It is to avoid this shame that she commits what we would think is a series of far more terrible crimes: she murders the princess Creusa whom Jason is to marry and she then murders her children. Her speech before she murders her children reflects, in its tortured and fragmented syntax, the difficulty of the decision. She twists and turns in her plans – 'Goodbye to my former plans! I shall take my children from the land. Why should I, as I seek to pain their father through their sufferings, win twice as much agony for myself?' – only to change her mind once again: 'But what is wrong with me? Do I want to make myself ridiculous [*gelōta*] by letting my enemies go unpunished?' (1044–50; Morwood translation). As she steels herself to do the deed, she fractures her being into different anatomical parts – 'My hand will not weaken'; 'Ah, do not, my heart, do not do this' (1055, 1056) – dramatising the radical self-alienation process she is undergoing.[13]

At the end of the play, Medea becomes a goddess. Like Oedipus, she has transgressed the mortal realm by the extreme nature of her crimes and thus, paradoxically, touches upon the immortal. Modern theatre productions in particular have had difficulties accepting and staging Medea's divinity. The production of the play, directed by Deborah Warner in 2001, removed the gods altogether and finished with Medea (Fiona Shaw) sitting dazed with her murdered children in their paddling pool before flirting with Jason in a whimsical and ironic attempt to recuperate the relationship after the slaughter.[14]

City

According to Jean-Pierre Vernant and Pierre Vidal-Naquet, fifth-century Athens marked the historical collision of two very different cultures. On the way out was the old society which looked back to the heroic past, myths and belief in the gods; on the way in was a new secular society governed by law, logic and democratic practice. The confusion and overlap between the two ways of thinking produced the doubts and questions animating tragedy. The consequent ambiguity runs through all aspects of Greek tragedy, from its treatment of the gods and moral responsibility to its use of ambivalent language and its scrutiny of the changing meaning of words and stories. But one area, these writers argue, which was particularly open to uncertainty was the democratic city and the individual's place within it. How was the individual to fit into the collective? Since radical democracy in Athens had only been established in 462 BC, four years before the first performance of Aeschylus' *Oresteia*, ideas about debate, decision-making and consensus were relatively new and insecure. Vernant argues that these questions were raised in tragedy through the relation between the individual actor and the chorus. 'The tragic technique exploits a polarity between two of its elements: on the one hand the chorus, an anonymous and collective being whose role is to express, through its fears, hopes and judgements, the feelings of the spectators who make up the civic community; on the other the individualised figure whose action forms the centre of the drama and who is seen as a hero from another age, always more or less alien to the ordinary condition of the citizen.'[15]

Certainly the chorus does, in Simon Goldhill's words, 'stand in opposition to, or in judgement on, the hero of the drama' and, as such, it evokes the 'tension between the individual and the collective which is integral to democratic theory and practice'.[16] It voices opinions which were key to Greek civic life: moderation, humility, good judgement, consensus. The chorus of Theban elders, for example, in *Antigone*, sings of the importance of 'learning some wisdom' from both sides, of 'showing reverence towards the gods' and not being 'madly defiant'. While the heroes needed to test certain principles to extremes lengths, the chorus tried to adopt a middle position, representing the central ground of the city.

But the difficulty with this theory is that the members of the chorus are often marginal, dispossessed characters themselves. The choruses of *Oedipus at*

Colonus, Women of Trachis, Electra and *Antigone, The Trojan Women, Hippolytus* and *Hecuba* are women, for example, who were not citizens of Athens. The choruses in the three plays of Aeschylus' trilogy, the *Oresteia*, are men too old to fight in Troy, women in mourning and the vengeful but eventually defeated Furies. While many of these groups might sing of civic duties and peaceful security at the heart of the city, they are all at some degree removed from the centre of power. Indeed we can sense the powerlessness of the chorus at the end of Aeschylus' *Agamemnon*, the first play in the *Oresteia* trilogy, when it attempts to stand up to Aegisthus:

> CHORUS No man of Argos will bend his neck to a dog.
> AEGISTHUS But they shall bend their necks to one who will whip them like dogs. (1665–6; Ted Hughes translation)[17]

The effect of the uncertainty over the relationship between the chorus and the city is twofold. The first consequence is that the extent to which the audience identifies with the chorus is ambivalent. The tension in the relationship between audience and chorus is all part of the wider oscillation between sympathy and distance in the watching experience. The second consequence is that there is arguably a power vacuum at the heart of Greek tragedy. In some plays this means that no one group prevails or can be said to represent the city and that events occur frighteningly at random and without a fixed standard of judgement. This happens, for example, in Euripides' *Phoenician Women* where members of the chorus are women who happen to be passing through Thebes on their way from Tyre to Delphi. Described as 'A crowd of women, like confusion in the city' (196–7), they are diverted by the war between Eteocles and Polyneices and have to take temporary sanctuary in the city, effectively as political refugees. It is while they are witnessing events that Creon's son, Menoeceus, is called upon to be sacrificed to the gods in order, supposedly, that the city will be saved from defeat by Polyneices. Although Creon tries to resist the demand from the prophet that this should happen, Menoeceus voluntarily allows himself to be killed (throws himself from the battlements) in the belief that the sacrifice of his life will save his land from ruin. However, because there is no centre to the community and therefore no fixed set of values or consensus, it is not clear that Menoeceus' sacrifice makes any difference at all to the fortunes of the city. Jocasta describes Creon as having a 'public blessing but a private grief' (1206–7). Consequently the relationship between the 'public' and the 'private', which, according to Vernant, is normally reflected and confirmed by the dialogue between chorus and actor, is subjected to radical doubt in this play. The public, stable collective, in the form of the chorus, is missing, substituted by a temporary, migratory and bewildered group. Jocasta, Creon and Menoeceus cannot see how their private experience can impact upon public events or how public pressures can make sense of private grief, and, as a result, individual responsibility becomes opened up to tragic cynicism.

In other plays, the collective mass of the people is invoked to justify certain actions. We see this happening particularly in Euripides' *Iphigenia in Aulis*, when the leaders make decisions under the palpable pressure of the massive Greek army, which is frustrated at being kept back from war by the lack of wind. Agamemnon tells of the 'ineluctable clutches of fate' (*avagkaias tuchas*: the Greek speaks of impersonal necessity) which compel him to sacrifice his own daughter, Iphigenia, to appease Artemis so that she will allow the wind to blow the sailboats to Troy (511). But when his brother Menelaus questions him on the source of this necessity, Agamemnon is forced to admit that it is the 'whole crowd of the Achaean army' (514). When later he considers withdrawing from the plan to sacrifice Iphigenia, Odysseus tells him that it is impossible to back down now because the army has heard of the sacrifice and will insist on its execution in order to guarantee the wind and the departure for Troy. The unseen ranks of sailors hold power over the weak, hapless Agamemnon. Yet this group is not represented on stage according to the Euripidean text; the chorus is made up of women. So the army becomes an empty power which can be invoked by any calculating individual to insist upon particular events. The invisible force (the Greek uses the word *ochlos* or 'crowd' here, like the description of the *ochlos* in the *Phoenician Women*) becomes all the more dominating and dangerous precisely because it cannot be confronted, named or known.

When Clytemnestra arrives with Iphigenia, she is quick to notice the political climate in Aulis. 'I am come', she says, 'a woman to this lawless crowd of military sailors' (913–14). (The word in Greek translated here as 'lawless' is *anarchon*, 'anarchy'.) In the political vacuum in which these shadowy unseen forces hold sway, there is no law or constraint on activity; anything is terrifyingly possible. And it is in this climate that Iphigenia makes her pointless sacrifice. Like Menoeceus, she finally goes to her death voluntarily. 'I give my body to Greece. Sacrifice me and sack Troy', she says. 'It is right that Greeks rule barbarians, and not barbarians, Greeks. For they are slaves and we are free' (1397–1401). But these words are rendered ironic by the context, in which the Greeks themselves seem 'lawless' and 'barbaric'. And they are further challenged by subsequent events. According to the messenger's report, Iphigenia's body was substituted by a goat at the last moment, as the axe was about to fall upon her neck. So she was saved and all the anxiety and grief was supposedly for nothing. He tells Clytemnestra that she should be pleased that Iphigenia was saved. But Clytemnestra's response is very interesting:

> Child, have you become a trick of the gods? [*klemma*]
> How can I speak to you? how can I be sure that I am not
> being soothed by an idle story [*tousde matēn muthous*],
> to stop my bitter grief for you?   (1615–18)

Instead of relief, Clytemnestra feels that she has been tricked or cheated by the gods. (The word in Greek here is *klemma*, which literally means something stolen or a theft.) Has Clytemnestra's belief or trust in anything or anyone been stolen from her? Does the 'lawless' or 'barbaric' world of the Greeks mean that nothing can be relied upon? Certainly Clytemnestra's reference to an 'idle story' suggests she thinks this. For the Greek word translated here as 'idle' is *matēn* which literally means 'in vain', 'senselessly', or 'at random'. Since power is distributed 'randomly' and unaccountably in Aulis, there can be no 'sense' and no faith in anything.

Critics are divided in their interpretation of Iphigenia's sacrifice. The fact that the end of the play may have been an addition by a later author means that, as Helene Foley puts it, 'any reading of the text remains speculative'.[18] She concludes that the ending is not ironic but through the ritual of sacrifice, 'rituals shared by all Greeks despite their political differences', Euripides enables the 'symbolic restoration and definition of Panhellenic culture'.[19] But the bleakly cynical view of Iphigenia's death, which I have been proposing, is confirmed by one of the great cinematic versions of the play, the Greek film-maker Michael Cacoyannis' film *Iphigenia* (1976). The film, made just after the military junta in Greece ended, conveys well the aggressive threat of the Greek army and the unaccountability of its power. In contrast, Iphigenia (played by the actress Tatiana Papamoschou) appears all the more vulnerable and innocent. As she ascends towards the altar for the sacrifice, a breeze starts to stir the grasses. But, when she hesitates, the priest comes forward to lead her away to death. There can be no more cynical representation of the pointlessness of her sacrifice and the fact that it is unrelated causally to the wind. The army starts to cheer and rushes down to the ships. The men have been rewarded with their primitive need for one girl's blood and they are hastening to Troy to seek more blood and destruction.

Place

One of the difficulties about identifying the democratic city of Athens in Greek tragedy is the fact that the majority of the plays are set in Thebes and only one extant play (the *Eumenides*) is actually set in Athens (for the second half). According to Froma Zeitlin, 'Thebes ... provides the negative model to Athens' manifest image of itself with regard to its notions of the proper management of city, society and self'.[20] Tragedy therefore offered an alternative 'site of displacement', very different from the environment of democratic Athens. Zeitlin's view of tragic place offers useful insights into the significance of the various references to sanctuary in Athens which recur in the plays (for example, *Oedipus at Colonus, Medea,* Aeschylus' *The Suppliant Women* and Euripides' *Electra*). But Vernant, Vidal-Naquet and Goldhill insist that the city of Athens is still being indirectly represented in the plays, despite the ostensible setting in Thebes or elsewhere. Just as the mythical world of gods and heroes is opened up to the scrutiny of the new, secular logic in Greek tragedy, so the setting of Thebes with its monarchical system coexists, in the plays, with the culture and concerns of the new Athenian democracy.

The result is an uneasy tension between different cultures and different locations, which reflects the general uncertainty and ambiguity of tragedy. This tension is possible to maintain in Greek tragedy, because the treatment of space is so complex. It is at once both literal and yet also metaphorical. Antigone, for example, refers to the unresolved nature of her death with the image of homelessness. 'I have no home on earth and none below, not with the living, not with the breathless dead' (941–2; Fagles translation), she says. Her lack of home is both physical – she will be walled up alive in a tomb, so will be neither in the world of the living or the dead – and also metaphorical, in the sense that, because of her tragic transgression, she no longer has a recognisable identity. Her image of homelessness also carries a contemporary political reference. For the word Antigone uses to describe herself is '*metoikos*': 'I go to my rockbound prison, strange new tomb / always a stranger [*metoikos*]' (939–40). The 'metics' (*metoikoi*) were a group in Athens who were neither citizen nor slave, who were migrant workers without a stake in the community. Like the Athenian 'metics', Antigone has also lost her stake in the city of Thebes and is estranged by her fate.

One of the most vivid examples of the simultaneous literal and metaphorical spaces in Greek tragedy occurs in Sophocles' play, *Philoctetes.* The island of Lemnos is an image for a state of mind, as well as Philoctetes' prison and home. Initially the island is described by Odysseus as 'untrodden on [*astiptos*] and uninhabited' (2). The deserted nature of the island seems to mirror the dejected state of Philoctetes' mind. He calls both his island and himself 'deserted' (228, 487). Significantly the word in Greek which Philoctetes uses is '*eremos*' (deserted), which recalls in its etymology the Greek verb '*ereo*' meaning to 'ask', 'search', 'explore'. It is as if the metaphorical, mental bewilderment and anxious self-enquiry haunts the literal bare landscape of the island. As the play develops, however, the society of Neoptolemus and Odysseus seems more manipulative and corrupt and the place which Philoctetes has established for himself on the island seems more attractive. Philoctetes transforms the island, in his description, from being deserted to being his home. Recalling Odysseus' opening words, he has in fact 'set his mark' – *stiptos* – upon the island, making it a place to which he belongs. As Philoctetes becomes more stubborn in his determination not to comply with Neoptolemus, Neoptolemus becomes more confused. He is said to be '*aporos*' which means literally to have 'no way out' but would be translated here 'at a loss what to say' (897). It is the same word, *aporia*, which Plato uses at the end of various Socratic dialogues, when the men discussing conventional ideas and definitions realise that all their previous fixed assumptions are wrong and they no longer know what to think or what to say. So Neoptolemus' bewilderment, when all that he has previously been taught by Odysseus has been challenged by Philoctetes' determined integrity, is figured in this image of geographical impasse: 'no way out'. It is only after the god Heracles has appeared, in order to impose a compromise between the entrenched parties, that the *aporia* is replaced with an image of maritime exploration. 'Let's all go', the final chorus sings, 'praying to the sea nymphs that we may arrive safely at a sanctuary at the end of our voyage' (*nostou sōtēras hikesthai*) (1469–71).

Films afford a productive medium in which to explore Greek tragedy's particular combination of physical and metaphorical space. Pasolini's movie, *Oedipe Re* (1967), is an interesting example. The film begins and ends in Italy: Oedipus' father Laius is a general in Mussolini's army and, at the close, Oedipus sits, a blind beggar, on the steps of a church in 1960s Bologna. But the central part of the film, in which Oedipus enquires into – and thereby relives – the secret of his origins, is set in Africa. It was filmed in Morocco, but might have been intended also to suggest Abyssinia (the modern Ethiopia), which was invaded by Mussolini in 1935.[21] Pasolini implies, by his choice of locations, that Oedipus' search into his private past is also a search into the origins of his civilisation, since Italy has been bound up with Africa in various shameful and exploitative ways. What Oedipus finds in that search is perhaps just as disturbing for Italy's (and by extension the West's) sense of itself as it is for his own identity.

The theatre, both ancient and modern, also provides a space which can dramatise the overlap of physical and metaphorical location in Greek tragedy. In recent years critics have been becoming increasingly interested in the physical dimensions of the Greek stage. They argue that knowing about the performance conditions of Greek drama can add to our understanding of the plays. So Ruth Padel focuses upon the central doors at the back of the stage, as a demarcating boundary between what can be seen and known and what remains unseen. 'Tragedy uses the vocabulary of house and door to demarcate self from other', she writes. 'A human being has a door to the interior, to the soul. The mouth is traditionally a fenced door. The background illusory house is important not just in itself, but as a structure parallel to the individual self. The *skene*, and what it stands for, is an image of the unseen interior of a human being.'[22] David Wiles counters this theory, by putting emphasis not upon what is off stage and interior, but upon the movements of the actors around the stage, or the 'blocking'. For him the most powerful place on the Greek stage was not at the back in front of the doors but in the centre. This centre becomes the centre of the home (the hearth), the centre of religious power (the altar), the centre of the city. And as actors move to and from that centre, they dramatise the tensions and oscillations of power in the tragedies. So in *Oedipus*, for example, the king begins at the centre, at the hearth: 'if by any chance he proves to be an intimate of our house, here at my hearth [*zunestios*], with my full knowledge, may the curse I just called down on him strike me!' (284–7; Fagles translation), he says, potentially cursing himself, as he thinks, for simply harbouring the murderer. Later he finds that he himself is the murderer and that his own hearth will curse and expel him. According to Wiles, the subtle movement of actor around the stage in *Oedipus* shows that 'god replaces man as the dominant force commanding the centre, within the microcosm of the performance space'.[23]

Pity

As well as the movement of actors and chorus in the Greek theatre, the other crucial element in Greek tragic performance was, of course, the audience. How far can we reconstruct the audience's response to ancient tragedy? As far as scholars have been able to glean information about the audience at the City Dionysia festival, it seems as if the spectators sat in the theatre in the same configuration as they sat in the democratic assembly. That is to say, the male citizens of Athens were divided into ten tribes and kept within those same tribal groups in the political and theatrical arena. This would suggest that only male citizens could attend the theatre; women and slaves could not be present. The implications of this are that Athenians considered attending the theatre to be a civic duty, sharing common concerns with the work in the assembly.

But whereas in the assembly citizens might be moved to decision-making and action, in the theatre they seem to have been moved to pity. The Greek notion of pity appears to have been very different from our concept of sympathy, which owes its origins to eighteenth-century thought. Homer offers a useful picture of the operation of pity at the end of the *Iliad*. The Trojan king Priam comes secretly to Achilles' tent to ransom the body of his son Hector. He reminds Achilles of how his own father is destined to mourn his death in time. The two enemies, the Trojan Priam and the Greek Achilles, are described weeping together, not in sympathy for the other's fate but sparked into grieving for their own. So pity is an emotion bound up in one's own preservation and insecurity, not in an abandonment of self. Aristotle suggests something similar when he writes that 'all the things which we dread for ourselves, excite our pity when they happen to others' (*Rhetoric*, 2.8.13). Pity for others coexists with a simultaneous relief that there is no threat to the self. Once the viewer can rest assured that he is not implicated in the experience of suffering, he can begin to extract some educative emotion from events depicted in front of him.

This economy of pity, where the self gains from the feeling of pity for the other's loss, has been described well by the Euripidean critic, Pietro Pucci. According to him, pity causes a 'split that tears the self between a part of it that suffers for the other's griefs and a part of it that desires to take control over that "alien" suffering.'[24] So in Euripides' tragic world, where there is no order and where power can be arbitrarily appropriated by different mortals or gods, characters are either victims or victors. '*Pathos* and *tyche* constitute the main aspects of life's brutality. The passivity of suffering [*pathos*] combines with the arbitrariness of events [*tyche*] to weave the scandalous texture of our life', explains Pucci (p. 58). The individual must try to gain power over another, even if only by the feeling of pity, if he is not to be overwhelmed by the 'arbitrariness of events' and become a victim himself. 'Under the semblance of recording and repeating the discourse of the other, for whom the pitier suffers, the pitier in reality gains control over this other, and listens to his own voice', Pucci claims (p. 16).

The power dynamics of pity, which Pucci identifies, are well dramatised in *Medea*. At the beginning of the play, Medea is described by the nurse as an object of pity: 'She lies there eating nothing, surrendering her body to her sorrows, pining away in tears unceasingly since she learned that her husband had wronged her. She will not look up, will not lift her face from the ground, but listens to her friends as they give advice no more than if she were a rock or a wave of the sea' (24–9; Morwood translation). It seems as if she will be overwhelmed by the cruelty of the world. But she steels herself to gain control over her situation, by splitting off the domestic, loving aspect of her character and killing her own children, thereby metaphorically mutilating herself. The chorus at the end of the play transforms the nurse's opening image of Medea into a very different type of stone, one that has been hardened by the experience of 'gaining control': 'Cruel woman, you must be stone or iron – for you will kill your children' (1280–1).

However, beyond the tightly structured economy of pity and victimisation, Euripides includes moments of pointless grief which appear to be surplus to requirements. These expressions of sorrow, which exceed the requirements of the plot and are not necessary for the dynamics of power and control in the play, focus upon the poignancy of the physical body which is suffering or about to suffer. As Medea bids her children farewell, for example, before killing them, she draws attention to each aspect of their innocent bodies: 'Give me your right hands, children, give them to your mother to kiss. O dearest of hands, dearest of lips to me, o children, so noble in appearance and so beautiful, may you find joy – but elsewhere. Your father took away your chance of happiness here. O the sweet pressure of my children's embraces, O the softness of your skin and the delicious fragrance of your breath' (1069–75; Morwood translation). And as Hecuba mourns Astyanax's pointless murder in the *Trojan Women*, she concentrates not on the political or metaphysical injustice but on the unbearable beauty of his dead body: 'O these hands, lying all broken at the joints, such sweet remembrances of your father's hands! This dear mouth was once so free with braggart promises, but it is silent now' (1178–80). Pucci's account of pity in Greek tragedy is very logical. But these depictions of sorrow appeal to an intuitive, somatic instinct, which lies beyond rational explanation. When all other structures of belief and trust and meaning have been undermined in Euripides' tragedies, it seems that the physical, tangible body, for Euripides' characters and for his audience witnessing the drama, is the only image upon which one can depend with certainty. It is appropriate then that at the end of the bleakest of tragedies, *The Trojan Women*, after everything has been destroyed and abandoned – city, gods, law, hope – Hecuba crosses the stage, drawing the audience's attention to her own body in pointless, excess sorrow: 'Oh, oh, my trembling, trembling limbs, support my steps' (1328–9).

2.2 Seneca and Racine

To some, it might appear strange to pair Seneca and Racine together in a single chapter. One man, Seneca, wrote plays to be read – and perhaps performed privately – by a small coterie of friends around the first century AD when the Roman Empire was governed by Nero; the other, Racine, produced tragedies, 1,600 years later, to be performed very publicly at the Théâtre de l'Hôtel de Bourgogne in Paris and (in the case of *Iphigenie* in 1675) at the court of Louis XIV in Versailles. What is more, Seneca's plays focus upon the depiction of physical violence and went on to influence the sensational excesses of Jacobean revenge tragedy, including plays such as Shakespeare's *Titus Andronicus* or Tourneur's *Revenger's Tragedy*. Racine, in contrast, is commonly associated with decorum and restraint, a reaction to what he considered the wild, unruliness of Seneca and Shakespeare. Certainly he denied any connection with Seneca, 'toning down the ferocity of Pyrrhus', in his play *Andromache*, 'which Seneca in his *Troades* . . . carried much farther than I felt I ought', and asserting that his source for *Phèdre* was Euripides rather than Seneca.[25] In any case the Roman playwrights had become deeply unfashionable by the second half of the seventeenth century in France. According to Racine's contemporaries, Seneca exemplified 'la foiblesse latine', understood the heart less well than the Greeks and was guilty of bombast, failing in his writing to make the word suit the action appropriately.[26]

Seneca and Racine were united, however, in their concern with the need to confront the past. The past was symbolised for them specifically by the mythic past of ancient Greece and by the generic precedent of Greek tragedy. Yet the concern with literary precedent came to represent the more general pressure of the past upon the present and its implications for tragedy. Both writers arguably saw the progress of history as cyclical, and believed that the past was bound to repeat itself. The necessity of confronting and escaping from the past was therefore coupled in their work with a simultaneous recognition of the virtual impossibility of ever moving on into the future. Theirs, in fact, is a world in which the tragic crisis is already predetermined and in which there is very little room for manoeuvre. Indeed it is possible to argue, as William Levitan has done most convincingly, that Seneca's specific place in Racine's work represents Racine's problematic engagement with the past. Levitan describes the 'struggle' in Racine's plays between 'a literary present and a literary past which can never be completely assimilated to it – between neoclassicism and Senecanism, the doctrines of order and violation, of nature and of monstrosity'.[27] Sometimes, when Racine alludes to Seneca's plays he manages to modify the references in order to imagine a different progress of history. 'For the sake of a future which the past itself would sacrifice to sustain its own privilege, Racine challenged the traditions of the past, and challenged them specifically in the most ruthless form they take in the tragedies of Seneca', Levitan observes.[28] But other times, for example at the end of *Phèdre*, he admits that Racine was unable to smooth over the ruptures and discontinuities in historical tradition. The monster from the deep which tears Hippolyte apart violently comes to represent the monstrous, alien quality of Senecan tragedy – 'a textual tradition not of a unified and continuous nature, but of another nature – indeed of an *other* or Seneca nature' (p. 210) – which lies within the Racinian, calm present.

Both writers were also concerned with the competing demands of reason and passion. Seneca explored the consequences of abandoning reason, of clouding the good judgement with physical appetite and base desire. For him, it was as if the clarity of reason which he believed lay at the foundation of every human mind was temporarily muddied over during the course of tragic events. Passion therefore seemed to be a man-made force, projected by our desires and weaknesses. 'We aren't afraid of the light; we have made everything into darkness for ourselves', he noted in a letter.[29] In contrast, Racine exposes a world in which reason can barely organise and restrain the unruly passions which drive each character. Underneath the decorum and restraint, according to one critic, spins a 'spiralling whirlwind of desire and aggression'.[30] Indeed, it can be argued that Racinian reason even paradoxically produces a form of irrationality. What Barthes has called Racine's 'elaborate book-keeping', in which there is a 'constant calculation of favours and obligations', leads to the terrible, uncontrollable feelings of jealousy, hate, infatuation and entrapment.[31] Quoting Pascal's comment on Descartes, that 'too much light darkens the mind', Lucien Goldmann suggests, in contrast to Seneca, that rationalism can actually make seeing or understanding more difficult.[32] And so it is that with searing precision and clarity, Racine's plays produce the turbulent agonies of imprisonment and despair driving his heroes and heroines.

The comparison between Seneca and Racine, therefore, is illuminating. It exposes the ambivalent relationship between theory and practice, or between reason and emotion, which lies at the heart of their plays and which of course is one of the central concerns of tragedy in general. By its exposure of irra-tionality, delusion and compulsion, the comparison between the writers high-lights the issue of metaphysical scepticism which dogs the tragic sense. And, finally, it raises the question of the connection between ancient and modern tragedy and the continuity of the tragic tradition. In their engagement with ancient Greek tragedy, and with each other, both playwrights interrogate the relevance of the tragic legacy to contemporary concerns. Can ancient tragedy continue to resonate today? How can we return to it? And how can we progress from it?

Seneca and Stoic reason

Seneca's two careers, as a philosopher and as a tragic playwright, have puzzled critics. How could the advocate of Stoicism – the belief that the gods were impervious to human dilemmas and therefore one should let reason guide the soul, free from emotional anxiety – be the same man who wrote the plays full of blood and guts? How could a rational philosopher create dramas which dealt with irrational passion and violent revenge? The connection between philosophy and drama becomes more understandable, however, when one recognises the strangely cerebral nature of Seneca's plays. These were plays written to be read rather than performed, and as result they become mental theatre, rather than physically enacted. Peter Brook, who directed a production of Seneca's *Oedipus* at London's Old Vic in 1968, explained the implications of the fact that Seneca's plays may never have been publicly performed:

> Seneca's play has no external action whatsoever . . . It takes place nowhere, the people are not people, and the vivid action, as it moves through the verbal images, leaps forward and back with the technique of the cinema and with a freedom beyond film. So this is theatre liberated from scenery, liberated from costume, liberated from stage moves, gestures and business.[33]

Supposedly 'liberated' from the demands of physical theatre, the characters in Seneca's plays are able to reveal their 'inner dynamism'. They struggle to become good, stoic citizens against the temptation to yield to atavistic hatred and desire. Each play focuses upon a character who might be described, in Latin, as a *proficiens*, a novice Stoic. He is tested and tempted, during the course of the play, to abandon Stoic teaching. And since the tragedies arguably teach readers through negative example, we witness, in each case, the *proficiens* abandoning the lessons of philosophy.[34] In *Thyestes*, there are several examples of a *proficiens* -type character. At the beginning, the ghost of Tantalus attempts to resist the Fury, only to succumb despite his better judgement: 'My belly / Aches with the agony of my old hunger / Awakened at thy bidding' (97–8; Watling translation). A scene later, Atreus himself voices some reluctance before he gives in to irrational desire to carry out his brutal act of vengeance:

> My heart is shaken with a storm
> Of passion that confounds it to its centre.
> I am compelled, although I know not whither,
> I am compelled by forces . . .   (260–2)

But the most dramatic example of the *proficiens* is Thyestes, who agonises over the decision to return to his brother Atreus: 'Why should my fear have limits, when his power is boundless as his hate' (483–4). His fear of Atreus is based upon irrational instinct ('boundless', immeasurable) and also upon a judicious calculation of Atreus' vengeful character. But he is finally persuaded to return, not so much out of reasonable willingness to imagine a reconciliation (as his son suggests) but rather out of a greedy desire to share the throne. In other words, he allows the lust for worldly power to overcome his better, Stoical judgement, and from then on, he is abandoned to his fate.

Senecan darkness

The forces which overwhelm the reason, in Seneca's plays, emanate from a mysterious, unfathomable source, impenetrable to scrutiny or analysis. Reason can only hope to control or repress these forces, not to understand them. They are figured, in the plays, by the image of darkness. Repeatedly the disappearance of reason is symbolised by the shadowing over of the sun and the onset of darkness. *Oedipus*, for example, opens with the unnatural shadiness of the sun:

> The night is at an end; but dimly yet
> The Lord Sun shows his face – a dull glow rising
> Out of a dusky cloud. It is a torch
> Of evil omen, this pale fire he brings
> With which to scan our plague-polluted homes.
>
>   (1–5)

This opening image becomes particularly significant when one recognises Seneca's departure from Sophocles' version, in which the process of bringing the secret past out into the light becomes so important. 'Anyone searching for the truth, my king, might learn it from the prophet, clear as day' (*ekmathoi saphestata*: 286), says the chorus, in Sophocles' *Oedipus Tyrannus*. But in Seneca, nothing is clear and nothing can be learnt, because evil is illogical, murky and chaotic. Oedipus discovers about his terrible past, not through his own powers of deduction, as in Sophocles, but from the ghost of his father, who is summoned from the 'everlasting night' of the Underworld. Moreover, darkness allows irrational, violent atrocities to happen. Since, according to Stoicism, the rational man could not commit acts of passion, the only explanation for evil is that reason was somehow occluded, darkness overwhelmed the judgement. So we see characters invoking the night in order to license the crimes they long to commit. In a speech which gets picked up again in Shakespeare's *Macbeth*, the Fury in *Thyestes* demands darkness so that the events of the subsequent play can proceed:

> FURY What right have stars to twinkle in the sky?
>   Why need their lights still ornament the world?
>   Let night be black, let there be no more day.
>   Let havoc rule this house; call blood and strife
>   And death; let every corner of this place
>   Be filled with the revenge of Tantalus!
>
>   (49–53)

The external world becomes no more than a projection of the internal mental state: both dark, both indistinct.

The events of the plays occur in a dark world, in which reason has departed and instinctual forces have been let loose. There are, therefore, no causes and consequences that can be analysed. Ghosts and furies prove to be adequate motivation; gut-wrenching fear is dramatic effect. Tantalus describes the passion for vengeance as a 'fire of thirst' coursing through his body. And Thyestes vividly feels the sin of his cannibalism of his own children as a physical nausea: 'My stomach moves; the sin within me strives / To find escape – cannot escape its prison' (1041–2). The lack of rational causation means that there is no sense, in Seneca, of the progress of history, of a before and after. Everything is reduced to a nightmarish present, in which fate is predestined, the atrocity has effectively already happened. The image of Thyestes feasting on his children, their body parts already in his stomach, figures precisely this hellish sense of enclosure, the literal absorption of past, present and future into the sickening compulsion of appetite. Indeed in the 1994 Royal Court Theatre's production of Caryl Churchill's translation of the play, the actors playing the ghosts of Tantalus and the Fury also doubled as Thyestes and his son, the Young Tantalus, thus emphasising this sense of claustrophobic repetition across generations.[35]

Seneca's nightmarish present, bereft of historical progress by the departure of reason and by the darkness, drags up past and future as mirages, in a demonic cycle. The past is recalled as a curse or a ghost; the future is conjured up as a picture of a theatrical scene to come. One might say that Seneca is cinematic in his capacity to imagine a montage of scenes, cutting and splicing simultaneously. So the messenger, in the *Troades*, describes the sacrifice of Polixena as a theatrical tragedy, which might be screened sometime in the future (1123–6).[36] And Atreus, when plotting his revenge in *Thyestes*, sees a picture of it in his mind, as if it has already happened: 'A picture of the murder, done, complete, / Rises before my eyes . . . the father's mouth / Devouring his lamented little ones . . .' (281–3). The messenger, when describing the event, also conjures up the scene in his mind, like a cinematic flashback: 'A picture of the brutal deed still floats / Before my eyes' (635–6). As in the cinema, he is absorbed by the spectacle, unable to rationalise what he saw but only to live again the fear as a traumatic recollection.

The conclusions of Seneca's plays resolve nothing. The present, after all, is apparently limitless and endlessly repeating, and so the future will just be a continuation of this. Thyestes returns to the darkness, to join the other ghosts and furies. The past, after all, was symbolised by a mythological precedent, which was never adequately explained but which was just given an overwhelming irrational force in the drama. And the future, back in the Underworld with those mythological beings, will just continue that mysterious turbulence. We are left, as William Levitan puts it, with 'the hallucination of the world as an endless theatre of action', in which images are conjured up and disappear and mythological precedent is 'internalized as a principle of absolute necessity'.[37]

Racine's light

While Seneca's plays open with the darkening of the sun and the anticipation of sinister night, Racine's begin with the sunrise. Bright clarity, however, is no comfort. The sun is the source of powerful fate, the guarantor of terrifying inevitability. *Iphigenie*, for example, begins in the pre-dawn darkness, as Agamemnon tries to reverse the anticipated course of events by warning his wife and daughter not to come to Aulis. But by the end of the first scene, the sun has risen, symbolising the unstoppable chain of events to come. 'Now the day is dawning, it is lighter. / Men are about. Someone is coming here; / It is Achilles' (158–60), says Agamemnon, realising that, with Achilles' arrival, his attempt to forestall the plot to ensnare his daughter has failed. Later Clytemnestra, picking up a reference to Seneca's *Thyestes*, begs the sun to become unnatural and thus to avert the course of fate:

> And you, O sun! who in this land behold
> The heir and true son of Atreus, who
> Did not dare shine upon the father's feast,
> Go back! They taught you this unhallowed path.
>   (1689–92; Cairncross translation)

'Generally born with the tragedy itself (which is a day), the Sun becomes murderous along with it', commented Barthes. 'The Sun's daily appearance is a wound inflicted upon the natural milieu of the night.'[38]

The lucidity of the sun also takes on a judgemental, punitive force. It witnesses everything. While in Seneca, the darkness gave licence to limitless violence, in Racine the light is equally horrific because it allows nothing to escape its interrogation and enforces an unceasing sense of guilt. Nowhere is this sense of the constant gaze which one must endure articulated more vividly than in Phèdre's agonised speech:

> My forebears fill the sky, the universe.
> Where can I hide? In dark infernal night?
> No, there my father holds the urn of doom.
>   (1276–78; Cairncross translation)

The clarity of the gaze simply reveals the imprisonment and guilt of the tragic hero. But, anticipating Foucault's reading of Bentham's Panopticon, it arguably also produces it. For just as the prisoner internalises the gaze of the prison guard, according to Foucault, and disciplines his behaviour to comply with the imagined guard's wishes, so Phèdre is riveted by the permanent, unseen gaze of the spectator, whether that is the audience in the theatre, the sun in the sky or all the gods in the universe.[39] The clarity of vision, focused upon her, enforces the rules.

In a similar way, the formal style and logical structure of the plays constitute a type of lucidity which controls unruliness. The poise of the Alexandrine verse is always held in tension with the physical disintegration of characters. We watch 'the most disruptive emotions being organized into a rational pattern', according to one critic, Richard Parrish, and this process forces a self-consciousness about theatre's potential upon the audience: 'We are protected from the primary experience through the safeguard of the fiction, the lie in other words, that is myth, that is theatre, that is dramatic text'.[40] So Racine's theatre has always been associated with a special rhetoric of performance. In the seventeenth century, this rhetoric was evident in the 'grand gestures' of the actors and the way in which they recited the verse, making it exaggerated, larger than life.[41] Recently, the New York avant-garde theatre company, the Wooster Group, experimented, in its adaptation of *Phèdre* entitled *To You The Birdie*, with a modern, technological rhetoric, in which the actors' voices were replaced with microphoned synch, and their bodies substituted by body images on video screens. 'The space is saturated with things that are coming apart from their sources', wrote one reviewer, Steven Connor.[42] Radically preventing any natural engagement between the audience and actors, because all the technology impeded the view, the Wooster Group well exemplified the capacity for rational form, in Racine, to contain and simultaneously dismember the irrational body.

Racinian lucid constraint

The Racinian stage itself, as Barthes has pointed out, becomes a form of constraint, regulating the actors' movements so that they are left virtually immobile. This stasis is visibly literal, in that no character really does anything or goes anywhere in a Racine play. There is instead a series of promised but unrealised departures. *Berenice*, for example, opens with Antiochus' anticipated exit: 'I come only to say . . . I leave, still faithful, though all hope is gone' (40, 46; Cairncross translation). And *Phèdre* begins with Hippolytus' decision to depart, only for all the rest of the play's events to thwart this: 'It is resolved, Theramenes. I go. I will depart from Troezen's pleasant land' (1–2).

But the immobility is also to be detected on a more metaphorical level. Characters are held in place by their dependence upon others, by the network

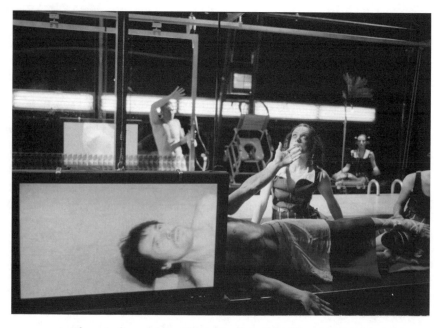

4. Theseus dismembered by technology. The Wooster Group's production of *To You the Birdie* (Racine's *Phèdre*), 2002. © Geraint Lewis

of relationships which structure the plots. These form, as one critic has put it, a 'perfect balance of terror'. *Andromaque* offers a good example. Each character loves somebody and is in turn loved by somebody else, in a chain of infatuation and unrequited love. Andromache is committed to her dead husband Hector and is in turn sought by Pyrrhus; Pyrrhus himself is pursued by Hermione; Hermione is loved by Orestes. Each relationship is carefully balanced between love and hate, according to whether the beloved object encourages or spurns the lover, and minute changes of attitude can tip the balance dramatically. In the course of just one speech to his friend Pylades, Orestes fluctuates between desire for Hermione, then hate after he has been rejected and he learns that she has been scorned by somebody else, and then back inevitably to softening love again; so infatuated is Orestes that his sense of morality becomes governed by Hermione's whims. He is prepared to kill Pyrrhus, because he thinks it will please Hermione, since she has been spurned by him. But of course, Hermione's temporary annoyance at Pyrrhus quickly converts back to love. The rules change with Hermione's heart. Orestes finds himself confused, uncertain on what stable set of values or imperatives he can depend. I quote from Douglas Dunn's fine translation:

Hermione? Could it be you I heard
And saw? For whom, then, was the King murdered,
Stabbed through until his blood flowed in the gutter?
Oh, if it's true, then I'm a murderer!
Did Pyrrhus die? Am I still who I was?
I suffocate lucidity because
The truth's unbearable – I've killed a King
And with that deed I've wiped out everything.

(1565–70)

Even Andromache, who commits suicide to join her dead husband, has compromised that unchanging commitment by marrying Pyrrhus first, to ensure the future safety of her son, Astyanax. Orestes is right, then, to question his ethics and identity. Despite the apparent regulation and stable restraints, what is there remaining on which to pin one's beliefs?

The third level of regulation, beside the literal stage performance and the metaphorical social structures, is the metaphysical: the judicial and punitive gaze of God. Many critics, most notably Lucien Goldmann, have pointed out the influence of Jansenist beliefs on Racine's theological context for his plays. The Jansenists were a very reclusive sect of the Protestant Church in France with doctrines similar to Calvinism in Scotland. Crucially, they believed that people were predestined to be either saved or condemned and they could do nothing to change God's favour. But paradoxically the fate of each person was unknown and unknowable and thus it was each person's duty to act as if he or she could win God's grace. Pascal, one of the best-known Jansenist writers and Racine's contemporary, explains:

> All men are compelled to believe, but with a belief mingled with fear and not accompanied by certainty, that they belong to the small number of the Elect whom Jesus Christ wishes to save; and that they should never place any man now alive, however wicked and impious he may be, for as long as he has a moment of life, elsewhere than in the ranks of the Predestined, leaving the distinction between the Elect and the Reprobate as part of the impenetrable secret of God.[43]

The important feature of Jansenist doctrine, from Racine's point of view, was its emphasis upon the 'impenetrable secret of God', upon the limits of human understanding and the unknowable mind of God. He was a 'hidden God', according to Goldmann, all powerful and yet inscrutable. People therefore had to operate according to a set of demands or a code of ethics which were, by necessity, unknown. They had to guess the mind of God, operate constantly as if they were both favoured and also guilty. It was like walking a tightrope stretched across a chasm whose boundaries and hazards were opaque. 'Nature has placed us so exactly at the very centre of things that we cannot move to one side without upsetting the balance', noted Pascal, highlighting how the metaphysical uncertainty led paradoxically to fixed and self-regulated immobility.[44] The uncertainty about the 'hidden God' and its implications for Racine's tragedies have been interpreted very differently by Racinian critics. According to Goldmann, Racine's dramas exemplify Jansenist doctrine faithfully. In other words, the action is presided over by a hidden God. Some characters are blinded by the illusion that they are free to make choices and act independently; the main heroines, however, realise that they are 'called', see the 'truth' of God's judgement, and must therefore depart this world and this life simultaneously. Racine's tragic vision is thus 'the radical opposition between, on the one hand, a world of beings lacking in authentic awareness and human greatness and, on the other, the tragic characters whose greatness lies precisely in the fact that they refuse this world and this life'.[45] In contrast, Roland Barthes suggests that Racine opens up Jansenist belief to a radical scepticism. The unknowability of God means that characters substitute their own fears, desire and pangs of guilt for the truth about God. They prefer to ascribe motivation to the structure of things, to the compulsion of Destiny as figured by the plot, to their own internalised guilt, rather than seeing God as the prime cause. 'Destiny permits the tragic hero partially to blind himself as to the source of his misfortune', explains Barthes. The tragic hero 'experiences [Destiny] as a form . . . and this formalism permits him modestly to avoid God without, all the same, abandoning him'.[46]

Phèdre

An analysis of *Phèdre*, the tragedy which raises the issue of guilt and condemnation more acutely than any other, should illustrate the debate between Goldmann and Barthes. In this play, speech is as dreadful and incriminating as action. Phèdre, after being prepared to die rather than reveal the cause of her agony at the beginning, is persuaded by her confidante, Oenone, to disclose her love to her stepson, Hippolytus. Rejected by him, she feels as if she is already guilty of incest, as if the declaration were tantamount to the act. Again, as in *Andromaque*, Phèdre's sense of morality is determined by the minute fluctuations in circumstance, by Hippolytus' encouragement or discouragement and by whether her husband, Theseus, is dead or alive. 'I to Hippolytus have bared my shame, And hope, despite me, has seduced my heart' (767–8), she confesses, charting this oscillation between hope and despair. She does nothing, even allowing Oenone to tell the lie about Hippolytus' incestuous pursuit of her rather than activating that deception herself. But the overwhelming guilt which she feels is internalised, self-generated, because it begins in the heart, not with the hands. As Racine comments in the preface to the play, 'The very thought of crime is regarded with as much horror as crime itself'. The question is: how does Phaedra know that she is guilty?

According to Goldmann, Phèdre recognises the truth of her tragic election by God. Finally divested of all hope and illusion, she comes to an intimation of the punitive, hidden God who presides over everything. This accords with her terrifying recognition that she cannot escape condemnation:

> I reek with foulest incest and deceit,
> My hands, that strain for murder and revenge,
> Burn with desire to plunge in guiltless blood.
> Wretch! and I live and can endure the gaze
> Of the most sacred sun from which I spring.
> My grandsire is the lord of all the gods;
> My forebears fill the sky, the universe.
> Where can I hide? In dark infernal night?
> No, there my father holds the urn of doom
> Destiny placed it in his ruthless hands.
> Minos judges in hell the trembling dead.
> Ah! how his horror-stricken shade will start
> To see before him his own daughter stand,
> Forced to admit to such a host of sins
> And some, perhaps, unknown even in hell!
> What, father, will you say to that dread sight?
>
> (1270–85)

With heroic courage, Phèdre confronts and 'endures the gaze' of the objective, hidden God, terrifying though that is. All other worldly concerns fall away, while the fact that the gaze never falters is strangely reassuring.

According to Barthes, however, Phèdre's paranoia, creating her sense of guilt and condemnation before anything has been enacted or is known, reveals the extent to which justice, destiny and metaphysical judgement are mental projections in Racine's world, to compensate for the vacuum which is a knowable God. 'We might say that every tragic hero is born innocent: he becomes guilty in order to save God', observes Barthes. 'Racinian theology is an inverted redemption; it is man who atones for God' (p. 46). Since guilt seems to be synonymous with speech, it is the structure of secrecy and avowal which forms the evil in the play, not the adultery or incest itself which, as Phèdre acknowledges regretfully, never happens: 'Alas, my sad heart never has enjoyed / The fruits of crimes whose dark shame follows me' (1291–2). So Barthes maintains that the logic of repression paradoxically engenders Phèdre's guilt and agony: 'Phaedra's objective guilt . . . is actually an artificial construction, intended to naturalise the suffering of the secret, to change form into content usefully . . . Evil is terrible to the very degree that it is empty, man suffers from a *form* . . . Phaedra's entire effort consists in fulfilling her transgression, that is, in absolving God' (p. 124).

Racinian logic, then, paradoxically produces passion, terror, paranoia and guilt. It leaves its protagonists locked in a solipsistic world, uncertain whether it is ultimately presided over by a malicious, punitive God or whether that God is just a negative projection of the structure of their mental lives. And so Racine's plays end arguably as claustrophobically as Seneca's. There is a circularity to his view of history too; the present will not evolve into the future. In *Andromaque*, Orestes will die rather than escape to Epirus and Hermione will be forever locked in guilt. In *Berenice*, all three lovers will spend the rest of their days in recollection of the other, unable to live together but equally unable to relinquish each other. They form a monument to mental stasis and blackmail:

> Let us, all three, exemplify
> The most devoted, tender, ill-starred love
> Whose grievous history time will e'er record.
>   (1502–4)

It has been suggested that Racine's plays bear witness to the development of a new order, that new types of economy or kinship are depicted in the plays and seem to be predicted for the future.[47] So, for example, in *Andromaque*, Astyanax represents a new type of future based on other relationship connections rather than looking back to dead Hector. And in *Iphigenie*, Iphigenie lives while Eriphyle dies, so that her priorities – social relationships, duty to one's father and community – prevail over commitment to the tragic, hidden God of Pascal.

But this interpretation, it seems to me, pins too much emphasis upon the possibilities of rational choice and the logic of historical progress in Racine. Rather, the experience of watching Racine is to open oneself up to the terrifying illogic of rational, theological belief, to the ruptures and discontinuities in the world which are exacerbated by compression and repression. For this reason, the monster which seizes Hippolytus at the end of *Phèdre*, drawn straight from Seneca's version of the play, is a crucial reminder of the impossibility of making a clean break with the past and of understanding clearly our relationship with it. I finish with the striking description of the monster's eruption from the sea, in Ted Hughes' appropriately visceral translation:

A sudden skull-splitting roar,
An indescribable, terrible, tearing voice,
Like lightning flash and thunderclap together,
Made us all duck and cower.
It came out of the sea, as if the whole sea
Had bellowed.
And then, like an echo to it,
Another roaring groan, subterranean,
As if something that groaned were trying to scream,
Rolled through the earth under our feet.[48]

2.3 Shakespeare

Critics have commented repeatedly that it is difficult to write about Shakespearean tragedy. A. P. Rossiter, for example, remarked on the 'sense of mystery which all critics agree to find in Shakespearean tragedy' and which defies definition or characterisation.[49] According to recent critic Tom McAlindon, it is perhaps easier to write about various tragedies by Shakespeare than to sum up the quintessential component of Shakespearean tragedy.[50] The particular difficulty in defining Shakespearean tragedy could be derived from the fact that all Shakespeare's tragedies challenged existing generic conventions, whether it be the revenge tragedy, the fall of kings, the evil of tyranny or doomed love. In the climate of late sixteenth- and early seventeenth-century Renaissance England, which was witnessing changes in political, religious and philosophical thinking prompted in part by the Reformation, the old models for tragedy inherited from medieval or early Renaissance traditions no longer seemed relevant or appropriate. Shakespeare's experiments with different dramatic structures and ideas could be considered responses to the confusion and uncertainty of his times but it means that the standards by which we can judge the nature of his tragic sense were invented, or at least developed, by the playwright himself.

The second reason why it is difficult to write about Shakespearean tragedy is that Shakespeare combined tragedy and comedy in his plays. This 'mungrell form' earned a degree of opprobrium at the time (Philip Sidney scorned Shakespeare's mixture of high and low genres) but garnered admiration a century later. 'Shakespeare's plays are not in the rigorous and critical sense either tragedies or comedies, but compositions of a distinct kind; exhibiting the real state of sublunary nature, which partakes of good and evil, joy and sorrow, mingled with endless variety of proportion and innumerable modes of combination', observed Samuel Johnson.[51] Each play contains elements of the tragic and the comic, regardless of whether it was originally designated in

Heming's and Condell's First Folio edition of 1623 as a 'tragedie', a 'comedie', a 'historie' or a 'romance'. Indeed, because of the mixed generic character of Shakespeare's plays, there is no fixed tragic canon and it is by no means clear which plays should be included in a discussion of 'Shakespearean tragedy'. Can one bring 'comedies' like *The Merchant of Venice* or *Love's Labour's Lost* into the debate? Should one also consider 'histories' like *Richard II* or the *Henry VI* trilogy? Is it indeed right to include *Hamlet* which A. P. Rossiter regarded more as a 'problem play' than a 'tragedy'? And what, indeed, are we to make of the 'problem plays' like *Measure for Measure* or *All's Well That Ends Well* ? When analysing Shakespeare, it is inevitable that the critic must range across his work, thinking about elements of the tragic which are evident in many different plays and pondering the very fine distinctions between tragedy and comedy.

Finally it is difficult to write about Shakespearean tragedy because of the particular simultaneously creative and destructive vision inherent in the language of the plays. Repeatedly, Shakespeare's characters, who are alive to the magical power of theatre, create, through their vivid language, what Coriolanus calls a 'world elsewhere', a realm of different perspectives and values to which they can escape or which can be invoked to intervene in this world. This world of the imagination, which Ibsen arguably inherited from Shakespeare, tantalises by its equivocal existence in reality, transgressing fixed definition until, as Macbeth says, 'nothing is but what is not'. The loss of this vision at different moments in the plays is a cause both for sorrow and joy, and replicates the ambiguous status of theatre itself.

However these three areas of difficulty in Shakespeare are also paradoxically the source of his power. It is in the nature of his tragic sense to defy explanation and to confound categorisation. It is for this reason that audiences and critics have been compelled by his plays, because, in its perennial need to understand the cause of things, each generation believes it can get to the heart of Shakespeare as never before and is consequently drawn into the complexity of Macbeth's conscience or the tangled motivation of a Iago.

Political change

Shakespeare's challenge to the traditional concept of tragedy was intimately bound up with the transformation of the political, religious and philosophical ideas of his day. In the sixteenth century, the authority of the king was believed to be derived from God. The medieval view that 'a king was to be seen as God's deputy on earth, ruling with the same loving care that a father showed for his family' still largely prevailed and was in fact useful to the Tudors, since their original claim to the throne, after the Wars of the Roses, was disputed.[52] According to this medieval theory, the king's place in the court replicated God's role in the universe, and political order in the state mirrored the natural order of the cosmos. The classic account of this notion of natural order is articulated by Ulysses in Shakespeare's *Troilus and Cressida*:

> The heavens themselves, the planets, and this centre
> Observe degree, priority, and place,
> Infixture, course, proportion, season, form,
> Office and custom, in all line of order.
> And therefore is the glorious planet Sol
> In noble eminence enthroned and sphered
> Amidst the other, whose med'cinable eye
> Corrects the ill aspects of planets evil
> And posts like the commandment of a king,
> Sans check, to good and bad.   (I.iii.85–94)

If anything went wrong, it was believed to be the fault of individuals and not that of the unchanging natural order. So George Puttenham could argue that tragedy was caused by the rise and fall of an individual king, framed by a stable political system which remained constant throughout the 'dolefall falls of unfortunate and afflicted Princes'.[53]

But, as Jonathan Dollimore argues in *Radical Tragedy*, 'culture itself is not a unitary phenomenon' and though some preachers may have been declaiming the king as God's representative on earth, others were seriously questioning the link between secular and religious authority while still others were cynically exploiting the old 'World Picture' ideology as a 'creed of absolutism to bolster up a precarious monarchy which lacked a standing army or an efficient police force'.[54] Machiavelli had written that princes were made not by God but by the state and by their ability to seize power, while another Elizabethan had observed that a monarch could gain the throne through 'money, arms, counsel, friends, and fortune'.[55] Since the philosophers of the Reformation were claiming that communication with God could be conducted by each person alone without the intervention of the pope, bishop or monarch, the importance of the clerisy was becoming undermined. Moreover in England, religious change had coincided with the ascension of different monarchs to the throne, as the country lurched between Protestantism and Catholicism depending on whether Edward VI, Mary or Elizabeth was sovereign. The result was to destabilise a fixed sense of the unchanging authority of the monarch and his or her link with God.

The cause of tragedy could therefore be attributed either to the king, with his fatal flaw, or to the fluctuating state of the world. Early Renaissance attempts to define tragedy respond to this confusion, by giving contradictory accounts of the genre. Philip Sidney, for example, observed in the *Defence of Poesy* that tragedy made 'Kinges feare to be Tyrants, and Tyrants manifest their tirannicall humors', thus suggesting that the cause of tragedy was the rise and fall of the individual monarch. But he also noted that tragedy 'teacheth the uncertainty of this world, and upon how weak foundations gilden roofs are builded'.[56] The contradictions inherent in these early Renaissance accounts can be detected in the modern critical debate about the cause of Shakespearean tragedy, which pits the view, promoted first by Bradley, that the downfall of Shakespeare's tragic heroes is caused by a 'flaw' in their character, against Rossiter's claim that the tragic flaw argument 'shifts all blame from the universe', by suggesting, as Cassius does in *Julius Caesar*, that the 'fault lies . . . in ourselves' and not in the unstable, political system.[57]

Puttenham's or Sidney's accounts of the tragic rise and fall of princes, while they may have been set in a context of 'the uncertainty of this world', depended upon a fixed sense of the identity of the prince. It was precisely this stable sense of the self, as evidenced in the identity of the king, which Shakespeare's plays challenged. Admittedly Christopher Marlowe, the leading playwright in London when Shakespeare first arrived there from Stratford, celebrated in his plays the glorious opportunism which the more fluid Machiavellian political system appeared to afford him, but he never questioned the coherent, stable figure of the monarch himself. His anti-hero Tamburlaine, for example, snatches at the chances for self-aggrandisement which the new chaos of the times seems to allow:

> Nature, that fram'd us of four elements,
> Warring within our breasts for regiment,
> Doth teach us all to have aspiring minds.
>   (Part One, II.vii.18–20)

He becomes the most awe-inspiring tyrant, feeling no qualms of conscience as he conquers vast sections of the known world. The flamboyant and exciting language, which Marlowe gives his anti-hero, reflects the shifting value of individual aspiration and social-climbing and has led critics to view this as a subversive play, which challenges the political and religious orthodoxy.[58] 'Come, let us march against the powers of heaven, / And set black streamers in the firmament, / To signify the slaughter of the gods' (Part Two, V.iii.48–50), Tamburlaine declares even as his body is wasting away with disease. At one point, just before the end, Tamburlaine questions the purpose of his life of conquest, in a Macbeth-like existential moment. Looking at a map with his sons, he considers how much of the world lies outside his empire: 'And shall I die, and this unconquered?' (Part Two, V.iii.151). Yet the nature of Tamburlaine's tyranny is never left open to doubt in Marlowe's two plays and, at the end, his son Amyras is crowned to continue the family business: 'Heavens witness me with what a broken heart / And damned spirit I ascend this seat' (Part Two, V.iii.207–8).

By contrast, in Shakespeare's plays the divine status of the monarch is radically questioned and the doubt over the king's identity results in terrifying, violent chaos. The possibility for individual ambition, which in Marlowe was the source of powerful desire, becomes in Shakespeare the cause of great anxiety and alters the generic tragic pattern of the 'fall of princes' altogether. This anxiety – sparked by the question of whether the king was quintessentially monarchical or simply performed a functional role as head of state – is evident in the long *Henry VI* trilogy, in which warring lords battle to gain control of the kingdom, while the ineffective king grieves over the violence attendant on such power vacuums. It is evident too in the contrast between Hotspur, with his excellent leadership skills but non-royal background, and the irresponsible prince-in-waiting Hal, in *Henry IV* Part I. 'O, that it could be proved / That some night-tripping fairy had exchanged / In cradle clothes our children where they lay, / And called mine Percy, his Plantagenet!' (I.i.85–8), says his father, suggesting that the natural order might have been magically inverted and that his real heir could be the admirable Henry Hotspur, Lord Percy. Hal, of course, confesses that he is only acting the part of a dissolute – 'herein will I imitate the sun / Who doth permit the base contagious clouds / To smother up his beauty from the world' (I.ii.175–7) – but, given the fact that his father seized the throne and that England has experienced several generations of internecine wrangling over the monarchy, the divine nature of the sovereign is still seriously interrogated.

Richard II poses the question even more directly when the king abdicates, asking us to 'mark me how I will undo myself' (IV.i.193). In stripping himself of the accessories of the king (crown and sceptre), the king believes himself to be fragmenting internally, until he becomes 'nothing'. Since, under the traditional belief in the divine right of kings, public and private man are intimately connected, internecine political strife is replicated in the disintegration of the king's person:[59]

> Thus play I in one person many people,
> And none contented. Sometimes am I king;
> Then treason makes me wish myself a beggar,
> And so I am. Then crushing penury
> Persuades me I was better when a king.
> Then am I kinged again, and by and by
> Think that I am unkinged by Bolingbroke,
> And straight am nothing.   (V.v.31–8)

Richard, in prison, creates a world in his imagination, peopled with his thoughts. But since he plays all parts in his head, he is both monarch and subject, king and traitor, radically split by internal, political contradictions.

Macbeth, the most classical of Shakespeare's tragedies, might at first appear to work according to the traditional generic definition. We witness the hero becoming a tyrant, butchering most of Scotland. We hear of the various signs that the natural order of things, described lovingly by Duncan before entering Macbeth's castle, has been perverted: horses eating each other, falcons killed by mousing owls, and so on. As the play progresses, we watch the forces of good closing in around Macbeth and his evil deeds catching up with him. The unequivocal good is to be witnessed at King Edward's English court, where one touch from the king miraculously cures disease. This is a play in which judgement 'returns to plague the inventor'. It is a society in which each Thane should, in Lady Macbeth's words, 'know [his] own degree', a world which is rocked by Macbeth's ambitious over-reaching. 'Take but degree away', says Ulysses in *Troilus and Cressida*, 'untune that string, / And hark what discord follows' (I.iii.109–10).

Yet even in *Macbeth*, there can be no easy explanation. For in his efforts to will himself into the role of king, Macbeth is prepared, unlike Marlowe's Tamburlaine, to unite or fragment parts of himself which otherwise will not fit into the simple narrative of self-aggrandisement. The eye must wink at the hand; the light must not see into his dark desires; the life to come must be jumped. While Macbeth cannot acknowledge the parts of himself now given over to evil, he is willing to condense other parts which might still be alive to moral scruple. 'From this moment / The very firstlings of my heart shall be / The firstlings of my hand' (IV.i.162–4), he says, after hearing of the failure of his plan to kill Macduff, following the witches' warning. Supernatural soliciting equivocates with him, leading him on with one hand and holding him back with the other. Just as, according to the drunken porter, drink 'provokes the desire but takes away the performance' (II.iii.27–8), so thought and deed are hopelessly disconnected in the play's narrative. 'Art thou afeard / To be the same in thine own act and valour / As thou art in desire?' (I.vii.39–41), Lady Macbeth taunts her husband, but being the 'same' in word and deed is revealed, in the equivocal climate of Scotland, to be almost impossible.

Ambition is actually rewarded in Macbeth's Scotland, not to mention the capacity to act with the rapidity of thought. Macbeth, for example, is praised by Duncan for his brave and speedy thinking in the thick of battle, while Banquo is rewarded for keeping his own mind undefiled, despite the fact that he admits to lapsing occasionally into thoughts of murder himself: 'restrain in me the cursed thoughts that nature / Gives way to in repose' (II.i.8–9). In this climate of ambiguous incentive and prohibition, it is not surprising that Macbeth and Banquo might feel a little confused when an invitation to alter their status apparently presents itself to them. Why should one act of brave butchery be rewarded and another be fatally damned?

So the mutability of fortune which Sidney originally defined as essential to tragedy becomes a more nebulous mutability, in Stephen Greenblatt's words, of 'meltings, category confusions and liminal states'.[60] In *Macbeth*, these confusions arise on the border between fantasy and reality, between the demonic world of the witches and the secular world of civil warfare and political treachery. Fantasy daggers, weird sisters and the equivocal promises of the fiend possess an external reality and yet also proceed from the 'heat-oppressed brain'. In *Hamlet*, the prince's private dilemma is set against the background of Fortinbras' invasion to reclaim lands wrongly seized from his father by old King Hamlet. The general upheaval of this war, which arguably challenges the legitimacy of the Danish monarchy, only exacerbates the murkiness of the Danish justice system, which leaves unpunished and uninvestigated the old king's murder. Revenge tragedies before *Hamlet*, such as Thomas Kyd's *The Spanish Tragedy*, had shown that the demand for private revenge arose when faith in the public justice system had been eroded; *Hamlet* continues this tradition with Marcellus' statement, when the ghost appears, that 'something is rotten in the state of Denmark' (I.iv.67). It is perhaps no wonder that the philosophical Hamlet extends the political confusion already threatening the country to consider the epistemological confusion between form and formlessness, significance and insignificance. Man, according to him, is nothing more than a 'quintessence of dust' (II.ii.298); the air 'appears no other thing to me but a foul and pestilent congregation of vapours' (II.ii.293). Everything is rotting and disintegrating, in a 'fine revolution' (V.i.82–3) from birth to death to birth again, as it is gathered into dust and dispersed. As Hamlet contemplates the skull of Yorick, the king's jester, unearthed from the grave, he wonders whether anything can retain value or significance when it is going to end up decomposing in the ground.

Religious scepticism

Hamlet's observations at Ophelia's grave go to the heart of the religious ambiguity in Shakespeare's tragedies. On the one hand, the stories of Hamlet, Macbeth, Othello and others are set in a theological context, in which evil is condemned and repentance is granted grace. Yet on the other hand, repeatedly the plays also voice an existential sense of nihilism, as if there were no God and nothing actually mattered.

The contradictions in the religious belief which lie behind Shakespeare's tragedies are a product of the radical transformation in faith at this time. During the Reformation, the Protestant challenge to orthodox Catholicism questioned the evidence for faith. It was argued that the existence of God should be justified by internal belief alone, not through external signs or acts of confession or through the intervention of the priest. Moreover Protestants claimed that, during the Eucharist celebration, the bread and wine was not turned literally into Christ's body and blood, as the Catholics believed, but only symbolically. And the belief in Purgatory, where the souls of the dead waited for a period of time to be purged of their sins, was outlawed, with the result that the living had no power over the dead to communicate with their ghosts or try through prayer to shorten their time in purgatory. These developments meant that all the commonly held ideas about the symbolic or literal representation of divinity, about miracles and magic, and about the relationship between the living and the dead, were undergoing radical change. So confusing were these shifts in understanding that in some cases Protestantism had the unintended effect of producing what Debora Shuger describes as 'a sense of the absence of God that verges on despair'.[61]

It is possible to see the impact of the Reformation ideas upon Shakespeare's dramatic imagination by comparing his play *Macbeth*, written in 1606, with that of Marlowe's *Doctor Faustus*, written probably about 1592–3. Both plays depict men who transgress profound taboos and who are destined for eternal damnation. Yet they are divided in their understanding of what damnation entails because of their differing responses to Reformation scepticism and uncertainty. Marlowe's play is, in many ways, a simple morality play in which Faustus makes a calculated bargain with the devil (his soul in return for twenty-four years of pleasure) and is punished for it. 'Regard his hellish fall' (V.iii.23), the didactic chorus says at the end. On the other hand, the play is defiantly heretical in its portrayal of Faustus' bravado. Faustus reproves Mephistopheles, for not showing sufficient 'manly fortitude' (I.iii.85) when deprived of God in hell, and Marlowe clearly relished Faustus' comic taunting of the pope (III.ii). The play thus is based upon a confident belief that divine judgement exists, while happily challenging it. It ends with the simultaneous sense of God's powerful presence and absence, in that Faustus' damnation is caused both by divine decree and yet also by his proud despair which prevents him from calling upon God for mercy. His self-condemnation, seeing God's grace streaming across the sky which he is unable to accept, is echoed at the end of *Othello*. Othello imagines that when he meets Desdemona at the last judgement, her glance will 'hurl my soul from heaven / And fiends will snatch at it' (V.ii.281–2). Condemned to hell already, he therefore has nothing to lose by committing suicide.

Marlowe depicts a deterministic universe and yet also one which allows a scornful individual to challenge heaven and lose, through despair, any chance of a relationship with God. But *Macbeth* is more sceptical and uncertain than *Faustus* because the hero's motivation is more opaque. Faustus lists the voluptuous experiences he wishes to have; Macbeth, in contrast, cannot even name what he desires. Similarly, Faustus knows the identity of Mephistopheles and strikes a quantifiable bargain with him; Macbeth, in contrast, is mystified by the witches, whose influence over his actions is ambiguous. Do they determine his murder of Duncan and all the subsequent action, or is the evil inherent within him and simply foretold by the witches? Is the supernatural external or simply conjured up by the black desires of the protagonists? So finally the sceptical depression of Faustus and Macbeth differs widely. Faustus' disappointment is focused upon external, quantifiable and specific matters. 'Was this the face that launched a thousand ships?' (V.i.97), he says on seeing Helen of Troy; have I sold my soul for this? The precise calculation of the bargain vividly highlights the tragic downfall and disenchantment. But Macbeth's final sense of emptiness and disillusion is both more widespread and also harder to pin down:

> Tomorrow, and tomorrow, and tomorrow
> Creeps in this petty pace from day to day
> To the last syllable of recorded time
> And all our yesterdays have lighted fools
> The way to dusty death. Out, out, brief candle.
> Life's but a walking shadow, a poor player
> That struts and frets his hour upon the stage,
> And then is heard no more. It is a tale,
> Told by an idiot, full of sound and fury,
> Signifying nothing. (V.v.18–27)

Despite Macbeth's certainty about hell and the condemnation of his soul, he can still wearily articulate a sense of the meaninglessness of life and the insubstantiality of his actions, as if they carried no judgement or repercussions. Rather than Faustus' empty rewards for his personal satanic transaction, Macbeth's disillusion implies a larger vision of universal nihilism.

Hamlet also is caught between the vestiges of the Catholic faith and a new scientific and philosophical scepticism born of the kind of scholarly research being conducted by Francis Bacon and, a little later, Thomas Browne. The ghost of Hamlet's father is trapped in purgatory, because he was murdered before he was able to purge his sins by his last act of confession. When he calls on Hamlet to revenge him, it is as if a voice from a land that has been officially abolished by authority has spoken and indeed Hamlet himself is concerned less the ghost be sent from the devil to tempt him into sinful murder.[62] His worry later about killing his uncle Claudius while he is praying, when he is 'fit and seasoned for his passage' is also prompted by a residual memory of Catholic beliefs in purgatory, confession and the need to unburden oneself of sin before death. Yet elsewhere in the play, and chiefly in the scene at Ophelia's grave, Hamlet articulates a nihilistic conception of the impermanence of things and the lack of any theological or metaphysical significance in the world. 'Why may not imagination trace the noble dust of Alexander till he find it stopping a bung-hole?' (V.i.187–9), Hamlet asks, echoing the morbid thoughts about the physicality of death which were current in the work of Francis Bacon, Thomas Dekker, John Donne and, later, Thomas Browne. 'When thou shall see, and be assured . . . that to morrow thou must be tumbled into a Mucke-pit', wrote Thomas Dekker during the 1603 London plague, which was raging when the text of *Hamlet* was first published, 'and prest with threescore dead men, lying slovenly upon thee . . . (and see howe they may be revenged, for the wormes that breed out of their putrefying carcasses, shall crawle in huge swarmes from them and quite devoure thee) what agonies will this straunge newes drive thee into?'.[63] The scenes of physical decay and burial in the earth, which Dekker describes here and which Shakespeare must have witnessed around the time he was writing his greatest tragedies, dramatically challenge the religious belief in the immortal soul and the unique preciousness of each human life.

The play which raises the question of a theological explanation for events more than any other is *King Lear*. Although it is set in pre-Christian England, its concerns are provoked by the early seventeenth-century religious controversy. The play asks, repeatedly, about the cause of suffering. 'Is there any cause in nature that makes these hard hearts?' (III.vi.71–2), asks Lear about his daughters. 'You have some cause [not to love me], they have not' (IV.vii.76), he tells Cordelia. 'No cause, no cause', she replies. Even the initial love test, invented by Lear as the basis for his abdication and division of his kingdom, attempts to justify or quantify what should be left without forensic explanation 'I love your majesty / According to my bond; nor more nor less' (I.i.91–2), is Cordelia's defiant answer, resisting the logic of the game. Gloucester is determined to blame the gods for his misfortune – 'As flies to wanton boys are we to the gods / They kill us for their sport' (IV.i.37–8). And although Edmund scoffs at his father – 'This is the excellent foppery of the world, that, when we are sick in fortune . . . we make guilty of our disasters the sun, the moon, and stars' (I.ii.109–11) – he nevertheless declares that 'nature' is his 'goddess', thus implying that being a 'bastard' or being 'natural' accounts for his evil 'nature'.

The play also asks about redemption. Both principal male characters are offered chances for redemption. Lear is taken 'out o' the grave' (IV.vii.45) by Cordelia; Gloucester is miraculously saved from his suicidal impulse. But in either case, the sacred image of redemption is compromised by the circumstances or subsequent events. The rescue of Gloucester is particularly troubling, for it demonstrates, apparently, that redemption is dependent upon a lie. The blind Gloucester is conned by his disguised son Edgar that he is standing on the edge of Dover cliff. Edgar describes the scene so vividly that even the audience believes that he is looking down at the beach far below and not just at the flat stage: 'The fishermen, that walk upon the beach, / Appear like mice' (IV.vi.17–18). We suspend our disbelief under the power of theatre. Thus when Gloucester attempts to throw himself off the cliff and falls forward on the stage, he believes he has been saved, not by the relative brevity of his fall but by God's miraculous intervention. Edgar comes rushing up, pretending to be a different character from the one who led Gloucester to the cliff. A fiend must have tempted him to suicide, he tells Gloucester. Now God has cushioned his fall and prevented the devil from capturing his soul:

> As I stood here below, methought his eyes
> Were two full moons; he had a thousand noses,
> Horns whelked and waved like the enridged sea:
> It was some fiend. Therefore, thou happy father,
> Think that the clearest gods, who make them honours
> Of men's impossibilities, have preserved thee.
>
> (IV.vi.69–74)

Thus Shakespeare suggests that, since Gloucester's faith is restored by Edgar's story, goodness is a deception, based upon a fiction. Theological belief, as one critic notes, is the product of 'human manipulation'.[64] Set in the context of the early seventeenth-century Protestant challenge to the Catholic Eucharist – which had been exposed as theatrical 'miracle minting' according to Stephen Greenblatt, because the congregation was forced to believe that the bread and wine literally became Jesus' body and blood – Gloucester's 'miraculous' rescue at 'Dover cliff' highlights the gullible capacity of people desperate to believe in religious and theatrical illusion.[65]

In the nineteenth century, critics responded to the theological questions which *King Lear* poses very differently, believing that Lear journeys towards redemption. At the beginning of the twentieth century, A. C. Bradley observed that the play should be renamed *The Redemption of King Lear*, and argued, in a way that was to prove most influential for subsequent interpretations of the play, that the business of the gods with Lear was 'neither to torment him, nor to teach him a "noble anger", but to lead him to attain through apparently hopeless failure the very end and aim of life'.[66] Even more recently C. L. Barber has maintained that the play leaves us with the 'final effect of affirmation along with tragic loss'.[67] He points to the image of Lear with Cordelia in his arms as a religious icon, a reversal of the *Pietà*, so that instead of Mary with her dead son, we witness a father with his dead daughter. Certainly Shakespeare's audiences would have been familiar with such images, from paintings to representations in the popular mystery cycle plays. But it seems as if the religious beliefs and rituals in *King Lear* are mocked and inverted by the play's persistent negative response – Lear's 'Never, never, never, never, never' – rather than reaffirmed. Current critical reception of the play and recent performances have consequently stressed the nihilistic, theological bleakness of the play, rather than any signs of hope for divine grace.[68]

Challenging genre

The confusion over traditional political and religious certainties seems to have prompted, in Shakespeare, a resistance to the kinds of explanation which conventional notions of tragedy appeared to offer. To put it simply, there were three theatrical traditions of tragedy before Shakespeare. The vernacular medieval performances of the mystery cycle plays, mostly focusing on the life of Christ and staged on wagons touring around the country, mingled sacred and secular characters and attributed Christ's self-sacrifice to divine will. Meanwhile, the medieval morality plays, in which an 'Everyman' character is tested by allegorical figures and either proves himself or succumbs to temptation, suggested that moral dilemma lay at the heart of tragedy but that divine providence existed to reward or condemn the individual appropriately. Finally the more recent Renaissance tradition, which had revived Seneca and its concept of classical tragedy, depicted the fall of an individual, crushed by the inevitable forces of an unjust world.[69]

Shakespeare evoked at times these traditional tragic forms, so that, for example, Richard III or Iago can be seen as typical villains from the medieval morality play, reminiscent of the Malus Angelus of *Everyman*. But these tragic expectations were aroused only to be undermined as sufficient explanations of the play's events. In recounting the source of his grievance, Iago skips over the logical steps of his reasoning and thus illustrates what Coleridge famously described as 'the motive-hunting of his motiveless malignity'. Othello, too, who, as F. R. Leavis pointed out, is as much the cause of the tragedy as Iago, cannot fully acknowledge to himself the reasons for his loss of faith in Desdemona and his decision to murder her:

It is the cause, it is the cause, my soul.
Let me not name it to you, you chaste stars.

(V.ii.1–2)

And Hamlet repeatedly challenges people to understand him, complaining that they would 'pluck out the heart of my mystery, . . . sound me from my lowest note to the top of my compass' (III.ii.335–6), more easily than they would play upon a pipe. The motivation of both Othello and Hamlet, and indeed Shakespeare's other tragic heroes, remains opaque to us, as closed to our scrutiny as indeed it may be to the characters themselves. The generic confusion of Shakespeare's tragedies consequently lies in part in the psychological complexity and inscrutability of the human mind.

Tragi-comedy

The Dover cliff scene in *King Lear* has become, for critics, a touchstone in the debate about the religious significance of Shakespeare's plays. It is at this moment when the illusions of theatre and the fiction of belief appear to be mutually dependent and thus acutely interrogated. But this scene has also become important for another critical debate: the place of grotesque comedy in Shakespearean tragedy. Jan Kott points out the difference between the illusion that Gloucester has really thrown himself from Dover Cliff and the realisation that he has just fallen forward on the stage. Gloucester's 'suicidal leap is tragic' but the pantomime he performs on stage is 'grotesque'. Since Gloucester believes in the gods, his decision to commit suicide can be said to be tragic. But as the gods do not exist in *King Lear* and Edgar has merely staged a piece of theatre for him, his attempted suicide is arguably grotesquely comic. It makes no difference and does not alter human fate or challenge the gods. There is no context by which to judge the action, and it becomes therefore meaningless and potentially laughable.

Gloucester's suicidal leap is an extreme example of the grotesque, but repeatedly in Shakespeare's plays, characters lose the serious context in which their actions may be judged and find their tragic dignity subverted by a comic perspective. Early comedies merely undermine the serious aspirations of the low characters. In *Love's Labour's Lost*, for example, the locals try to stage a dramatisation of the 'Nine Worthies' for the princess and her court, only to find themselves laughed off the stage. 'You have put me out of countenance' (V.ii.614), one actor, the pedantic schoolmaster, Holofernes complains, after the aristocratic Biron has repeatedly interrupted him with teasing banter. And he advises another actor, Mote, to 'keep some state in thy exit, and vanish'

(V.ii.588). The court merely laughs at the embarrassment and disappointment of the local theatricals, until the messenger Mercade 'interrupt'st our merriment' (V.ii.710) to bring news of the king's death. Meanwhile, *Twelfth Night* mocks the acute discomfort of another character, when Toby, Maria, Feste and others taunt Malvolio with the accusation of being mad. Cross-gartered under the mistaken illusion that his mistress has requested this, Malvolio is imprisoned in a darkened room and visited by Feste, disguised as a priest. 'They have here propertied me, keep me in darkness, send ministers to me, asses, and do all they can to face me out of my wits' (IV.ii.93–5), Malvolio complains, and even Toby begins to be troubled that the joke has gone too far.

'Keeping some state', maintaining 'face' or 'countenance', proves to be impossible not only for these serious characters who happen to find themselves in comedies, but even for tragic characters. 'No more a soldier. Bruised pieces, do' (IV.xv.42), says Anthony, as he disarms himself before attempting suicide. But he turns out to have lost his soldierly 'state' not only because he has unbuckled his shield but also because he cannot dispatch himself cleanly with the sword, but must be hoisted up to the monument, a physically heavy casualty, to die in Cleopatra's arms. Hamlet also denies Polonius a dignified death, emphasising instead the grossness of the corpse, 'lug[ging] the guts into the neighbour room' (III.iv.186) and joking about Polonius at supper, 'not where he eats, but where a is eaten' (IV.iii.20). Hamlet himself acts the role of the fool in the play, replying to Polonius' serious questions with witty, nonsensical answers. Just as he describes to Polonius the clouds changing their shape, from a camel to a weasel to a whale, so the play threatens to lose its generic shape. 'Our wooing doth not end like an old play. / Jack hath not his Jill' (V.ii.860–1), Biron says at the end of *Love's Labour's Lost*, when the expected marriages of comedy are postponed by the king's death. So too the play of *Hamlet* refuses to retain its tragic shape, extending itself into farcical slapstick and digressive, black humour. Only by the careful cutting of potentially comic scenes – the banter with Polonius, the whole Rosencrantz and Guildenstern subplot – was Lawrence Olivier able to control carefully the way we view his seriously reflective and romantic film version of the play.

The confusion over the distinctions between tragedy and comedy in Shakespeare is also exacerbated by the fact that the stuff of his comedies is actually quite dark. Love, for example, is far from unproblematic. In *Midsummer Night's Dream*, it is artificially stimulated by Puck's love juice; in *Much Ado About Nothing*, the match between Beatrice and Benedict is brought about by a fiction which is deliberately overheard. Helena forces Bertram to marry her by tricking him into bed with her and then presenting him subsequently with the facts, in *All's Well That Ends Well*, while the horse-trading of partners goes on even more openly in *Troilus and Cressida*. Indeed, so devastating is Troilus' discovery of Cressida's betrayal of him with Diomedes that, like the inversion of nature provoked by the fall of kings, it seems as if 'the bonds of heaven are slipped, dissolved and loosed' (V.ii.159).

The cynical devaluing of love in Shakespeare's plays means that what is traditionally comedy's solution – love, courtship, marriage – becomes instead the source of some of its most poignant, and arguably tragic, effects. *Measure for Measure* and *The Merchant of Venice*, designated comedies in the First Folio but nowadays known rather as 'problem' plays or tragic-comedies, highlight the tragic potential of devalued love most acutely. Both plays apparently view relationships and marriage as a calculated, commercial exchange. Angelo, of course, strikes a hard bargain with Isabella, demanding her body in exchange for his leniency and thereby forcing her to weigh her chastity against her brother in the moral scales. But the duke also appeals to some debt which Isabella owes him for rescuing her brother from execution when proposing marriage to her:

> If he be like your brother, for his sake
> Is he pardoned; and for your lovely sake
> Give me your hand, and say you will be mine.
>
> (V.i.489–91)

Meanwhile, Shylock's notorious comparison between the loss of his daughter and the loss of his ducats, which is the source of some anti-semitic jokes ('I never heard a passion so confused / So strange, outrageous, and so variable / As the dog Jew did utter in the streets. / 'My daughter! O, my ducats! O, my daughter!" (II.viii.12–15)), merely extends the commercialisation of love manifested at Christian Belmont. Portia's choice of husband according to which metal casket he selects and her testing of fidelity through the exchange of a ring shares in common with Shylock the monetary, material measurement of love. And as Shylock and Portia discover, such love can disappear as easily as a ring is slipped from a finger.[70] In both *Measure for Measure* and *The Merchant of Venice*, characters attempt to pin down the slipperiness of love's experience by the literal application of law (Angelo's punishment for fornication; Shylock's pursuit of Antonio's bond). And both plays counter the impossibility of applying the law literally by using mercy perversely as a form of punishment. Instead of being executed, Shylock is forcibly converted to Christianity; rather than lose his life, Angelo is compelled to marry Mariana. In a tragically satiric inversion of the traditional marriage at the end of comedy, Lucio, who is also forced by the duke to marry, protests that he would rather be executed: 'Marrying a punk, my lord, is pressing to death, whipping and hanging' (V.i.521–2).

Disintegrating language

There are a couple of Shakespearean tragedies, of course, in which love is not treated cynically but where it becomes the transcendent force driving the characters to sacrifice everything else for its sake. *Romeo and Juliet* and *Anthony and Cleopatra* retain a sense of love's value, right to the point of death, but they do this through the power of their language and imagery. In both plays, language itself becomes the source of power and delight but also dangerous in its capacity to seduce the protagonists. In *Romeo and Juliet*, for example, the famous balcony wooing scene sweeps the two young lovers into a lasting commitment to each other within minutes, through the power of the rhetoric. Indeed Juliet rightly worries that Romeo resorts to love's clichés all too easily – 'swear not by the moon, th' inconstant moon' (II.i.151) – and that their conversation has precipitated their love too speedily: 'I have no joy of this contract tonight. / It is too rash, too unadvised, too sudden' (II.i.159–60). But she grounds the exchange not by suggesting more restraint and time for reflection, but by proposing marriage:

> Three words, dear Romeo, and good night indeed.
> If that thy bent of love be honourable,
> Thy purpose marriage, send me word tomorrow,
> By one that I'll procure to come to thee,
> Where and what time thou wilt perform the rite,
> And all my fortunes at thy foot I'll lay,
> And follow thee, my lord, throughout the world.
>
> (II.i.184–90)

Anthony's and Cleopatra's relationship is similarly based upon fantasy, game-playing and what they choose to believe about each other:

> CLEOPATRA If it be love indeed, tell me how much.
> ANTHONY There's beggary in the love that can be reckoned.
> CLEOPATRA I'll set a bourn how far to be beloved.
> ANTHONY Then must thou needs find out new heaven, new
> earth. (I.i.14–17)

They live by exaggeration, by finding 'new heaven, new earth' to express their feelings for one another. Even when facing death, their capacity of eloquent, self-delusion is undiminished. Anthony announces that he will be 'a bridegroom in my death' (IV.xv.100) before bathetically failing to kill himself; Cleopatra imagines her assistant Iras stealing the first kiss from Anthony in the Underworld before the poisonous asp has had time to kill her. As Ibsen's tragic protagonists were to discover later (*Master Builder, Rosmersholm*), Cleopatra's attempt to transform death into a positive escape from this imprisoning world and to resist a tragic interpretation of her end through her imagination, is open to challenge and doubt. 'I dreamt there was an Emperor Anthony', she tells Dolabella, Caesar's envoy. 'His legs bestrid the ocean; his reared arm / Crested the world ... Think you there was, or might be, such a man / As this I dreamt of?' (V.ii.75; 81–2; 92–3). When Dolabella replies 'Gentle madam, no', she berates him for lack of imagination. But if her 'fancy' or 'dream' about the colossal Anthony is unfounded, so it seems that her vision of life after death in the arms of Anthony may just be an illusion too. Just as Solness' transcendent image of himself victoriously building castles in the air is belied by his literal fall from the church steeple (Ibsen's *Master Builder*), so the reality of Cleopatra's death may be very grimly different from her erotic portrayal of it. 'Dost thou not see my baby at my breast, / That sucks the nurse asleep ... As sweet as balm, as soft as air, as gentle. / O Antony!' (V.ii.304–6) are her dying words as the poisonous snake kills her with its bite. But 'this is an aspic's trail, / And these fig-leaves have slime upon them' (V.ii.344–5) observes the guard bluntly when he finds the body, and Caesar has the prosaic last word: 'Most probable / That so she died' (V.ii.347–8).

Shakespeare's language has the capacity to create worlds which can then just as easily disintegrate and disappear. Prospero vows to 'drown his book' (V.i.57) in *The Tempest*, which has allowed him to 'bedim the noontide sun' and to dictate the events of the play through his 'airy charm' and 'rough magic'. Indeed *The Tempest* and the other late play, *The Winter's Tale*, comment upon theatre's ability to bring creatures to life, and just as easily relinquish them again. Paulina points out the very fine line between the rejuvenating power of theatre and its capacity to betray one's trust, as she is about to show Leontes the 'statue' of Hermione, now restored to life through her art. In reflecting upon the equivocal nature of theatrical illusion, these plays could be said to be more meta-theatrical comments upon tragedy, than tragedies themselves.

But the consciousness of theatre, for good or ill, is latent in the earlier plays and lies at the heart of Shakespeare's tragic sense. For theatre both allows action to be brought to life and yet also stands as a metaphor for the tragic insubstantiality of life itself. Macbeth's bleak comment, quoted earlier, is worth repeating here, because it reveals sharply the connection, in Shakespeare's tragedies, between theatre and a kind of existential despair:

> Life's but a walking shadow, a poor player
> That struts and frets his hour upon the stage,
> And then is heard no more.   (V.v.23–5)

Since the Elizabethan theatre relied very little upon props and not at all upon scenery, it demanded from its audience an active exercise of the imagination to transport them to another place. The little O of the Globe theatre becomes, in the course of the play, Macbeth's Scotland, Othello's Cyprus or Lear's heath, if the audience will allow Shakespeare and his theatricals, 'ciphers to this great account, on your imaginary forces [to] work'.[71] But it can just as easily dispel that illusion at the end, leaving the audience with Macbeth's sense of futility.

The provisional nature of Shakespeare's theatre carries not only the despairing realisation of life's ephemeralness but also the sense that characters improvise their plots, rather than following a predestined course. The result of this apparently spontaneous improvisation, drawn from the medieval, vernacular tradition of street theatre, can be captivating and comic. Richard III, for example, seduces his audience by the continual confession of his plans as they progress. But Iago's similar confessions, as he hatches his strategy to trick Othello, carry far more sinister implications. He shows evil actively at work, enticed simply by the thrill of 'playing', in the sense both of playing a game and of performing in the theatre:

> Let me see now,
> To get his place, and to plume up my will
> In double knavery – how, how? Let's see . . . .
> . . . I ha't. It is ingendered. Hell and night
> Must bring this monstrous birth to the world's light.
>
> (I.iii.384–6; 395–6)

The flexibility of a world that can allow such 'knavery' to be 'ingendered', simply by the lightening speed of an active mind and an environment pliant to such creative energy, is one in which there appears terrifyingly to be no safeguards and no constraints.

Endings

From very fragmentary accounts of the original performances of Shakespeare's tragedies in the early seventeenth century, it seems as if they ended with the restoration of order and a sense of a life well concluded. We know that the Elizabethan tradition of the actors dancing a 'jig' immediately after the end of the play's action was continued by Shakespeare, since Will Kemp, Shakespeare's main clown until 1599, was said to dance a fine jig. It is likely that these dances were performed after the early tragedies as well as the comedies; 'now adayes they put at the end of everie Tragedie (as poyson into meat) a comedie or jigge', one contemporary theatre-goer complained.[72] It seems likely too that the drama of various tragedies would have closed with a funeral procession, drawing upon established funerary practice.[73] So when Fortinbras commanded 'Let four captains / Bear Hamlet like a soldier to the stage' (V.ii.349–50), he was probably directing the final choreography which would have seen Hamlet's body carried by mourners in a long procession and guided off the stage in solemn ceremony. These reminders of common rituals – the funeral ceremony, the dance – supposedly brought the audience back to a comforting sense of normality, which had been disturbed during the course of the play.

This early seventeenth-century performance practice reflected, to a certain extent, the conclusions in the extant texts themselves. In more-or-less each tragedy, the death of the hero is followed immediately by the arrival of a new leader, who promises to usher in a new regime of peace and stability. Malcolm overthrows Macbeth's tyrannous regime in Scotland and announces he will bring all those in exile back home; in *Othello*, the governor of Cyprus, other Venetian officers and officials make a sudden and belated entrance into the doomed bedroom, where Desdemona lies murdered, and vow to refer the private domestic tragedy to the public state of Venice to solve; *King Lear*, too, also appears to be ending conclusively with the arrival of Cordelia and the French army to crush the brutal English rulers, Goneril and Regan. In each case, too, the survivors pass judgement upon the tragic hero, giving him or her the consolation of a fitting epitaph. So unlike Ibsen's HEDDA GABLER, where the suicide is greeted anti-climatically by the puzzled response that 'people don't do things like that', the aftermath of Cleopatra's death is stage-managed by Caesar so that it reflects well both on her and on himself, the leader of the new order:

> No grave upon the earth shall clip in it
> A pair so famous. High events as these
> Strike those that make them, and their story is
> No less in pity than his glory which
> Brought them to be lamented.   (V.ii.353–7)

Caesar assumes a community here which links the past ('their story') with the future ('his glory') and which will be consistent in its judgement on the value of Anthony's and Cleopatra's lives. Here is another articulation of the significance of the tragic life, along the lines of Hecuba's claim in Euripides' *Trojan Women*, namely that individual loss and suffering can earn the compensation of immortal fame and everlasting understanding.

But while these events and speeches seem to be restoring order, in fact it becomes apparent that the problems and doubts exposed during the course of the plays will not be addressed by the new regimes and thus nothing will actually be resolved. In part this is due to the fact that, as I pointed out earlier, the notion of the 'natural order' itself is highly problematic and so it cannot easily be reimposed. Even Malcolm leaves the way open in Scotland for more civil strife and individual ambition, when, in promising to 'plant newly' (V.xi.31) his plans of reward and punishment, he recalls Duncan's early speech to Macbeth: 'I have begun to plant thee, and will labour / To make thee full of growing' (I.iv.28–9). It is probably in response to the potentially sinister undertones of the play's conclusion that Roman Polanski decided to end his film with Donalbain, Malcolm's brother, setting out to consult the witches. The lack of resolution at the end of Shakespeare's tragedies is also due in part to the opaque nature of the characters' motives discussed earlier. It is significant, for example, that when he is presented with a vision of the 'tragic loading of the bed', Iago refuses to speak: 'Demand me nothing. What you know, you know. / From this time forth I never will speak word' (V.ii.309–10).

Ultimately the questions which the tragic heroes raise during the course of the plays are too profound and transgressive to allow for a strong conclusion in which we can believe. In this respect, the ending of *King Lear* is most powerfully disturbing. It is a play in which the 'end', in the sense both of conclusion and of purpose – the Greek '*telos*' – itself becomes a source of debate. Edgar reflects, after seeing the stumbling figure of his blinded father, upon the fact that the play repeatedly exceeds one's expectations about the tolerable extent of anyone's sufferings: 'O gods! Who is't can say 'I am at the worst'? / I am worse than e'er I was . . . And worse I may be yet: the worst is not / So long as we can say "This is the worst"' (IV.i.26–9). And the structure of the play mirrors Edgar's sense that acceptable boundaries keep being exceeded by repeated atrocity. The traditional ending, in which the order is restored through the arrival of the French army, is exploded by the news of Cordelia's execution, with the result that the 'good' forces are lost along with the 'bad' ones. Lear's life has been extended by grief more than its natural course. 'He hates him much / That would upon the rack of this tough world / Stretch him out longer' (V.iii.312–14), observes Kent, evoking an image of torture to describe the excess of Lear's suffering. And Edgar continues to point out that one can never rest in the knowledge that the end has been reached, that there will be no more suffering and that something has therefore been resolved. 'Is this the promised end?' (V.iii.262), asks Kent, as Lear walks onto the stage bearing the dead Cordelia in his arms, and Edgar replies 'Or image of that horror?'. In a play which depicts the nihilistic absence of gods and the worrying lack of any obvious causation or purpose, it is only fitting that the end is more one of exhaustion than triumphant conclusion. Edgar's final words are suitably trite and cautious about the future, since nothing can be learnt from the action of the play and no safeguards or improvements therefore can be set in place:

The weight of this sad time we must obey;
Speak what we feel, not what we ought to say.
The oldest hath borne most; we that are young
Shall never see so much, nor live so long.

(V.iii.322–5)

Exhausted by the act of witnessing 'so much' atrocity and devoid of ideas for action, the only hope that Edgar and the others can cling onto is the fact of their endurance. The possibility of surviving tragedy, stripped of illusion, rhetoric and love, is the most we can expect from this, the bleakest of all Shakespeare's plays.

2.4 Romantic tragedy: Ibsen, Strindberg, Chekhov

Late nineteenth-century tragedy is haunted by the Romantic legacy. Even in Nora's obsession with freedom in Ibsen's *The Doll's House* ('When I've left this world behind, you will be free') or Solness' fantasy of transcendence in *The Master Builder* ('Haven't you noticed, Hilde, that the impossible – it, as it were, fascinates and calls to one'; Act II, p. 171), one can hear the echoes of Byron's *Manfred* or Goethe's *Faust*. Those plays established the basic Romantic dichotomy between the self and the rest of society, which was to structure the tragedies of the Scandinavians, Ibsen and Strindberg, and the Russian Chekhov. These writers, however, relocated this dichotomy to particular social contexts, with more parochial, specific concerns. They dramatised the conflict between the alienated individual, who aspires to some alternative world of the imagination, and narrow social conventions, designed to crush such aspirations.[74] In Ibsen, this conflict results in the death of the individual, but, since death also offers escape from the pressures of social conformity, its outcome is ambivalent and possibly much to be desired. Far more problematic in the development of post-Romantic tragedy is the fact that aspiration itself becomes fitful, open to doubt and ultimately illusory. In Strindberg and Chekhov, the Romantic dichotomy is more significant for its absence than its presence, existing merely as a dim memory in the name of which characters attempt to assert themselves.

Romantic legacy

The Romantic preoccupations with rebellion against society and psychological retreat into the private world of the imagination were themselves derived from the perception, in that period, of the Shakespearean and classical tragic tradition. The German rediscovery of Shakespeare, prompted by Wieland's translations and Schiller's imaginative response in his play *The Robbers*, was to change the way the British read their own Bard. Coleridge's interpretation of Hamlet, with its emphasis upon his internal life of the mind, was to prove particularly influential: 'The external world and all its incidents and objects were comparatively dim and of no interest in themselves, and began to interest [Hamlet] only when they were reflected in the mirror of his mind'.[75] Hamlet, for Coleridge, exhibited 'the aversion to action which prevails among such as have a world in themselves'. It is indeed possible to detect Coleridge's interpretation of *Hamlet* in Chekhov's *The Seagull*, which is filled with references to the Shakespeare play. Trepliov's solipsistic despair, which prevents him from understanding anyone outside his own mental world, arguably owes more to Coleridge's Romantic reinterpretation of the play than it does to Shakespeare himself.

Meanwhile, in his *Lectures on Dramatic Art and Literature*, A. W. Schlegel was focusing upon Aeschylus' *Prometheus Bound* as his prototypical tragedy: 'The other poems of the Greek tragedians are single tragedies; but this may be called tragedy itself'. He admired the play for its static depiction of defiance:

> It is . . . an image of human nature itself: endowed with a miserable foresight and bound down to a narrow existence, without an ally, and with nothing to oppose to the combined and inexorable powers of nature, but an unshaken will and the consciousness of elevated claims.[76]

The literal binding of Prometheus upon the rock in the Caucasus comes for Schlegel to serve as a metaphor for the condition of the individual in society, 'bound down to a narrow existence'. And the defiance which Prometheus shows for Zeus comes to stand for all resistance of political oppression and social constraint. The result is an emphasis less on an Aristotelian plot, with narrative, linear progression, and more on the static condition of implacable opposition, in which the only activity takes place in the mind, in the 'consciousness of elevated claims'. Both Goethe and Byron claimed that, in Byron's words, 'The Prometheus – if not exactly in my plan – has always been so much in my head – that I can easily conceive its influence over all or anything that I have written'.[77] Even Sophocles' *Antigone* was reinterpreted by Schlegel as a Romantic, Promethean drama of individual intransigence rather than a political clash between two equally justified powers.[78]

The Romantic reinvention of classical tragedy certainly informs Goethe's plays. His version of *Iphigenia in Tauris* focuses upon the internal dilemma of the heroine, who owes allegiance both to her brother and to the king who has sheltered her in Tauris. Iphigenia is given some wonderfully defiant lines when resisting the king's marriage proposals and orders to sacrifice her brother: 'Has man alone the privilege of daring? May only his heroic breast aspire to clasp the impossible?'. Rather than the cynical world which Euripides depicts, in which Athene intervenes in the mortals' affairs, Goethe's king Thoas is won over by Iphigenia's reason and 'noble soul'. Likewise Goethe's *Faust* updates earlier versions to become a study of the tragic consequences of Promethean aspiration and distorted idealism. Unlike Marlowe's Faust, Goethe's hero is an intellectual, a philosopher, who sells his soul not so that he can gain tangible rewards but because he is suffering from an existential *ennui* and craves any kind of alternative experience, good or bad:

> My heart, from learning's tyranny set free
> Shall no more shun distress, but take its toll
> Of all the hazards of humanity,
> And nourish mortal sadness in my soul.
> I'll sound the heights and depths that men can know.
>
> (Faust's study iii, pp. 89–90)

Consorting with Mephistopheles allows Faust to dispense with social conventions which he has come to despise – the demands of the university institution, the regulations governing sexual conduct – and to woo any woman he chooses. However the desire he feels for the innocent Gretchen and which, with Mephistopheles' diabolical help, he is able subversively to satisfy, paradoxically destroys her. Condemned by society for her sexual transgression, for inadvertently murdering her mother in order to further her affair with Faust and for drowning their illegitimate baby, Gretchen still feels mentally freed by her love for him. Yet she prefers to submit to public execution and divine judgement than to follow Faust into an amoral life of no responsibilities and no ties. The play raises questions about the merits of a private as opposed to public morality, about love as an alterative virtue to faith and about the human consequences of romantic aspiration. 'Gaze we for nought in one another's eyes' (Martha's garden, p. 153), answers Faust, when Gretchen asks him about his religious beliefs. The play (Part I) ends with the slim possibility that Gretchen's love for him might count for more than all her sins and transgressions. Mephistopheles announces sanguinely that 'she is condemned to die' but he is immediately answered by a voice echoing from above: 'Is redeemed on high' (Prison, p. 197). Like Bess in *Breaking the Waves* (see pp. 175–76), Gretchen's redemption, based upon her self-sacrifice for the sake of love, defies conventional morality in the name of some transcendent code of ethics.

Desire is central for self-assertion and political resistance in Romantic tragedy, and yet desire itself is forbidden. This paradox, dramatised in Goethe's *Faust*, is repeated in Byron's *Manfred* (1816), in which the hero is outlawed by a love so shameful that it cannot be precisely described. 'Thou lovedst me / Too much, as I loved thee', Manfred tells the ghost of his beloved Astarte. 'We were not made / To torture thus each other, though it were / The deadliest sin to love as we have loved' (II.iv.121–4). In this play, there is not even the excuse of Mephistopheles to justify the protagonist's transgression of social *mores*. Instead Manfred condemns himself, feeling the fluctuating emotions of defiant pleasure and anguished guilt. Impervious to society and unmoved by any human interaction other than his love for Astarte, which sets them apart, he internalises divine judgement until he becomes his own heaven and hell:

> . . . I bear within
> A torture which could nothing gain from thine;
> The mind which is immortal makes itself
> Requital for its good or evil thoughts —
> Is its own origin of ill and end . . .
>
> (III.iv.127–31)

When Manfred dies, it is uncertain whether he will go to heaven or to hell; Byron leaves the question of Manfred's redemption far more open than Goethe leaves the question of Faust's fate. The Abbot, shut out from understanding much of Manfred's last words, is left in bewilderment. In his baffled final speech, which cannot fathom the 'heights and depths' (to quote Faust) that Manfred's soul has 'sounded', we can hear, presaged, the confused response of Judge Brack to Hedda Gabler's suicide or Mrs Solness' grief at the Master Builder's fall.

Ibsen

Goethe's and Byron's plays are really poetic dramas or even dramatic poems, arguably not designed for performance. Byron himself confessed that he designed his plays for a 'mental theatre'. Ibsen's debt to these Romantic writers is apparent, not least in the fact that his early plays – *Peer Gynt* and *Brand* – were also poetic dramas and similarly metaphysical in form. (*Brand* was only first staged nineteen years after Ibsen wrote it). *Brand* also addresses many of the same questions as *Faust* and *Manfred*, exploring spiritual isolation and rejecting religious consolation. Brand's harsh version of religion, which allows no compromise, is both other-worldly and yet also destructive, causing misery for those he loves, his mother, his son and his wife. His argument is that all the sacrifices are worth it to achieve ultimate spiritual redemption. But the end of the play, like that of *Manfred*, is ambivalent. Spurned by the community and forced to flee higher and higher up the mountain to seek some support from God, Brand faces the possibility that his God has abandoned him, or at least is failing to answer. Finally he is buried in a avalanche, before he can hear the reply:

BRAND (*shrinks before the onrushing avalanche*)
Answer me, God, in the moment of death!
If not by Will, how can Man be redeemed?
The avalanche buries him, filling the whole valley.
A VOICE (*cries through the thunder*). He is the God of Love.

(Act v, p. 112)

This is either a benevolent or a cruelly ironic God. On the one hand, since God has replied to Brand's question, and confirmed his identity as a 'God of Love', it seems as if Brand will not be entirely abandoned but that he will be redeemed. But on the other hand, God (or the voice) waits until after Brand's death to reply and, if Love rather than Will is the route to redemption, God has cruelly remained silent while Brand erroneously sacrificed all those he loved to his mission. This is an ironic God, who claims to love while remaining harshly elusive.[79]

Brand raises the question of Ibsen's relation to the Romantic legacy: is he endorsing Romantic transcendence, as E. M. Forster believed[80] or ultimately ridiculing it?[81] It could of course be argued that Romantic tragedies (*Faust* and *Manfred*) are themselves highly ambivalent. At any rate, these questions about Romantic transcendence reoccur in Ibsen's later prose dramas, which move out of the cold, mountain location and into the claustrophobic Victorian drawing room. Placed in visibly cluttered nineteenth-century rooms described in lengthy set instructions, these plays counter the contemporary social conventions with the Romantic emphasis upon the creative will and the freedom of the imagination. Now the Romantic sensibility is only apparent in the symbolism or what John Northam has called 'visual suggestion'.[82] So the haunting footsteps of John Gabriel Borkman, the devastating revelation of sunlight in *Ghosts*, wounded birds diving to the sea-bed in *The Wild Duck*, the curtain and pistols in *Hedda Gabler* – all suggest some deeper, symbolic significance which the characters, embedded within constrained sensibilities, cannot fully articulate but which they can apprehend on this metaphorical level.[83]

At the heart of Ibsen's tragic sense is the conflict between individual, creative aspiration and an oppressive society which cannot even understand that aspiration. The tragedies repeatedly end in the failure of the individual protagonist but raise the question of whether that failure to conform is actually to be admired and whether the consequential death is a desired escape. During the conflict, the protagonist – usually an artist or architect – is often inspired by a woman, muse figure. So, for example, *The Master Builder* deals with the ambitions of the architect Solness, egged on by the mysterious Hilda, while *When We Dead Awaken* depicts the sculptor Rubek and his former model Irene. This relationship is sometimes viewed as exploitative, creating a tension, according to Ina Stina-Ewbank, 'between the man whose perceived "calling" is to create and the woman whose love he uses as enablement'.[84] Certainly Irene in *When We Dead Awaken* complains that Rubek puts 'the work of art first, and flesh and blood second' (Act I, p. 246), and it could be said that the play explores the tragic consequences of single-minded artistic ambition. But Hilda in the *Master Builder* creates a fantasy too which she shares with Solness:

> SOLNESS Why have you come?
> HILDE Because I want my kingdom. The time's up now.
> SOLNESS [*laughing involuntarily*] Well, you are an amazing person!
> HILDE [*merrily*] Hand over the kingdom, Mr Solness! [*Tapping with her fingers.*] The kingdom on the table!   (Act I, p. 152)

Unlike the chorus at the end of Greek tragedy or even the comments offered after the demise of the Shakespearean tragic hero, there is, in Ibsen, no consensus about the significance of the tragic gesture. The great acts of sacrifice which close many of Ibsen's plays go unheeded or misunderstood. The end of *The Master Builder*, in which Solness falls from the steeple, is a good example. Most characters consider the fall a pointless waste of life, but Hilda responds positively to Solness' metaphorical achievement of briefly rivalling the gods:

> RAGNAR Terrible business. So he couldn't manage it.
> HILDE [*as though in a quiet, bewildered triumph*] But he got right to the top. And I heard harps in the air.
> [*Swings the shawl up and cries with wild intensity*] My – my – master builder!   (Act III, p. 211)

Through the diverse reactions to Solness' death, we become aware of the fractured experience on stage. There are no longer any objective facts or values but rather each event is open to subjective interpretation. And this loss of faith in a shared meaning becomes itself a source of tragic despair.

Men, at least in Ibsen, have some outlet for their creative urge, even if its practical result is of ambivalent worth. The women, by contrast, possess only a flickering sense of a transcendent world. Yet it is only possible to understand the frustration of a heroine like Hedda Gabler if one sets the play in a Romantic context, recognising that, as in the late plays, 'the overruling agencies are no longer now the criticism of the world but the visions released from the depths of the soul in hours of lonely reflection'.[85] Hedda longs apparently for beauty, for some different kind of perspective upon her world. 'It's a release to know that in spite of everything a premeditated act of courage is still possible. Something with at least some spark of instinctive beauty' (Act III, p. 84), she tells Judge

Brack. But her motivation ultimately remains opaque, both to those around her and to the audience. Her husband Tesman admits that he does not really know her, and Hedda arguably does not even know or understand herself. Her only positive skill turns out to be destructively negative: 'I often think that there is only one thing in the world I have any talent for . . . Boring myself to death' (Act II, p. 42). The play is thus like *Hamlet* in its elision of motive and its resulting mystery, and early theatre-goers were 'at a loss' to understand it.[86]

It becomes more difficult to understand Hedda's vision because it has been distorted by her oppressive environment. While she is dissatisfied by society, she does in fact share many of its prejudices. Indeed her views upon marriage, social position and scandal are far more conventional than those of Thea Elvsted, who has abandoned her husband to run after the writer Eilert Lovborg. Moreover Hedda's so-called creative vision actually takes the form of destruction. She burns Lovborg's book, rather than helping to create it as Thea Elvsted does. And she is terrified at the prospect of motherhood. Even Lovborg's suicide is misdirected by her. She describes it as a creative act, controlling and terminating a life like a work of art: 'All I know is that Eilert Lovborg had the courage to live his life the way he wanted to live it. To its final great and beautiful achievement. When he had the strength and willpower to walk out on life . . . early' (Act III, p. 84). But in fact it turns out that Lovborg's death was probably a mistake, the result of a drunken tussle in a brothel, where he was accidentally shot in the stomach. It is only after this revelation that she realises the implications for all her endeavours: 'It's like some curse, everything I touch turns into something ludicrous and disgusting' (p. 85). Even her death, which is conducted dramatically by a pistol shot to the head – achieving a perverted form of courage in a way that Lovborg failed to do – is greeted with the deflating, banal comment: 'People don't do things like that!'

So Ibsen's two plays which are arguably most compelling – *Hedda Gabler* and *Little Eyolf* written four years later in 1894 – tackle the tragic absence of transcendence. Hedda's 'vine leaves' and Bacchic 'beauty', though uttered sincerely, jar with her other interests in scandal and jealousy, while, in *Little Eyolf*, the rhetoric of transcendence is overlaid with irony. 'Up, – to the mountain-tops. To the stars. And to the great stillness', declares Allmers at the end of the play, but nobody really believes his sudden visionary aspiration to develop a social conscience. Instead Allmers and Rita are guilty of a series of substitutions and evasions. Allmers avoids real responsibility by devoting years to writing a book on the subject; both parents neglect their son to indulge their own sexual passion; Eyolf embodies their guilt through his disability. Like *Hedda Gabler*, *Little Eyolf* works through implication, deriving its power from what is not said but only threateningly implied, like the imaginary eyes of the dead child Eyolf, looking up accusingly at his parents from the bottom of the fjord.[87] In this environment, in which desires are repressed and perverted, the revelation about the virtually incestuous relationship between Allmers and his half-sister Asta, which might otherwise appear melodramatic, becomes appropriately symptomatic of the play as a whole.

Strindberg

In Ibsen's plays, the subjective fantasy of the protagonist is supported, however validly, by the dramatic symbolism; in Strindberg, there is no such external corroboration but rather beliefs develop out of the twisted psychology of the characters. The Romantic imagination has become merely delusory, hypothetical, distorted. Even during what is known as his pre-Inferno period (before his mental collapse in 1894–7), the purchase on external reality depicted in Strindberg's plays is extremely extenuated. *The Father* contains echoes of Hamlet and Heracles, two male heroes arguably driven mad by women, but its male protagonist's 'madness' is based upon the suggestions of his wife Laura that he is not the father of his child, that he is a failed scientist and that he is insane. The illusion is deliberately manufactured, until finally a straitjacket is put on the Captain unawares. This visible sign, which caused outrage during the early performances, added to the psychological pressures already placed on him during the play, tips the Captain over the edge into insanity. *Dance of Death* (1900) has an obviously Romantic setting, in a remote tower on an island. Strindberg, an accomplished artist, in fact frequently painted seacliff tower and lighthouses, which he regarded as 'metaphors for his own isolated role in a hostile society'.[88] In keeping with this Romantic atmosphere, the Captain and his wife Alice encourage each other's fantasies and, like Faust or Manfred, the Captain is defiantly indifferent to the opinions of anyone else in the world. But we discover during the course of the play, that the Captain is actually quite cowardly and superstitious – he aggressively throws possessions out of the window but then is frightened by the wind rattling the panes – and his military duties are a charade which his wife helps him to maintain. Like Hedda Gabler, or Allmer and Rita in *Little Eyolf,* the Captain has diverted his Romantic will into a parasitic dependence upon other people, 'seizing hold of other people's destinies', as his wife Alice explains, 'sucking excitement out of other people's lives, ordering and arranging for others, because his own life is devoid of interest' (p. 152).[89]

In this atmosphere, games, however torturous, are easier to bear than the truth. Indeed, both the Captain and his wife engage in role playing and fantasy games, from the Captain claiming that he has drawn up divorce papers to Alice reporting on the Captain's supposed embezzlement. And, as Ibsen's John Gabriel Borkman also discovers, truth when it comes is both transcendent and nihilistic. Chastened by his visit to the doctor, the Captain confesses to Kurt, who has taken on the role of spectator for the husband's and wife's 'performance', that 'There comes a moment when the ability to invent, as you call it, ends. And then reality is revealed in all its nakedness!' (p. 167). The Captain's recognition of the truth, and momentary reluctance to 'invent', presages George's decision to end the game in Albee's *Who's Afraid of Virginia Woolf*. Indeed one can detect Strindberg's interest in role playing and the devastating revelation of reality in many of his major tragedies. Laura in *The Father* improvises her plot like a Iago or a Lady Macbeth, so that 'I've never reflected upon what has happened; things just glided along on rails, which you yourself laid down' (Act III, scene 7, pp. 50–1) But this ludic journey results in her husband's death from a heart attack caused by the pressure of his mental isolation. In *Miss Julie*, the heroine sees through her playful intoxication, after sex with her servant Jean, and recognises the grim reality of her scandalous fall from her elevated position in society. While the transgression may seem minor now to an early twenty-first-century audience, she describes it in apocalyptic terms.[90] 'Oh, what have I done? My God, my God!' (p. 89), she cries as she realises the full implications of her one-night stand, and 'That's true – I'm among the very last; I am the last' (p. 109) as she recognises that her planned suicide will mark the end of the family line and thus acquire millennial resonance.

In the absence of any higher purpose, the characters in Strindberg's plays torment each other. As in Euripides, the vacuum of the metaphysical realm is filled by the powerful demands of desire and cruelty. We might recall the disturbing combination of exploitation and sentimentality in the relationship of Faust and Gretchen, but the relationship explored in *Miss Julie*, in which the power dynamics between the sexes is complicated by class difference, is far more atavistically brutal and compelling. The couple compete in the cruel taunts they hurl at each other: 'I'd like to see your sex, swimming in a sea of blood . . . I do believe I could drink from your skull, I'd like to paddle my feet in your breast, I'd roast your heart and eat it whole!' (p. 103). While many of the lines are purely rhetorical, designed to hurt and excite the other in equal measure, there is also an underlying deep disappointment. Jean's confession, 'I'm sorry that what I was myself aspiring towards wasn't something higher or more worthwhile; I'm sorry to see you sunk so low that you're far beneath your cook' (p. 91), is a genuinely felt admission of regretful disillusion, and thus it darkens the whole play further. In *Dance of Death*, the game of torment takes on a metaphysical as well as natural reality. Here, the circular, repetitive structure of the play mimics the round shape of the tower, and both suggest the rings of hell. 'Hell is other people', says Garcin in Sartre's *Huis Clos*, and Strindberg appears to be anticipating him, in suggesting that even human care can take on the appearance of torture:

> ALICE And now I'm to be your nurse?
> CAPTAIN If you wish.
> ALICE What else can I do?
> CAPTAIN I don't know.
> ALICE [sits down apathetically, in despair] This must be everlasting hell! Is there no end, then?
> CAPTAIN Yes, if we're patient. Perhaps when death comes, life begins.
> ALICE If only that were so!   (p. 173)

Strindberg is less well known than Ibsen or Chekhov, possibly because readers and audiences have been rightly troubled by the misogyny which lies behind his creation of the Miss Julie or Laura characters and confused by the extreme fear of emasculation which motivates the anxiety of his male characters. For Strindberg, the loss of the Romantic ideal became caught up in a paranoiac concern about the loss of a notional male, heroic code. But this nostalgia is still resonant for us because it is instrumental in producing the modernist absurdity which informs Strindberg's plays and which was to prove so influential upon Sartre, Beckett, Ionesco and others. The Captain in his straitjacket haunts us like Winnie in Beckett's *Happy Days*. And *Dance of Death* recalls Beckett's *Endgame* in its depiction of a narrow world winding down, running out of food, burgundy, champagne, conversation, ideas:

> CAPTAIN Then I've run out of ideas. – Shall I dance for you?
> ALICE No, thanks. Your dancing days are over, remember.   (p. 122)

The grotesque tragic-comedy, which the play deteriorates into, is the result of a loss of purpose or significance, as it was to be later for Beckett. 'He'd be comic if he weren't tragic' (p. 145), Kurt says of the Captain, struggling to find contextual definition. Indeed, Strindberg's absurdity has been recognised from very early on by directors. The description of Max Reinhardt's 1912 production, for example – 'Alice and Edgar sitting far apart from each other, motionless and in silence, staring out into nothingness with their backs toward the audience' – reads like a stage direction for one of Beckett's bleakest dramas.

Chekhov

The combination of realist and absurdist theatre can be seen also in Chekhov's plays. Here the memory of Romantic transcendence meets contemporary existential meaninglessness, but this clash cannot even generate the tortured heat of Strindberg. *The Seagull* raises issues of male creativity and its female victims, the destructiveness of love, and the disillusion of Romantic hope. These issues have been evident as Romantic concerns since *Faust* and *Manfred*, but now they are expressed through the emptying out of symbols, not through the flickering sense, as in *Hedda Gabler*, that symbols might be the only remaining means of articulating despair. So Trepliov's dead seagull, which he flings melodramatically on stage claiming it represents his wasted life, is appropriated by both the writer Trigorin and Nina, only for it ultimately to be dismissed as an inadequate representation of life's futility:

> NINA I'm a seagull. No, that's not it again . . . Do you remember you shot a seagull? A man came along by chance, saw it and destroyed it, just to pass the time . . . A subject for a short story . . . . That's not it (Act IV, p. 181)

By rejecting the Romantic symbol of the seagull, with all its burden of profound meaning, Nina and Chekhov were rejecting an old type of theatre, with its over-theatrical style of acting, and ushering what was thought to be naturalism.[91]

Chekhov's later plays – *The Three Sisters* (1901) and *The Cherry Orchard* (1904) – while commonly considered 'naturalist', can also be seen as post-Romantic and nihilistic. Moscow in *The Three Sisters* becomes, like Ibsen's mountains or the sea, the transcendent place, the location of hopeful fantasy. But it becomes meaningless. Olga states firmly towards the end that 'we shan't be going to live in Moscow' and Vershinin replies a few moments later, 'In the old days the human race was always making war, its entire existence was taken up with campaigns, advances, retreats, victories . . . But now all that's out of date, and in its place there's a huge vacuum, clamouring to be filled' (Act IV, p. 325). The 'vacuum' here stands for all significance in the play, 'clamouring to be filled'. And similarly the cherry orchard assumes a symbolic role as the source of beauty, hope and memory, only for it to be traded and chopped down. The stage directions at the very end demand that 'silence ensues, broken only by the sound of an axe striking a tree in the orchard far away'.

Under these circumstances, history becomes the only reassurance for these characters that they 'matter' and that they will be 'remembered'. They must 'suffer' in order to create a future life of happiness for their descendents. But in the climate of amnesia that washes around the provincial Russia Chekhov portrays, even that reassurance is not fail-safe. 'The years will pass, and we shall all be gone for good and quite forgotten', says Olga at the end of *The Three*

Sisters. 'Maybe, if we wait a little longer, we shall find out why we live, why we suffer . . . Oh, if we only knew, if only we knew!' (pp. 329–30).

The loss of significant symbols and reliable purpose in Chekhov's plays results in a form of existential absurdity. Indeed, it is only through recognising the potential for existential absurdity that we can begin to understand the function of comedy in Chekhov's writing. Chekhov himself raised the question of tragic definition, provocatively terming his plays either 'comedy or 'drama' and even removing the gunshot, that ended his earlier plays, from *The Cherry Orchard.* But since many of the characters speak 'through tears', it is hard to see the comic nature of the plays unless one focuses upon their similarity to modern, absurdist drama. As in many Beckett plays, the plays are structured around a series of dependent pairs and self-contained dialogues. There is also a similar uncertainty about whether real communication or understanding between characters actually occurs. The conversation between one Beckettian pair, Andrey and Ferapont in *The Three Sisters,* is a good example. Ferapont says to Andrey at one point, 'I'm sorry, I can't tell you. I don't hear very well', and Andrey replies 'If you could hear properly I don't think I'd be talking to you like this' (Act II, p. 274). In this exchange of simultaneous dependency and incomprehension, we can hear the echoes of Hamm and Clov, or Winnie and the silent Willie.

But unlike Beckett, these plays have some external reference. The history that will not remember them, the society which is moving on, are placed specifically at the beginning of the twentieth century. These nineteenth-century characters who will be forgotten come to represent the marginal, everyday voices not normally recorded by history, those who are overlooked or often silent, too unimportant to register their experience or suffering. More than anyone, Chekhov developed the tragedy of understatement, of yearning and of missed opportunities. He overturned the need for dramatic gesture and metaphysical crisis in great tragedy. From now on, tragedy was to be located in what was missing, what was left unspoken. Feers, the old retainer left behind at the end of *The Cherry Orchard,* evokes the poignancy of this new tragic sensibility:

> FEERS [*walks up to the middle door and tries the handle*] Locked.
> They've gone. . . . [*Sits down on a sofa.*] They forgot about me. Never mind.
> . . . I'll sit here for a bit. I don't suppose Leonid Andryeevich put on his fur coat, I expect he's gone in his light one. . . . [*Sighs, preoccupied*]. I didn't see to it.   (Act IV, p. 398)

2.5 American tragedy

If we accept Jean-Pierre Vernant's account of tragedy, that it emerges in a society which is undergoing a period of historical transition, then America in the twentieth century might seem to be the obvious environment for the flowering of tragic drama. This was a society caught between the old and the new world, a people who perhaps one generation back had lived in Europe but who had arrived as immigrants in Ellis Island, anxious to establish themselves in their new country. It was a culture buoyed up by an old set of beliefs, the religious faith of the puritan Founding Fathers or the Catholicism of the Irish or Italian immigrant family, or even just the optimism which motivates the immigrant to break free from the past and bravely start anew in a different country. But it was also a culture facing challenges to those beliefs as the context for them changed. Struggling to establish a new identity, Americans found that old assumptions and expectations might no longer be relevant and that new structures of faith and value would need to be developed. This general sense of confusion and potential disillusion was ripe for tragic exploration.

While the historical, cultural context of twentieth-century America bears some comparison with that of fifth-century Athens, with its similar confusion between traditional and avant-garde beliefs and its development of new political, social systems, the form of tragic drama manifests a distinct departure. Indeed, American playwrights had to find a form which was appropriate to their particular social and cultural conditions. They had inherited the European traditions of tragic drama: the Greeks, Shakespeare, Ibsen, Strindberg. But they needed to invent a new dramatic language which probed American dilemmas with equal profundity and power to those classically explored in the past. One can, indeed, detect a certain awkwardness in early American drama about its status and its relationship with the European generic tradition (see, for example, *Mourning Becomes Electra*) before a distinct tragic practice was, to adopt a term used by Jean Chothia, 'forged'.[92]

The prime focus of American tragedy has been the family. It must be granted that a separate tradition has developed which sets its dramas in the town bar, in the drunken saloon. (Think, for example, of Eugene O'Neill's *Night of the Iguana* or *The Iceman Cometh*.) But one of the main traditions has centred upon the family house, the yard, the living room. The family is to provide the community since the new country or environment remains confusing to the immigrant. Dramas have focused upon these enclosed, private spaces and upon the very boundaries themselves which protect or shut off these places, the walls and the fences and the fire escapes. For the attention upon the family and its boundaries is a means of exploring the relationship between the private family and the wider society, the connections between the small group of people witnessed by us on stage and the imagined wider society beyond those walls, that fence, the theatre itself.

In a well-known essay 'Tragedy and the Common Man', published in the *New York Times* in 1949 shortly after his play, *Death of a Salesman,* first opened in New York, Arthur Miller justified his use of an ordinary man as the hero of his tragedy. He argued that Willy Loman's downfall was as dramatic and his sacrifice as great as that of the kings in ancient Greek tragedy, since the common man was as representative of American society as great leaders like Oedipus or Agamemnon were of Greece: 'We never hesitate to attribute to the well-placed and the exalted the very same mental processes as the lowly'.[93] Miller's essay was an important and necessary intervention, since criticism of the ordinary Willy Loman was rife. But nearly sixty years on, what seems problematic in Miller's essay is not so much the notion that the central character in a tragedy could be said to be 'common' (we now take this for granted) as that he can be 'representative' of society. For what the American tragedies, from O'Neill and Miller onwards, seem to question repeatedly, with their stage sets of tidy fences and enclosing walls, is the assumption that there is a connection between the bourgeois family and society, that, as one critic put it, 'beyond the family is the family of mankind'. Can the nuclear family be considered a microcosm of society? Or is it isolated from it, unique in its misery? Does it bear a private grief? And is the atomisation of society one source of that grief?

Eugene O'Neill

If society does have a bearing upon the individual characters in dramas by play-wrights such as O'Neill and Miller, it is to be found in the beliefs and illusions which the characters hold. The outside world has penetrated the imaginative life of these people in the form of aspirations, expectations and constraints. As he was arguably just developing his dramatic skills in *Mourning Becomes Electra,* O'Neill portrayed this outside world literally in the form of the towns-folk who gossip about the Mannon family at the beginning of each play in the trilogy. Since O'Neill intended the trilogy to be a reworking of Aeschylus' *Oresteia,* relocated from the Trojan aftermath to an American civil war context, these townsfolk represent the ancient Greek chorus, as O'Neill is careful to point out to us in the stage directions. It is their chatter about the mysterious Mrs Mannon at the beginning of *The Homecoming* or their anxiety about the ghosts in the house in *The Haunted* which provides the context for the concerns of the plays' protagonists. It is these people who supposedly would be the readers of Orin's scandalous history of his family, which he threatens to disclose in the final play of the trilogy.

But in fact this chorus does not reappear after the opening five minutes of each play and the pressure of its reaction to events is never really brought to bear upon the action. Instead the characters are constrained by their own psychological desires and hatreds. 'God won't leave us alone. He twists and wrings and tortures our lives with others' lives until – we poison each other to death' (Act I, p. 66), says Christine Mannon in the second play, *The Hunted*. Enthralled by a dance of cruelty and intense desire, which recalls the power games of Strindberg's *Dance of Death*, the Mannon family is concerned only with torturing and testing the feelings of other family members, in a power struggle which, by its very perverse nature, must shut off the outside world. The relationships between the characters which dominate the trilogy's action can be seen as a series of Oedipal conflicts. Orin is tied to his mother, to the extent that he is motivated by murderous rage against any rival in her affection; Vinnie, close to her father, maintains a jealous battle against her mother but cannot help feeling an erotic attraction to her mother's lover, both because of unacknowledged identification with her mother and because of his physical likeness to her father. In this complex Oedipal narrative, in which incestuous love and hate are closely entwined, the family lineage determines the course of action. It becomes, in other words, a form of fate. As Oswald, in Ibsen's *Ghosts*, inherits his father's fate along with the physical symptoms of syphilis, so the curse of the Mannon family is assumed to be genetic – influenced by physiological appearance which evokes desire and hate – rather than simply generic.

It could, however, be argued that the motivation of characters in the trilogy is imposed somewhat heavy-handedly by O'Neill in the form of the Aeschylean model. The twists and turn of the plot, with its melodramatic crises of poisonings and revenge killings and incestuous blackmail, are derived from the classical Greek precedent with its emphasis upon action. But in Vinnie's final decision to deny herself the happy escape of marriage to Peter and to imprison herself in the Mannon mansion, we can see a concerted effort to forge a psychological integrity, albeit psychotic, independent both of American society and of classical precedent:

> Don't be afraid. I'm not going the way Mother and Orin went. That's escaping punishment. And there's no one left to punish me. I'm the last Mannon. I've got to punish myself! Living alone here with the dead is a worse act of justice than death or prison! I'll never go out or see anyone! I'll have the shutters nailed close so no sunlight can ever get in.[94]

In contrast, in *Long Day's Journey Into Night*, the local community outside the tight Tyrone family is unseen. Jamie, the elder son, is concerned about what the rest of the town thinks of them. He worries about people seeing him reduced to having to clip his own hedge, about them noticing the second-hand Packard car he drives. And both he and his younger brother Edmund worry about how Tyrone's decision to send the consumptive Edmund to a state-run, cheap sanatorium will be interpreted by the town:

> To think when it's a question of your son having consumption, you can show yourself up before the whole town as a stinking old tightwad! Don't you know Hardy will talk and the whole damned town will know? Jesus, Papa, haven't you any pride or shame?   (Act IV, p. 88)

But in fact Edmund's concerns here about the rest of society are superseded by the fears over the limited extent to which the Tyrone family can communicate with one another and scrutinise themselves. Fog always threatens to envelop the family. Foghorns have kept Mary Tyrone awake all night before the play opens and, while the fog has lifted at the start of the drama, it is always in danger of returning. Indeed foghorns sound periodically throughout the play's proceedings. In one comic moment, Jamie, returning home drunk after a night on the town, accuses the fog of tripping him up:

> The fron' steps tried to trample on me. Took advantage of the fog to waylay me. Ought to be a lighthouse out there.   (Act IV, p. 95)

That is an example of the physical fog operating literally to block the entrance to the house. But the fog swirling outside the house is also metaphorical of the characters' state of mind. It acts as a metaphor for Mary's morphine addiction which craves the drug to block out feeling. Mary says to her son Edmund 'strangely', as O'Neill writes in the stage directions, that 'the only way is to make yourself not care' (p. 32). By the end of the play, after she has been dosing herself continually upstairs in the bedroom, Tyrone speaks of her 'drowning herself' (p. 109) in it, as if it, the fog, had condensed its water droplets into a sea of forgetfulness.

The fog suggests metaphorically the inability of the characters to communicate one with another. Each character deceives the others in one way or the other, whether it be the simple act of topping up the whisky bottle with water to disguise the amount of liquor consumed or Jamie's more complex, psychological deception of encouraging his brother to drink so that he will also make a mess of his life. The characters fluctuate between shielding themselves from the truth by lying – Edmund does not really have consumption, Mary is only taking medicine for her rheumatic hands – and breaking out into rough acts of confession or aggressive accusation. This repeated desire for self-deception or confession even affects the style of speaking in the play. Each character interrupts others and breaks off his or her own speech. It is partly for this reason that each character's final monologue has such dramatic power, because it is the first and only time we hear each speaking without interruption. 'In vino veritas', says Tyrone, before launching into his self-revelation to Edmund. We have, under the influence of alcohol, both the ultimate of self-justificatory illusions and yet also an illuminating truth.

What emerges from these moments of revelation is the difficult experience of the immigrant from which each has suffered. Tyrone tells the story of Irish poverty and his need to relinquish his dramatic ambitions in order to make ends meet. And, in the most powerful moment of the play, Mary, now 'drowned' in morphine, relives her desire to become a nun and her marriage instead to Tyrone, when she lost her Catholic faith, her family roots and her grasp upon reality simultaneously. Alcohol and drugs in O'Neill's tragic drama seduce characters into losing touch with reality and yet also confront them with an alternative, revelatory truth. Its ambivalence probably derives from a heady combination of Prohibition propaganda about the demon drink and Nietzschean celebration of the Dionysiac in tragedy. A combination, in other words, of new world and old world attitudes.

Edward Albee

This certainly seems to be the case in the drink-fuelled action of Edward Albee's *Who's Afraid of Virginia Woolf*, which Albee admitted was heavily indebted to O'Neill. Here the Nietzschean undertones are suggested quite overtly in the German titles to each act – *Walpurgisnacht* etc. – and in the portrayal of George as a Dionysus-like master of ceremonies, actively encouraging the others to 'torture their lives with others' lives', to coin Christine Mannon's phrase, and urging on the stripping of their illusions. Unlike *Long Day's Journey Into Night*, where no character is fully self-aware or able to manage the downward spiral of events, George, the university professor, treats the process of unravelling the deceits upon which the two marriages are built as an intellectual game, a type of performance. In *Long Day's Journey*, Jamie might quote extracts from poetry or knowingly greet his mother's final entrance with the ironic 'The Mad Scene. Enter Ophelia!', but this, as O'Neill points out, is 'self-defensively sardonic', a way of deflecting an examination of his own emotional response. In contrast, George is fully aware of the implications of Martha's final revelation, that they have no child. He knows that they have rules and that these have been broken.

The fiction which George wishes to challenge in *Who's Afraid of Virginia Woolf* is that of the perfect marriage and the perfect family. George and Martha's guests for the evening, the new professor Nick and his wife Honey, seem to fit the stereotype happy couple familiar from advertising in the 1950s and 1960s. But as the evening progresses and the characters antagonise or attract one another, it is revealed that Nick and Honey have very little in common. Like Honey's phantom pregnancy, which forced them to marry in haste to avoid social scandal, their marriage is an empty sham. Similarly George and Martha have to invent the nuclear family, the child, which they have actually failed to produce, in order to measure up to the expected notion of happiness both have imbibed. However, in their capacity to play with their self-deception, to invent rules and then knowingly to break them, George and Martha might be said to be able to detach themselves from the action sufficiently to get through the trauma. The ending – in which Martha responds to George's song ('Who's Afraid of Virginia Woolf?') with the confession 'I am' – leaves the audience with a glimmer of hope. Martha might be frightened but at least she has confronted the problem at the heart of their marriage and is facing the future with open eyes.[95]

Arthur Miller

The ubiquitous pressure on families to be happy in America in the mid-twentieth century produced some explosive tragedies, because of the gap between the commercial fiction and the wide-spread reality of disappointment and bewilderment. Albee is in fact surprisingly optimistic in *Who's Afraid of Virginia Woolf.* Much more typical and iconic in its influence on subsequent drama is Arthur Miller's *Death of a Salesman.* In this play, the level of illusion and self-deception is so high that Willy Loman is losing touch with reality altogether. He stumbles through a kaleidoscope of past and present, reliving his lost business opportunities with a shadowy brother and revisiting his earlier ambitions for his sons, while facing repeated disappointment now. At the heart of his delusion is the notion that for success one needs to be 'well liked'. And to be 'well liked', one should simply look smart and feel good. In other words, one must 'sell' oneself. Willy Loman, thirty-six years in the business, should know all about the art of selling in America in the mid-twentieth century, how it just involves radiating confidence and convincing people that buying certain products will allow them to be similarly confident and happy. But he has reached a crisis in which he is no longer a good salesman and cannot even convince himself:

> WILLY Sure, sure. I am building something with this firm, Ben, and if a man is building something he must be on the right track, mustn't he?
>
> BEN What are you building? Lay your hand on it. Where is it?
>
> WILLY [*hesitantly*] That's true, Linda, there's nothing.
>
> (Act II, pp. 183–4)

The person who could strip Willy of his illusions and prove to him that his dreams are 'nothing' in the way that George strips Martha of her fantasy, is Willy's son Biff. He is, on the one hand, the product of Willy's empty promotion. Puffed up throughout his childhood with talk about his talent and future success, he still half-believes the fiction that he will make it big in business one day and cannot, as a result, hold down a job in the lowly position for which his actual qualifications equip him. Yet he has also gone through the revelation that, as he puts it, his father is a 'fraud' when he finds him in Boston with his mistress. While he cannot actually do anything positive as a result of this understanding, at least he has the clarity of vision to state that 'I'm one dollar an hour' and that 'I'm nothing' (Act II, p. 217).

Tennessee Williams

The plays which I have been discussing so far posit the bourgeois family as the framework within which individual success or failure may be measured. While the notion that the family shares unproblematically the aspirations and perceptions of society is challenged in the course of the plays with disturbing effect, the model of the family itself as a measurement of value is unquestioned. O'Neill's families may torture each other, psychologically, to death but they remain bound together, standing as the context for each individual's grief. So too the Loman family, who have failed to live up to American public aspirations, remain steadfast as Willy Loman's chief mourners, the benchmark of his success or failure as a new, 'common' hero.

But some American tragedies, particularly more recently, gain their power partly through their critique of the bourgeois family as a 'tragic community'. Tennessee Williams, for example, presents various conventional families only to blow them apart through the course of the dramatic action. *Sweet Bird of Youth* appears to present a conventional narrative, the stuff of romantic tragedy. A father has prevented his daughter from marrying the man she loves; the man comes back into town years later to try to reclaim her again. But in the course of the play, we discover that the father, Boss Finley, has an almost incestuous, possessive affection for his daughter, which prevents her having any normal relationships. And the hero, Chance Wayne, realises that the only relationship left for him in the future is with an ageing movie actress who is deluded by her own celebrity. Just as Tom, in *The Glass Menagerie*, seeks escape from the family in the movies every night, so Chance is going to bury his despair over his lost youth and lost opportunities for love in the arms of the Princess Kosmonopolis.

A Streetcar Named Desire also replaces family relationships with alternative support systems during the course of the drama. Blanche arrives in

New Orleans, seeking refuge with her newly married sister, Stella. It emerges during the course of the drama that, for all her pretensions at glamour and grandeur, Blanche has fallen on hard times and been forced to become the notorious woman of the town, taking money from men in return for favours. In these circumstances, her family seems the one group of people she can trust and she comes to find help from her sister. But that hope is shattered as her brother-in-law Stanley strips the paper lantern, with which Blanche has attempted to improve the room, off the naked light bulb and then pursues her into the bedroom with the threat of sexual violence. We are not shown the rape. In the movie version, directed by Elia Kazan, the camera fades on Blanche's (Vivian Leigh's) agonised face reflected in a mirror cracked symbolically by Stanley (Marlon Brando). But we can sense the betrayal when Stella prefers to believe her husband's denial of the event than her sister's testimony:

> STELLA I couldn't believe her story and go on living with Stanley
> EUNICE Don't ever believe it. Life has got to go on. No matter what
> happens you've got to keep on going.   (scene 11, p. 217)

Blanche's final appearance on stage, as she is committed to psychiatric care and led out of the house by the doctor and nurse, recalls Mary Tyrone's 'mad Ophelia' scene with its ambivalent combination of naïve raving and uncomfortable, revelatory insight. Yet madness in *Long Day's Journey Into Night* is guarded within the family, for the duration of the play at least. In contrast, Blanche appears to realise that she must now place more trust in impersonal institutions – the doctors, nurses and hospitals – than in her own family: 'Whoever you are – I have always depended on the kindness of strangers' (p. 255). To emphasise this shift in allegiance, Eunice places the baby in Stella's arms, after Blanche has been led away by the medics. The message is clear. The baby has replaced Blanche in Stella's affections. Indeed, it was supposedly for the baby's sake that Blanche was removed from the household. The stereotypical family – Stella, Stanley and baby – is predicated on such acts of sacrifice, betrayal and deception. Every perfect family unit, in other words, is achieved at some cost, repressing or erasing a tragic narrative like Blanche's.

The families in Tennessee Williams' plays are inward-looking and insular, even as they are revealed to be based upon fiction and self-deception. Repeatedly external historical events are referenced, only to seem more illusory than the delusions of the family. Does Williams endorse this apolitical, narcissistic outlook? Or can we perhaps detect a critique of the family in the references to lynchings in the South, ignored or excused by Boss Finley (*Sweet Bird of Youth*), or the extreme poverty in Spain and Morocco recounted by Big Daddy, which makes no impact upon Brick, benumbed as he is by alcohol (*Cat on a Hot Tin*

Roof). If these characters could concern themselves with external events, perhaps they could escape the downward spiral of their own lives, locked as they are in psychological confusion and self-deception. Nowhere does this seem to be more the case than in *The Glass Menagerie*, which figures the harmful solipsism of the family in the entrancing, glass animal collection of Laura. As the play's events progress – the disappointment over Laura's ability to hold down a job or typing course, the excitement over the gentleman caller, the sad realisation that he is engaged to be married and that Laura is condemned to a life indoors – Tom reads about the crisis in the Spanish Civil War: 'In Spain there was Guernica! But here there was only hot swing music and liquor' (scene 5, p. 265). The war is as distant and irrelevant as the movies Tom escapes to and nothing, other than the momentary shattering of Laura's glass unicorn when Jim, the gentleman caller, wakens her sexually, is going to impact upon their lives and fantasies. The tragedy of these plays is that the family which should become a microcosm of the wider society, which is confusing and disorientating enough, is utterly disconnected from it. Moreover, even the fantasy which holds the family together is deceptive and pernicious. History goes on elsewhere while these characters drink themselves to oblivion or worry about their private worlds of 'mendacity' (*Cat*) or 'dreams' (*Glass Menagerie*).

August Wilson

In contrast, the African American playwright, August Wilson, proposed that the family at the centre of each of his plays is absolutely representative of history. Wilson's large project of ten plays, one for each decade of the twentieth century, was based on the assumption that the story of each family could stand for the general trends of history in that particular period. What he challenged is not so much the model of the bourgeois family but the question of whose history they might represent. Aimed at raising African American consciousness of their own neglected history, Wilson's plays are not, on the face of it, tragedies. According to the major Wilson critic, Sandra G. Shannon, he aimed to 'inspire healthy spiritual and attitudinal adjustments within his people'.[96] But in the way that Brecht attempted to stimulate political awareness in his audience by dramatising the tragic oppression inherent within capitalism, so Wilson tries to provoke his audience by portraying the injustices and prejudices from which African Americans have suffered over the century. What results is arguably tragic.

While Wilson declared that he had not read the tragic canonical writers, like Shakespeare, Miller or O'Neill, and that he wrote not so much in the tradition of Western (white) drama as in the black tradition of the blues, one can recognise common tragic themes throughout his work. *The Piano Lesson*, for example, with its focus upon the significance of the piano in the history of Berniece's and Boy Willie's family and the arguments for and against selling it, recalls the ambivalent implications of Chekhov's *Cherry Orchard*. Even more striking and interesting are the comparisons which can be drawn between *Fences* and *Death Of A Salesman*. As in Miller's play, *Fences* portrays one family: a father, two sons, a wife and a mistress. It revolves similarly around the two pressing concerns of the typical American family, the home and the sports-field. The first represents security and responsibility. 'I'm gonna build me as fence around this yard. See? I'm gonna build a fence around what belongs to me' (Act II, scene 2, p. 77), says the Willy Loman character, Troy Maxson. The second, the sports-field, represents the father's aspirations and ambitions. Is Troy still able to hit a homerun? Can he steal second base? Through the metaphor of baseball he is able to articulate his hopes for his own life and that of his children.

But unlike Willy Loman, Troy Maxson's dreams and illusions are distorted by the history of racial prejudice. Rather than dreaming, self-deceptively, that his son is going to be the star of the football team, Troy actively prevents his son Cory from progressing in sports because 'the white man ain't gonna let you get nowhere with that football noway' (Act I, scene 3, p. 35). Having been unsuccessful himself in baseball because of racial prejudice, as he believes, he does not want the same experience repeated for his son. His wife, Rose, however points out that it was probably his age which hampered his chance in the team (he spent his youth in jail) and that times have changed in any case and black players are getting into the team. But Troy, who is locked into his own world without progression – 'I get up Monday morning . . . Make my way . . . Find my strength to carry me through to the next Friday' (Act I, scene 3, p. 40) – is unable to visualise a life and set of historical conditions which might be different from his own. While trying to make his son's life better than his own – 'I don't want him to be like me! I want him to move as far away from my life as he can get' (p. 39) – he actually ensures that his own experience of disappointment and alienation from his father is repeated. He refuses to sign the papers allowing Cory to be recruited for the sports scholarship to college, prevents him from playing in the team and eventually throws him out of the house.

The end of *Fences* has proved quite controversial. When the play was initially transferring to New York for the first time in 1987, the producer, Carol Shorenstein, waged a campaign to change the final scene, in which Troy's brother Gabriel attempts to play his trumpet at Troy's funeral. She felt that Gabriel was a ridiculous figure who took away from the seriousness of the play. But

Wilson and the cast welcomed the funny and cathartic close to the drama: 'The audience was already dealing with the fact that this man they had experienced for close to two hours was dead . . . What they needed was something that would give them this release.'[97] Sandra Shannon also maintains that the fact that Cory has a good job at the close and that the family has come together at Troy's funeral leaves us with hope about the progress of history. It is true that Troy's commitment to his love-child Raynell and the relationship between his widow Rose and Raynell are positive suggestions, at the play's close, that some aspects of African American family life have improved, that families will remain tightly bonded despite external pressures. But it seems to me that, in other respects, the play ends very bleakly. Cory, who has missed his chance to get to college with a sports scholarship, has been recruited into the US Marines. Since it is 1965 and we know that the worst years of the Vietnam conflict are about to happen – over 14,000 Marines were killed in action – the sacrifice of Cory to his father's distorted ambitions is all too poignant. And Gabriel, half of whose head was blown away in the last war and who has been committed to hospital so that his brother Troy can make use of his invalid pension, provides a tragically ironic comment upon military heroism and private faith when he attempts to play his trumpet. His trumpet has no mouthpiece and makes no sound and the fanfare which will supposedly warn St Peter to open the gates of heaven is no trumpet blast but a howl. Like the end of *Long Day's Journey* or *Streetcar*, this is the bleakly illuminating revelation from the mad. 'There is a weight of impossible description that falls away and leaves him bare and exposed to a frightful realization', writes Wilson in what must be one of the least stageable stage directions. 'It is a trauma that a sane and normal mind would be unable to withstand' (Act II, scene 5, p. 101).

Tony Kushner

Wilson's tragic dramas are in fact quite orthodox in form. They take up traditional tragic themes in order to reset them in an African American context and thus to critique them. But the most radical consideration of the place of tragedy in American culture or history in recent times can be found in Tony Kushner's epic drama, *Angels in America*. History by this stage is about to 'crack wide open'. It is global in reach and apocalyptic in nature. Facing the end of the millennium, the characters face suitably millennial anxieties: plague (or, in other words, AIDS); irrevocable environmental damage; rampant exploitative capitalism and a widespread loss of religious faith. And matching this worldwide sense of history in crisis, the plays' focus is more diffuse. Gone is the stereotypical family of traditional American tragedy, surviving in this play only in the plastic model family of the Mormon diorama.[98] Instead Kushner posits a set of alternative relationships: gay male partnerships, nurses and patients, even the new alternative Mormon family:

> PRIOR (*looks at* HANNAH, *then*) This is my ex-lover's lover's
>   Mormon mother.
>   *Little pause.*
> EMILY Even in New York, in the Eighties, *that* is strange. ·
>   (Act IV, scene 6, p. 66)

In the context of a new, queer 'family', Kushner poses some of the questions familiar from the tradition of American tragic drama. Overwhelmingly, this is a play about the potential threat to love in the Reaganite climate of aggressive individualism. Louis abandons his lover Prior when he discovers that he is falling sick with AIDS. The Mormon Joe leaves his wife. Hannah, his mother, cannot understand or communicate properly with her son. And most dramatically, Roy Cohn casts his shadow over the whole epic, his words to Joe apparently prophetic of the condition of late modernity:

> Love; that's a trap. Responsibility; that's a trap too. Like a father to a son I
> tell you this: Life is full of horror; nobody escapes, nobody; save yourself.
> Whatever pulls on you, whatever needs from you, threatens you. Don't
> be afraid; people are so afraid; don't be afraid to live in the raw wind,
> naked, alone . . . (*Millennium Approaches*, Act II, scene 4, p. 42)

The 'raw wind' of the late twentieth century strips away all the protective beliefs and fantasies with which earlier dramatists like O'Neill and Williams were concerned. Harper, Joe's agoraphobic wife who is addicted to valium, follows a great tragic tradition of combining escapist illusion and revelatory insight. She sees the symbolic significance of the break in the ozone layer, a 'shell of safety for life itself'. 'Something just fell apart' (Act 1, scene 7, p. 22), she tells Prior in a hallucinating dream. And the angels, who attempt to intervene through prophecy and who are derived from the great Puritan tradition of divine witness, are shown to be necessarily artificial. 'It's OK if the wires show', Tony Kushner notes at the start of the published text, 'and maybe it's good that they do'.[99] If faith is still possible in Kushner's tragic world, it can be achieved only through a camp and comic irony. Heaven, for example, looks like San Francisco after the 1906 earthquake.

Yet despite the isolation of characters, the many AIDS-related deaths and the prevailing scepticism, there are signs, as in Aeschylus' *Oresteia*, of hope and redemption. The turning point of the epic occurs halfway through the second play, *Perestroika*. Following the hated Roy Cohn's death, his nurse Belize (who is arguably an angelic character himself) summons Louis to say kaddish over his dead body. The ghost of Ethel Rosenberg joins him in the recitation. It is a striking moment of forgiveness and it results in the delivery of all Cohn's AZT tablets to the very ill Prior. With the aid of these pills, Prior is still surviving five years later in the final, epilogue scene by the Bethesda fountain in Central Park. The Bethesda angel offers healing. The end of the Cold War shows the progress of history. And meanwhile, Harper has just had her vision of redemptive healing on a night flight to San Francisco:

> Souls were rising, from the earth far below, souls of the dead, of people who had perished, from famine, from war, from the plague, and they floated up, like skydivers in reverse, limbs all akimbo, wheeling and spinning. And the souls of these departed joined hands, clasped ankles, and formed a web, a great net of souls, and the souls were three-atom oxygen molecules, of the stuff of ozone, and the outer rim absorbed them, and was repaired. Nothing's lost forever. In this world, there is a kind of painful progress. Longing for what we've left behind, and dreaming ahead. (Act 5, scene 10, p. 96)

Earlier Harper has voiced the stale circulation of history and our imagination. Even our fantasies are second-hand reworkings of what we already know. But in this final vision that circulation has redemptive qualities. The world can 'repair' itself; nothing is 'lost forever'.

A valium addict and a haggard AIDS patient just hanging onto life courtesy of some pills might be a bleak prospect on which to pin the hopes of America in the twenty-first century. But there is an honesty and a camaraderie between the characters in the final epilogue of Kushner's play which might provide an answer to O'Neill's and Miller's and Williams' and Albee's tortured self-delusions.

2.6 Post-colonial tragedy

Tragedy has traditionally been considered a Western genre. Invented by the Greeks, the art form has supposedly been haunted by the precepts of Aristotle and the dramatic structure developed by Aeschylus, Sophocles and Euripides. Even tragic dramas which depart from this orthodoxy can only be appreciated fully when it is understood how far they question or challenge the expected dramatic structures. Moreover, some critics such as George Steiner maintain that traditional tragic concerns – the plight of the individual, moral or ethical choice, the consciousness of guilt – are confined solely to Western culture.[100]

Some post-colonial writers have appeared to endorse Steiner's view by suggesting that the subaltern response to classical, Western tragedy should be one of comic resistance. If Western tragedy, in the form of Shakespeare or classical Greek tragedy, has been exported to the empire as part of the imperial, canonical legacy, then the post-colonial counter-discourse would logically attempt to dismantle that canon through various strategies, such as mimicry, burlesque, carnival or, in Helen Gilbert's words, 'performative intervention'.[101] According to this argument, Western tragedy concentrates upon the single unity of Aristotelian tragedy; the post-colonial drama allows other, previously repressed voices to express themselves in 'dialectic' with the colonial (Bakhtin's term) or in an uncategorisable 'hybrid' (Homi Bhabha). Following this strategy, post-colonial stagings of Western tragedy and also modern adaptations of traditional texts repeatedly invert the normal genre of a play, so that what is conventionally played as tragic becomes comic and vice versa. So, for example, Derek Walcott's play, *A Branch of the Blue Nile*, combines Shakespeare's language with his native Creole traditions to produce what becomes a comically debunking version of *Anthony and Cleopatra* (itself, of course, quite a comic tragedy). In contrast, productions of *The Tempest* now regularly emphasise the colonial injury inflicted upon Caliban and Sycorax by Prospero with the result that the happy ending is overshadowed by the injustice suffered by the island's original inhabitants. Sam Mendes' RSC production, in which Simon Russell Beale's Ariel spat in Prospero's face at the play's close, is just one example of what is becoming almost an orthodox reading of the play as tragic in its portrayal of colonialist exploitation.[102]

But in the last fifty years, since decolonisation, there has been a rise in theatre productions of classical tragedy in different, non-Western settings, which offer an alternative perspective on this debate. These productions place ancient Greek tragedy or Shakespearean tragedy in new post-colonial contexts in order to explore the relevance of the classical tradition to other cultures and the relationship between very different concepts of the tragic. In some cases, playwrights are paradoxically finding analogies between classical tragedy and their own culture, by exploring their own native traditions while divesting themselves of Western expectations. In other cases, dramatists, influenced by European artists like Brecht, are attempting meta-theatrical stagings of tragedy, which ponder the function of theatre and expose, through performance, the sorrow of their contemporary situation. There are, of course, alternative traditions of theatre altogether, in Japan or in India, which have been ignored until very recently and which challenge Steiner's Eurocentric assumptions. This Asian theatre is beginning to make an impact upon Western productions of tragedy and thus to broaden our understanding of the genre.

Analogy: Wole Soyinka

According to Ketu Katrak, there is no African tradition of tragedy. Citing Anthony Graham White's book, *The Drama of Black Africa*, he argues that 'there appears to be an ancient and anti-tragic superstition that to express sorrow was "somehow to invite it"'.[103] But in recuperating Yoruba rituals and beliefs and drawing also upon his knowledge of European theatre, Nigerian playwright Wole Soyinka has attempted to offer a new, distinctively African tragedy. He implicitly draws an analogy between his perception of ancient Greek society and that of traditional Nigerian society. Like the Greeks, the Yoruba people place great importance upon the community, upon its rituals and collective decision-making. There are correspondences between Greek ideas about fate and Yoruba beliefs about destiny, and both cultures were or are not very concerned with individual introspection, believing that the self is determined by society. But while Greek tragedy reflected the democratic context of its performance, ancient Yoruba society was aristocratic and feudal.

Another Nigerian playwright, Ola Rotimi, explored some of these points of comparison and contrast in his version of *Oedipus, The Gods Are Not to Blame* (first performed in 1968). The play substitutes an elite council of chiefs for Sophocles' Theban citizens, and the priest of Ogun directs the dialogue which leads to Odewale's (Oedipus) discovery of the truth, with the townspeople only arriving near the end to 'kneel or crouch in final deference to the man whose tragedy is also their tragedy', according to the stage directions.[104] As a result, Rotimi focuses upon the religious aspect of the play, rather than the political as in the Sophoclean original.

Continuing this emphasis upon Greek and Yoruba religion, Soyinka draws an analogy, in his essay 'The Fourth Stage', between the Greek god of theatre, Dionysus, and the Yoruba god of creativity, Ogun. Like Dionysus, Ogun is worshipped by sacrificing animals and drinking wine, and, like Dionysus, he is believed to be fearsome and terrible in his revenge. As the god of iron who is thought to have built the first road, he is considered to combine creativity and destruction. But he is also Promethean in his capacity for self-sacrifice. The Yoruba legend is that the gods were troubled by their separation from mortals and longed to recover their original unity. Ogun took it upon himself to bridge the gulf, by hacking his way, with his iron machete, through primordial chaos, across the barrier of mortality and death, to the world of the living. Thus he himself experienced a form of death or disintegration in order to re-emerge whole, with the connection between men and gods renewed. Soyinka, in making the comparison between Dionysus and Ogun, is influenced by Nietzsche's account of the Dionysiac in *The Birth of Tragedy*, with its account of the Apollonian and Dionysiac principles and the ecstatic destruction of the self. But, as Soyinka points out, Nietzsche's abyss or 'primordial oneness' is masked by art and illusion, whereas the abyss for the Yoruba constitutes simply the essential state of the world, in which gods and mortals or the living and the dead are held together in eternal 'cosmic struggle'.[105]

So the world, according to the Yoruba religion, is basically tragic in the sense that it undergoes a continual cycle of destruction and renewal, a continual 'cosmic struggle'. Performance, however, adds a further element of tragedy, because we witness the protagonist re-enacting Ogun's sacrifice, by himself plunging into the abyss, making the 'transition' between the world of the living and the world of the dead. On the one hand, the protagonist is believed initially to resist the demands of the gods, attempting to avert the moment of his death or 'the final step towards complete annihilation' (p. 28). His anguish at the point of death is channelled, according to Soyinka, into a form of music, the 'soul's despairing cry which proves its own solace'.[106] But on the other hand, the protagonist also needs to exert a superhuman strength of will in order to emulate Ogun's machete-hacking journey across the abyss between life and death. So the activity of the hero shifts between resisting his fate and paradoxically hastening it on. This emphasis upon self-sacrifice for the good of the community or the cosmic relation between men and gods is the aspect of Yoruba tragedy which is most alien to the Western imagination. For Soyinka develops this belief into an explanation of the redemptive purpose of ritual, sacrifice and tragedy, which is arguably at odds with the radical questions raised by Greek tragedy or the haunting scepticism found in Shakespeare. By the destruction of the individual, who emulates Ogun's first sacrifice, the balance of the world is supposedly restored, the bridge between men and gods rebuilt and the totality of the cosmos re-created.

The redemptive conclusion of Soyinka's *Bacchae*, commissioned by the National Theatre, London, in 1973, has proved to be the most controversial aspect of the play for critics and reviewers. Earlier in the drama, Dionysus' African concerns do not seem to conflict with the Greek original. His emphasis upon the power of magic (unlike the original Euripides' version he convinces Pentheus that he is arming himself for battle when he is really donning women's clothes as disguise) and his politics of emancipation (he inspires a chorus of liberated slaves) are understandable even within the Greek context. But the end of the play forces the audience to ponder the limits of the comparison between Greek and African drama and the very different significance of Ogun and tragedy in the Yoruba tradition. In contrast to the Euripides version, where Dionysus reappears after Pentheus' murder to vaunt his petty revenge to the detriment of his supposed divine nobility, in Soyinka's play, the fact that Dionysus is unseen and heard only as his 'theme music' suggests that his punishment of Pentheus is endorsed by the cosmic order. Even more problematically, the landscape, which before was harsh and rocky, is now irrigated by Pentheus' blood. 'Moisture oozes up at every step' (p. 307), says Teiresias. As if to confirm this statement, Pentheus' severed head starts to spout wine instead of blood. 'Dream-like', according to the stage directions (p. 307), Agave, Kadmos and others move towards the head, cup their hands and drink. Pentheus has emulated Ogun in allowing himself to be torn apart for the good of the community and Thebes, fertilised by his blood, is the beneficiary.

Besides the adaptation of Greek tragedy, Soyinka has produced original plays which continue his preoccupation with ritual, sacrifice and redemption. In each case, the drama revolves around the relationship between the individual and his community, as the main protagonist finds himself emulating, in traditional ritual, the 'transition' of Ogun across the abyss for the good of his people. In *The Strong Breed*, for example, we see a typical ritual, in which somebody is sacrificed for the village. The outsider, Eman, offers himself as a sacrificial victim to protect the idiot Ifada, who would otherwise be killed. After trying to elude his killers for a time, Eman finally decides to yield to his destiny, willing himself to die and making the 'transition', in emulation of Ogun, from this world to the next. But the interest of the play lies in the moments when rituals are challenged and the specific historical circumstances in which the hero finds himself intervene. So, for example, in one of the three flashbacks in the play, we learn that Eman was forced to travel away from his original community and become an outsider because he refused to participate in their male initiation rites. He resisted his family destiny, the 'strong breed', who were expected traditionally to sacrifice themselves to purge the community's sin. But in the end he appears to accept this destiny, because although he sacrifices himself for a different village, he is led on to his death as much by the ghost of his father as by village elders who are pursuing him. Most disturbing is the account of the sacrifice itself. Instead of appreciating the fact that the killing of Eman is for the benefit of the community, the villagers receive it in silence: 'One and all they looked up at the man and words died in their throats', Jaguna, one of the village elders, reports (p. 146). Eman has potentially died for nothing. The play questions the very purpose of the ritual, for a society apparently in a state of flux. 'It is a sorry world to live in', says Jaguna (p. 146), disappointed by the community's indifference during the sacrifice.

The tragic confusion produced by historical change is even more evident in Soyinka's best-known play, *Death and the King's Horseman*. The play again deals with a failed sacrifice, but this time the sacrifice is thwarted not by the community's reluctance to respond to the victim's demise, but by the confusions of modernity and the disruptions brought about by colonialism. According to the local tradition dramatised by the play, when the king dies, his horseman must die too in order to accompany him across the abyss to the world of the dead. So Elesin, at the play's opening, prepares to voluntarily allow himself to die out of sheer, courageous will-power. But, seduced by the pulsing life of the market and the beauty of its women, he persuades the community to let him delay his death by a few hours so that he may marry a young bride and sow the seed for a new generation to succeed him. It is arguable that Elesin exploits his sacred role as sacrificial victim to satisfy his selfish, carnal desires, perverting traditional religious beliefs in a way which is comparable to the actions of some of Soyinka's other characters – The Professor (*The Road*) or The Old Man (*Madmen and Specialists*). As a result, his divinely inspired will to die is weakened or corrupted. In any case, the colonial District Officer, Pilkings, intervenes to prevent the suicide, supposedly in the attempt to rescue Elesin from a barbaric fate. However, despite Pilkings' well-meaning intentions, the result is tragic confusion and ignominy. Elesin, under Pilkings' custody, is taunted by the market-woman, Iyaloja, for the fact that he 'dared not open the door to a new existence' and thus he, their leader, betrayed their hopes (scene 5, p. 55). In one of the great *coups de théâtre*, Iyaloja produces the body of Elesin's son, Olunde, who has sacrificed himself in his father's place (p. 61). Shamed by his son's greater power of will and horrified at this perversion of nature (for the son to die before the father is, for the Yoruba, a perversion), Elesin strangles himself by the chain which shackles him in prison, recalling, in the disgrace of his suicide, the hanging body of Okonkwo in Chinua Achebe's novel, *Things Fall Apart*.

Soyinka's celebration of ancient Yoruba culture, his apparent endorsement of ritual suicide and belief in the gods have attracted some criticism. For him, the focus of the drama is the 'transition' from history to ritual, as the actor sloughs off contemporary concerns and thinks only in terms of spiritual dimensions. So he insists, for example, that *Death and the King's Horsemen* is not about the clash between African and Western imperial culture but about a 'largely metaphysical' confrontation which is contained in 'the universe of the Yoruba mind'.[107] But for Western audiences and for some of Soyinka's critics, it is actually the mismatch between individual and community, or between history and ritual, which offers the main interest of the play. One of his main critics, Biodun Jeyifo, has complained that Soyinka adopts a 'metaphysics which idealises and effaces the conflicts and contradictions in African societies, which rationalises the rule of the dazzling FEW (such as Elesin) over the deceived MANY'.[108] Another critic, the younger Nigerian playwright, Femi Osofisan, deconstructs Soyinka's tragic universe and opens up an alternative politics of progress beyond a tragic past. Approaching the Yoruba gods more as metaphors than as literal deities, he revises Soyinka's plays like *The Strong Breed*, by suggesting, at the end of his play *No More the Wasted Breed*, that non-human sacrifices to the gods would be more appropriate. And in *Another Raft*, he implies that the Yoruba gods and traditional rituals are used cynically and covertly by the ruling class to justify their system of oppression and exploitation.[109] But it can be argued that while plays like *Death and the King's Horseman* do focus upon the inner, spiritual life of the protagonist and its attempt to cleanse itself from the 'material of drama', nevertheless Elesin's consciousness, in Adebeyo Williams' words, 'has been determined by the dialectic of his material and political circumstances'.[110] In other words, the protagonist's determination to sacrifice himself for the good of the community is weakened by the confusing demands of a society under occupation. While Okonkwo in *Things Fall Apart* might hold on, like Sophocles' *Ajax*, steadfastly to traditional values while the world around him adapts to colonialism, Elesin, in contrast, finds his personal commitment to ritual challenged by historical circumstances despite the continuing fervent beliefs of his society. We witness the tragedy of his self-doubt, exacerbated by the injustice and absurdity of colonialism.

The critical debate over Soyinka's plays goes to the heart of the question of what we expect from tragedy. For Soyinka, it is supposedly enough that the plays offer the 'dramatization of a ritual' (Katrak's words), since, for the Yoruba, the distinction between ritual and performance is blurred. The ritual itself is tragic, in that it repeatedly demonstrates the necessary destruction of the individual prior to the community renewal. But for both Western and many African critics, tragedy must attend to the historical moment, both the time which is represented in the drama and the specific temporal space of performance. So it matters to them that each play situates the sacrificial ritual at a particular time and place and considers the historical conflicts and ambiguities which intervene in that ritual practice. These conflicts are for them the source of the tragedy, rather than the unchanging ritual.

Meta-theatrical performance: Athol Fugard

The most fruitful way for post-colonial playwrights to situate traditional or classical ritual in a contemporary context is through metatheatrical performance (staging a 'play-within-the-play'). This allows the ritual which is performed or the text which is staged to be critiqued by the modern setting. A critical perspective is opened up which can, in Helen Gilbert's words, 'remind us that any performance stages the necessary provisionality of representation' but which can also reveal tragic conflict or uncertainty.[111]

One of the most influential metatheatrical versions of Greek tragedy in Africa was staged by the South African playwright, Athol Fugard. Fugard, a white liberal Afrikaner, worked closely with the theatre company, The Serpent Players, in Port Elizabeth during the dark days of apartheid in the 1960s, devising, through improvisation workshops, various versions of classical drama, such as *Antigone* and *Orestes*. But it was his creative association with two black actors, John Kani and Winston Ntshona, from about 1970, which resulted in the most groundbreaking production of *The Island*. This version of *Antigone*, devised by all three men and set in the prison of Robben Island where Nelson Mandela was incarcerated, opened in June 1973 at the Space Theatre, Cape Town. It later transferred to London in December 1973 and to New York the following year. Restrictions upon black South Africans were so great under the apartheid regime that Kani and Ntshona had to be classified as Fugard's servants rather than actors in order to be able to travel outside the country. It meant that just staging the play at all became an act of political resistance.

This is the main question – the purpose of staging a play – which *The Island* poses. The drama opens with 'John' and 'Winston' (the actors retained their names as characters) digging sand as punitive hard labour on the island prison and returning each evening, exhausted and beaten by harsh guards, to their basic cell. There they comfort each other, play imaginative games to escape the narrow confinement of their lives, and begin to plan their performance for the prison concert in a week's time. John wants to perform *Antigone* but Winston is reluctant, partly because he must play the part of a woman but also because he cannot see the relevance of the story to their lives:

> Go to hell, man. Only last night you tell me that this Antigone is a bloody . . . what you call it . . . legend! A Greek one at that. Bloody thing never happened. Not even history! Look, brother, I've got no time for bullshit. Fuck legends. Me? . . . I live my life here! I know why I am here, and it's history, not legends. I had my chat with a magistrate in Cradock and now I'm here. Your Antigone is a child's play, man.   (p. 210)

Winston's speech could be regarded as a classic articulation of the subaltern rejection of Western tradition. How can some old Greek legend bear any relation to the experience of political prisoners in South Africa?

But as the drama progresses, the relevance of Antigone becomes increasingly apparent, both to Winston and to the audience. Her speech to Creon, pointing out the injustice of his laws and the prior authority of the gods over men, is the centre-piece of the prisoners' performance. Indeed they end the play at the point when Antigone is led to prison ('I must leave the light of day forever, for the Island, strange and cold, to be lost between life and death'), and omit the second half, in which Creon is compelled to confront his transgression. By emphasising Antigone's defiance in this way, John and Winston also challenge the unjust laws of the apartheid regime under which they were sent to Robben Island. For those laws too were made by men, not by god, and serve one particular interest. The analogy between Antigone's situation and Winston's is made all the more pointed by his reference to Antigone's prison as an 'island', rather than a rock tomb, and by removing his 'costume' (a rope wig, false breasts and a nail necklace) to deliver the final words of their play as Winston, not Antigone: 'Time waits no longer. I go now to my living death, because I honoured those things to which honour belongs' (p. 227).

Beyond the strong words of Antigone, which Winston delivers powerfully, the very activity of staging a play in prison becomes an act of defiance. From meagre supplies in prison – rope, tin mugs – the actors are able to transform their cell into a theatre and their brutalisation at the hands of the prison authorities into independent creativity. The transformation is crucial. For Fugard suggests, like Camus (see pp. 133–34), that to attain a consciousness of one's oppression is to gain a tragic victory over it, even if that victory is only in the form of mental freedom rather than physical. The hard labour on the island to which Winston and John are condemned – digging sand from one part of the beach to deposit it in another – recalls the punishment of Sisyphus, who was doomed for eternity to push a rock to the top of a hill only for the rock to roll back to the bottom again. When John hears that his sentence has been shortened and he will be freed in three months, Winston suddenly becomes aware of the absurdity of their lives in the prison. Like Sisyphus, they are engaged in a futile task everyday without the prospect of an end. Like Camus' account of Sisyphus, they can lose all perspective until, like one prisoner Harry, they actually 'love the stone' in the labour quarry, they love the regime's instruments of torture. For a moment, it seems as if Winston is yielding to the prospect of this mindless existence. But then he stands up, according to the stage directions, speaking in the 'voice of a man who has come to terms with his fate, massively compassionate' (p. 221). At this point, he makes the decisive commitment to perform Antigone. It marks the moment when, according to critic Albert Wertheim, 'the plight of Sisyphus can be connected with and transformed into the power of Antigone', which allows freedom to be measured against 'the absurdity of incarceration'.[112]

So Fugard marries local traditions of story-telling and actual known performances of tragedy in Robben Island with Western European drama and philosophy, to create a play which addresses self-consciously the function of theatre in 1970s South Africa. The performance of ancient tragedy both reflects and resists the contemporary situation of injustice. Role-playing is revealed to have a transformative effect. Fugard, John Kani and Winston Ntshona continued this idea with their next workshopped play, *Sizwe Bansi is Dead* (often performed in a double bill with *The Island*), in which identities are assumed not on the makeshift stage but in the photographer's studio. 'This is a strong-room of dreams', says the photographer Styles in his studio, explaining his capacity to give ordinary people memories, photographs, something of significance to leave behind them when they die since apartheid South Africa 'and its laws, allows us nothing, except ourselves'.[113] But the play reveals that even that photograph or memory can be compromised by the apartheid system. Sizwe Bansi must leave Port Elizabeth and return to the rural, impoverished Transkei, where there is no prospect of work, because his pass book, allowing him to remain in the city, has expired. Encouraged by Styles, he takes the pass book of a man who has just died and fakes a new identity for himself, with a new photograph and the dead man's name. He is now called Robert Zwelinzima; as he explains to his wife in a letter, Sizwe Bansi is dead.

The play originally had a specific purpose, to expose the injustice of the pass book laws under the apartheid regime. But, in a time now of increasing migration of peoples and the ever-stricter laws about visas and passports, the issues it raises about the political control of individual identity continues to be universally relevant and powerful. Sizwe Bansi's assumption of a new identity to thwart the system has a bitter-sweet effect. For in his efforts to survive, he has lost the one thing which Styles says belongs to each man under apartheid: his identity. His amusing worry over the name of the person now married to his wife reveals an underlying tragic self-doubt: who is he? and what name will he leave behind?

Alternative traditions: Noh theatre

The post-colonial plays discussed so far draw their power from the clash of cultures. They explore the doubts and contradictions each culture can bring to the other, and find, in that encounter, a source of tragic poignancy or understanding. But it is instructive to think about dramatic traditions which are outside the Western canonical legacy altogether. The Noh theatre in Japan developed completely independently of European drama around the fourteenth century; it raises the question of whether tragedy as a genre is specific to the West or whether it can be deemed universal. Certainly Noh plays emphasise the sorrowful aspect of life. They dramatise lament: of lovers for dead loves, of families for lost homes, of warriors for defeated causes. They elegise the past, in the form of ghosts and haunted landscapes. But the form of the drama does not fulfil the Aristotelian expectations of the West. Since the story often involves a ghost, who tells his or her story, the past and present are condensed in a single image which negates the need for narrative plot and all the reversals and moments of decision which go with that. And as the story is frequently told by several characters, voicing the personal narrative communally, there is no possibility for the development of individual character or psychological introspection. Instead, the performance is poetic and symbolic, in a way which is hard for a Western audience to understand. Character is delineated by mask, so that the protagonist (*shite*) wears the *shite* mask, and the travelling character, who arrives at the scene to hear the story, wears the *waki* (traveller) mask. Each positions himself or herself at particular places on the stage, which have developed symbolic meaning, and enact the poetic story.

But the tragic import of the plays, which are far briefer than classical Greek tragedy, appears to lie in their capacity to dramatise powerfully the sense of thwarted hope and the claustrophobic memory of trauma. To take just one example, which has haunted subsequent writers and film-makers, *Motomezuka* (*The Sought-For Grave*) opens with a priest arriving at the village of Ikuta and enquiring about a woman's grave which has become the source of legend. The woman who shows him the grave turns out to be the ghost of Unai, buried there. She was courted by two suitors, but, unable to decide between them, she drowned herself and they killed each other. Now she continues to be tormented by guilt. 'If you abandon this evil obsession, you surely can escape eternal punishment', the priest tells her.[114] But she is imprisoned in an everlasting hell of self-imposed recrimination, figured in the 'Burning House' of her tomb, and she vanishes back into the ground, still screaming with the torment. The fact that Ikuta means 'field of life' and the women at the beginning are picking the first flowers of spring adds a grimly ironic comment on Unai's tragic inability to let go of winter and to renew a sense of hope.

The horribly confining nature of traumatic memory is evoked in Noh by the focus upon place: the tomb, the 'field of life'. Despite the fact that Noh theatre was codified and arguably stultified as an art form in the sixteenth century, it is possible to see the continuation of Noh conventions in modern Japanese theatre and cinema. Kurosawa's *Throne of Blood* (1957), a Noh version of *Macbeth*, opens and closes with the misty, ruined castle of Washizu (the Macbeth character) and the words:

> Behold within this now deserted place
> There once stood a mighty fortress
> There once lived a proud warrior
> Who was murdered by ambition.
> Still his spirit walks, his fame is known.
> For once was so, now still is true.
> Murderous ambition will pursue
> Beyond the grave to give its due.

Washizu's story is inextricably linked to the ruins. Instead of voicing the trauma of guilt with words such as 'O full of scorpions is my mind', Kurosawa suggests Washizu's guilt and entrapment by the visual images of the shadowy castle and his body at the end riddled with arrows. Meanwhile the Lady Macbeth character, Asaji, recalls Unai's ghost in that she does not die but is left in an endless traumatic loop of hellish hand-washing.

Ghosts play an important role in the other great Japanese film of the 1950s, Mizoguchi's *Ugetsu*. As with *Throne of Blood*, the traumatic memory of the Second World War and Japan's fatal imperialist aspirations probably lie behind the film's concern with ambition. Two country men go to the city to seek their fortunes – to win money, fame, honour and glamour – only to destroy their lives and sacrifice the happiness of their families. But Mizoguchi tells the story through the conventions of Noh. The hero Genjuro is seduced by the ghost of a courtly lady, Lady Watsaki, who has cast him in her spell so that she can know the pleasure of love for the first time. Only once he has lost faith in her and flailed wildly at the ghost with a sword does time condense so that her house becomes a ruin and her life just a story in the past. He returns home to be greeted by another ghost, that of his wife, who was bayoneted by soldiers for some meagre rice-cakes. The film closes with the family living and working beside the wife's grave, watched by her loving ghost: 'Many things have happened. At last you have become the man of my ideals. Except I am no longer in the same world as you, except in spirit.'

While film-makers like Kurosawa and Mizoguchi have taken Western subjects and translated them into a Japanese context, a few Western writers have imported ideas back from Noh to express their ideas. W. B. Yeats, for example, who was introduced to Noh by Ezra Pound, responded to the Japanese connection between place and trauma. 'These Japanese poets feel for the tomb and wood the emotion, the sense of awe, that our Gaelic-speaking country-people will sometimes show when you speak to them of Castle Hackett or of some holy well', he observed, comparing implicitly Japanese courtly history and Irish colonialism.[115] His play *Purgatory* is perhaps the tragedy most influenced by Noh theatre in the West, which accounts for the bewildered reception and mixed success it has enjoyed here. The ruined house (based perhaps on the ruined Castle Hackett, home of an ancient Anglo-Irish aristocratic family) stages its tragic history of family conflict and murder repeatedly in a traumatic loop. The old man and the son come to visit the scene, as if they were the *waki* (travelling character), only to discover, in an inversion of Noh, that they are horribly implicated in the family history of the house. The old man stabs his son again and again to prevent the family curse (of son killing father) from continuing. But even as his son gasps out his last breath, his father hears the ominous sound of the curse repeating itself once more. Nothing can break the cycle of violence is the message of the play. Personal histories are bound up with national histories in Ireland, and both play out in a tortured loop of imprisoning memories, an Irish purgatory or the Japanese 'infinite tortures of the Eight Great Hells'.[116]

2.7 Beckett

Comic absurdity

Beckett's plays blur the distinction between comedy and tragedy according to a generic tradition which can be traced back to Shakespeare and Chekhov. Like Shakespeare, Beckett is concerned with figures and plots losing their shape to ambivalent effect. Vladimir and Estragon, for example, consider altering their body shape in *Waiting for Godot* in order to pass the empty passage of time on stage:

> VLADIMIR What do we do now?
> ESTRAGON Wait.
> VLADIMIR Yes, but while waiting.
> ESTRAGON What about hanging ourselves?
> VLADIMIR Hmm. It'd give us an erection!
> ESTRAGON [*Highly excited*] An erection!   (Act I, p. 18)

This classic sexual joke, which usually elicits laughter in performance, works through its recognition of the body's uncontrollable movements, in accordance with Bergson's description of comic business. Comedy, Bergson maintains, challenges 'a certain rigidity of body, mind and character, that society would still like to get rid of in order to obtain from its members the greatest possible degree of elasticity and sociability. This rigidity is the comic, and laughter is its corrective.'[117] But the imagined loss of Vladimir and Estragon's shape also recalls Hamlet's despairing, disintegrating vision of the world as a 'congregation of vapours' (II.ii.293), in which he can tease Polonius by imagining the clouds endlessly changing shape:

> HAMLET Do you see yonder cloud that's almost in shape of a camel?
> POLONIUS By th' mass, and 'tis: like a camel, indeed.
> HAMLET Methinks it is like a weasel.
> POLONIUS It is backed like a weasel.
> HAMLET Or like a whale.
> POLONIUS Very like a whale.   (III.ii.345–51)

This corporeal fluidity in both *Hamlet* and *Waiting for Godot* is mirrored by a structural shapelessness. Hamlet, Vladimir and Estragon worry about 'passing the time' (Act I, p. 46), improvising their entertainment on the stage to fill up the allotted time of the play, whether it be acting with the players (Hamlet) or telling jokes and stories (*Waiting for Godot*). In both cases, while the fluidity might recall comic digressive absurdity, it is prompted by the sense of tragic futility, in which ontologically nothing appears to carry any significance or to have any influential effect.

As in Chekhov's plays, 'passing the time' for Beckett involves recalling other times, nostalgically remembering past history. In *Endgame* Nagg and Nell look back wistfully to the early days of their relationship when they crashed their tandem in the Ardennes, or when they went rowing on Lake Como; in *Waiting for Godot* Vladimir and Estragon talk about having been together perhaps for 'fifty years' and recall the time when Estragon fell in the river Rhone and Vladimir 'fished [him] out'. In a similar vein, Olga, Masha and Irina, the 'three sisters' of Chekhov's play, remember their former, more exciting life and look forward to an imagined future in Moscow. Their concern over whether they will be remembered by future generations renders them simultaneously ridiculous and poignant. So both Chekhov's and Beckett's characters experience a form of existentialist absurdity, in the sense that their beliefs in objective reality and in unchanging, reliable meaning are shown to be an illusion. But Chekhov's absurdity is grounded in history, in the timely angst of the turn of the century when old certainties were being dashed and nothing appeared to be lasting or significant any longer. Beckett's absurdity, on the other hand, is rooted in the theatre, in a closed hermeneutic system in which the notions of representation and referentiality have been negated. Beckett's absurdity is a result of what Stanley Cavell calls a 'hidden literality', an economy in which words and symbols mean no more than their literal signification on the stage.[118] So, unlike Chekhov, Beckett's sense of history entails only the passage of time during the theatrical performance. The clock in *Endgame*, for example, 'is a real thing, empty of function and alarm'; the life of Didi and Gogo off stage in *Godot* is just that, the wings and corridors of the back-stage theatre.[119]

The emptiness and despair in Beckett, then, finds its *raison d'être* in the conditions of the theatre, which is both no more than a shadowy illusion, as in Shakespeare, and yet also not illusion at all but literally all that there is. But can plays which refuse to be grounded in reality be classed as tragic? For all their references to the great tragic canon, how are we to regard Beckett's plays? Assuming that tragedy revealed something about the condition of man in society, the Marxist critics Georg Lukacs and Raymond Williams expressed reservations about Beckett's apparently self-referential focus. For them, Beckett was guilty of reducing tragedy to a bourgeois aesthetic in which it was concerned purely with dramatic form and not with content. Lukacs attacked the 'modernists', including Beckett, for their 'negation of outward reality' and for portraying the 'ontological solitariness of the individual' which makes it 'impossible to determine theoretically the origin and goal of human existence'.[120] Williams, meanwhile, argued that the denial of objective reality in Beckett's plays led to a de-politicisation of tragedy. For him, Beckett offered a nihilistic form of theatre, without function or effect, 'converting a dynamism of form which had flirted with a dynamic of action to a repetitious, mutually misunderstanding stasis of condition'.[121]

Tragic meaning

Yet the self-enclosed nature of Beckett's plays can itself be considered tragic. The incapacity of the plays to mean anything more than they appear and the irrational compulsion behind their action may be considered tragically grotesque. According to the critic Jan Kott, 'the world of tragedy and the world of grotesque have a similar structure'.[122] Both worlds depict situations which are 'imposed, compulsory and inescapable' (p. 132) and both 'pose the same fundamental questions' (p. 141). In tragedy the question is answered by the absolute or God; in the grotesque it is answered by an 'absurd mechanism' which is actually 'set by man himself' (p. 133). Famously comparing *Endgame* to *King Lear*, Kott argued that the metaphysical absolute in both plays (in the form of the gods, justice, external significance) was revealed to be absent and that therefore the suffering endured was grotesquely absurd because it was justified by a non-existent reason. So Gloucester's suicide is 'only a somersault on an empty stage' and it 'does not solve or alter anything' (p. 149); so Hamm, still playing the king in his wheelchair throne, realises that suffering is merely a performance: 'Perhaps I could throw myself out on the floor' (p. 133). Clov looks out of the window to see what is 'happening' or 'how can it end?', and Vladimir and Estragon wait for Godot; in doing so they ask the same questions about the reasons for their current suffering as the great tragic heroes. But in our realisation that there is no significance beyond the characters' present experience, because there are only the words and events performed on stage, we encounter the grotesquely absurd foundation of any life or experience which is purely theatrical.

Yet actions on stage in Beckett, however ridiculous they may initially appear, do replicate aspects of modern life. In other words, Beckett's refusal to mean anything beyond the limits of his own plays does paradoxically carry wider, substantial implications. According to the Marxist critic Adorno, the fragmentation of the coherent self in Beckett actually testifies to the radically devastating effects of modern, capitalist society, which alienates and disempowers the individual. Characters literally trapped on stage in dustbins (*Endgame*) or in a mound of sand or earth (*Happy Days*) embody the feeling of powerlessness engendered by bureaucratic unaccountability or institutionalisation. Actors find themselves defined by objects on stage, whether it be the tape recorder in the case of *Krapp's Last Tape* or the contents of a handbag in the case of Winnie in *Happy Days*. This material definition replicates the condition of capitalism, in which one establishes a sense of self through the purchase of consumer goods. Stable identities disintegrate or radically split in Beckett under the alienating conditions of theatre, just as they do when people are divorced from the means of production. Hamm and Clov, polar opposites, are mutually dependant like two aspects of one self; Lucky's words bear no relation to his intention in *Godot* but are at the disposal of Pozzo; Mouth spews empty words uncontrollably in *Not I*. Beckett's characters are 'empty *personae*, truly mere masks through whom sound merely passes', comments Adorno.[123] Only the gaze of a silent witness appears to give comfort or significance to these empty, meaningless performances: 'So that I may say at all times, even when you do not answer and perhaps hear nothing, something of this is being heard, I am not merely talking to myself, that is in the wilderness, a thing I could never bear to do . . . That is what enables me to go on, go on talking that is' (p. 145), Winnie says to the silent Willie in *Happy Days*. But even that gaze appears to offer as much punitive compulsion and exploitation as comfort. The 'auditor' in *Not I* offers a minimal 'movement' when Mouth pauses in her relentless delivery but this 'gesture of helpless compassion' actually appears to force Mouth cruelly to continue.[124] Meanwhile, the player in *Act Without Words* is thrown back onto the stage by an unseen force from the wings each time he attempts to exit. In these cases the gaze of an unseen spectator, which might not actually see but appears necessary for the performance, enacts literally the absurd compulsion of theatre which Kott described. 'The absolute is transformed into a blind mechanism, a kind of automaton', which is 'not transcendental any more in relation to man . . . [but] a trap set by man himself into which he has fallen'.[125]

Adorno's claim about Beckett's necessary unintelligibility relies upon the notion that an essential sense of self is outmoded: 'the individual is revealed to be a historical category, the outcome of the capitalist process of alienation'.[126] According to this interpretation, the plays may be considered tragic parodies of modernity, in which any recognisable identity proves to be merely a performance. 'The discrepancy between [the] situation and behaviour' of Winnie, for example, 'suggests that her consciously enacted identity is a self-sustained fiction'.[127] The first productions of the plays in the 1950s appeared to confirm

Adorno's interpretation, by creating an effect in the audience of dislocation and bewilderment. They were originally written in French as well as English, and given premières in Paris and London.[128] Jokes in the plays often rely upon a bilingualism in the audience – puns about Godot, for example – and the linguistic disorientation arguably led to a hermeneutic disorientation too. But recent productions have challenged this critical tradition, rooting the plays in a time and a place: Ireland in the post-war period of '1950s consumerism and Cold War apocalyptic fear. So the Irish accents of Felicity Kendall's *Happy Days* or Michael Gambon's *Endgame* can be considered symptomatic of a critical interest in the implicit politics and place of Beckett's plays.[129] And with this awareness of time and place, there is a renewed sense of the physical reality of the characters. After all, the characters exhibit real physical needs in the plays, to which we are bound to respond with compassion too. Nagg is hungry and eats a biscuit even after his wife, Nell, has apparently died; Winnie complains of migraine; Gogo's feet ache because of uncomfortable boots. They weep and laugh at appropriate moments – Nagg cries after Nell dies – even if Nell says earlier that 'nothing is funnier than unhappiness' (p. 101).

Beckett's plays should not therefore be considered simply as commentaries on tragedy or as a reduction of tragic concerns to aesthetic form, despite the fact that his work has prompted a reconsideration of the tragic canon, both in academic criticism and in theatrical productions.[130] They should not be considered simply as tragic parodies of the modern alienated condition, either, despite the influential claims of Adorno and others. Rather, they present what survives a philosophical, dramatic deconstruction in accordance with a tragic tradition which goes right back to *The Trojan Women* or *King Lear*. While the onion layers, as Jan Kott puts it, of protective significance are stripped away, Beckett leaves us with some essential human instincts which invite our compassion and pre-rational understanding. We witness cruelty, tenderness, dependence and vulnerability evident in the characters on stage, based upon the fact that they are embodied as we are. And we see the determined quest to go on living and asking questions, despite the lack of answers, which lies at the heart of the tragic sense.

Case studies 1: Physical violence and dismemberment

'In the anguished, catastrophic times we live in', wrote theatre director Antonin Artaud in 1933, 'we feel an urgent need for theatre that . . . arouses deep echoes within us, . . . which upsets all our preconceptions, inspiring us with fiery, magnetic imagery and finally reacting on us after the manner of unforgettable soul therapy'.[131] According to Artaud, theatre had become either too escapist and diversionary or too cerebral. It needed instead to appeal equally to an audience's emotions and intelligence and to engage with the audience on a visceral level, if it were to fulfil its vital ethical, political role. He went on: 'One cannot separate body and mind, nor the senses from the intellect, particularly in a field where the unendingly repeated jading of our organs calls for sudden shocks to revive our understanding' (p. 66).

The Theatre of Cruelty, which Artaud was developing when he wrote these remarks, was driven by his demand for theatre which was physical and which would 'shock' an audience into reflection and 'understanding'. Contrary to popular belief, bloodshed, mutilation and atrocity were not essential to the form, but 'unrelenting necessity' and 'irreversible and absolute determination' most definitely were. Cruelty brought out the basic instincts of humanity – its passions, its brutality, its desperate struggle for survival – and therefore compelled an audience to face unpalatable truths. Physical cruelty depicted on stage also supposedly forced an audience to recoil in sympathetic horror, thus waking them up to the shared experience of the theatre in which both actors and audience participated. The Theatre of Cruelty thus achieved a heightened level of reality, which inflicted on the audience, according to Artaud, a 'kind of tangible laceration'.

Artaud's Theatre of Cruelty has important implications for tragedy and its particular life in performance. It presses the issue of the importance of the shared experience of theatre and the physical presence of the actors, performing in real time before the audience. And it raises the question of the emotional impact of theatre, which must shock an audience or at least appeal to it on a visceral level. Both these concerns – physicality and emotion – might be said to be crucial to the effect of tragic drama. But cruelty also gets to the heart of the problem of tragic performance. For it tests the bounds of theatre and what we find believable. Physical cruelty, after all, is hard to stage, and, instead of Artaud's heightened reality, might actually lead to heightened stylisation and audience alienation. Secondly, in testing the capacity of theatre, physical cruelty might also be thought to test the boundaries of genre, paradoxically turning shock to laughter rather than profound tragic sorrow. Central to the ambivalence of tragic performance, therefore, are those moments when we witness acts of violence and dismemberment, and are compelled to respond.

The atrocity of lopping off a limb on stage or tearing a body apart in front of an audience is very difficult to direct. How does one do it convincingly, so that the audience feels the horror appropriately? Innogen's discovery of Cloten's headless body, dressed in the clothes of Posthumus in *Cymbeline*, is intended to be 'senseless' and surreal:

INNOGEN O Posthumus, alas,
Where is thy head? Where's that? Ay me, where's that?
Pisanio might have killed thee at the heart
And left thy head on.[132]

In contrast, the blinding of Gloucester in *King Lear* continues to shock its audience, because we feel the fragility of the old man in the hands of the young. In keeping with the reductive nature of the play, which 'reasons the need' of everything and destroys it, Gloucester's eyes are described purely as physical objects. 'Out, vile jelly!' (III.vii.86), says Cornwall, as he gouges out the second eyeball. The shock is also exacerbated by the casual way in which the torture scene is conducted, unexpectedly early in the overall structure of the play and seemingly provoked spontaneously by the course of events and chance remarks. The altruistic servant, for example, who dies trying to protect Gloucester, apparently provokes the mutilation of Gloucester's second eye by his dying words: 'My lord, you have one eye left / To see some mischief on him' (III.vii.84–5). In the 1986 National Theatre production, directed by David Hare, Gloucester (Michael Bryant) was strapped to a chair and tilted back to the floor, so that he seemed more terrifyingly vulnerable. In other fringe productions, Regan has given Cornwall anything that comes to hand to use as a torture tool – a stiletto heel, a hair clasp – thus emphasising the improvised, evil nature of the scene. In all these cases the torturers crowd round the victim, simultaneously making him appear more at their mercy and also shielding the details from the possible disbelieving eyes of the audience.

Some plays make the question of the believability of theatrical representation paradoxically central to the horror they wish to stage. The scene in which the Duchess of Malfi kisses what she thinks is her husband's hand is a classic example of this issue. At first, in the dark, the duchess believes her husband is present before her, although she is concerned how cold the hand is. When the servants arrive with torches, she discovers the hand is severed from the rest of the body and, on being shown the 'artificial figures of Antonio and his children' and told that 'here's the piece from which 'twas ta'en' (IV.i.55), believes that she has indeed kissed the hand of her dead husband. It is only later that the audience discovers from Ferdinand that the bodies were merely waxworks, designed to 'bring her to despair' (IV.i.113). In the nineteenth-century productions, the duchess only kissed a ring held by Ferdinand, thus avoiding the risk of disturbing sensibilities through the suggestion of physical mutilation; in the 1980 Manchester Corn Exchange production, by contrast, Helen Mirren (the duchess) threw a very realistic looking hand into the audience in her horror.[133]

The point of this scene is to raise awareness of the deceptive illusion of theatre. Webster expects us to interpret the significance of the hand differently as the scene progresses, from living body part, to horrific atrocity, to theatrical prop of undisclosed origin. The cruel power which Ferdinand exercises over his sister's sanity, by teasing her with violent simulacra, is replicated by the power which Webster's theatre exercises over us. What are we to believe? How can we respond appropriately, taunted by various visions of horror, some staged and others supposedly real? To what extent does grotesque theatre, with its ambivalent reality, actually portray a world gone mad?

If *The Duchess of Malfi* presents us with horror, only to reveal later that the vision was merely one of waxworks, Euripides' *Bacchae* stages the reverse process. It suggests that the Dionysiac *sparagmos* (tearing apart the sacrificial victim) will only take place in ritual form and that Pentheus will be able to witness it at a safe distance, enjoying the security of invisibility just as the theatre audience is sheltered from the represented violence on stage by the conventions of theatrical performance. But the play goes on to explode that security. Dionysus himself allows the Bacchic women to pull Pentheus down from his position of safety high in a treetop. The presiding god of theatre, in other words, licenses the destruction of the trusted boundaries and safeguards of theatre. Pentheus is torn apart savagely, according to the messenger's report, and Agave comes in with the graphic result of this perverted *sparagmos*, the severed head of her son. The dialogue which follows, between Agave and her father Cadmus, during which Cadmus forces Agave to recognise what she has done, goes to the heart of question about ancient tragic performance. For Agave must acknowledge the significance of what she holds in her hands, that it is supposedly not the head of a lion but that of her son, even if it was only a tragic mask in ancient productions. 'What *prosōpon* is that in your hands?' (1277), Cadmus demands, the Greek word *prosōpon* meaning both face and mask and thus blurring realist, theatrical distinctions.[134] Once Agave realises that she has killed her son, she wishes to know the fate of his body. Can it be restored? The dialogue here is most poignantly telling:

> AGAVE   And the dear body of my son, father – where is it?
> CADMUS   I found it with difficulty, and have brought it here.
> AGAVE   Are all his limbs joined decently together? (*kalōs*)
> CADMUS   [missing line in text]   (1298–1301)

Agave's demand for 'decency' relies upon a continued distinction between the body of an actor and the body of her son to be lamented, between theatre and reality, between the sanctity of the human body and its cruel, fragmentation into physical pieces. But after Dionysus' tearing down of the safeguards of theatre,

5. Agave sits beside Pentheus' severed head/mask. National Theatre's *Bacchae*, directed by Peter Hall, 2002. © Geraint Lewis

no such distinction can be guaranteed. It seems grimly fitting that Cadmus' response to Agave's question is missing here, because of the disintegration of the manuscript.[135] For what reply could he give to her? Decency was a concept which disappeared with the savage dismemberment of Pentheus' body under the god of theatre's direction. Just as Bosola declares that justice disappeared with the Duchess of Malfi's death – 'Thou took'st from Justice her most equal balance / And left her nought but her sword' (V.v.38–9) – so Dionysus rid the world of 'decency'.

Cadmus' response to Agave's anxious question over the state of Pentheus' body is missing and one can only try to imagine what it might have been. The silence seems appropriate in this case. But the alternative, in *Titus Andronicus*, is to fill horror with rhetoric. Marcus finds his niece raped and mutilated, her tongue and hands cut off, and, far from being stunned into silence, responds with an elaborate forty-six-line speech:

> Speak, gentle niece, what stern ungentle hands
> Hath lopped and hewed and made thy body bare
> Of her two branches, those sweet ornaments
> Whose circling shadows kings have sought to sleep in. . . .
>
> (II.iv.16–19)

This 'appropriately inappropriate' speech, as Jonathan Bate describes it, attempts to respond to the unutterable horror of Lavinia's brutalisation.[136] The contorted level of the conceits of language is symptomatic of her physical contortion and mutilation. So some productions have staged this scene symbolically, to echo the rhetorical nature of Marcus' response. The groundbreaking production of Peter Brook, for example, cut Marcus' speech altogether and replaced Shakespeare's verbal stylisation with visual stylisation. Lavinia (Vivian Leigh) entered the stage in silence, red ribbons streaming from her mouth and wrists. In contrast, Deborah Warner's violently realistic version reinstated Marcus' speech and accompanied it with gruesome stage makeup, flagging up the horrible incongruities and transgressions at the heart of this play.[137]

The difficulty with staged physical violence, then, is to elicit the correct response, whether that be correctly appropriate or correctly inappropriate. The audience's capacity to be shocked by what it sees in the theatre carries implicit assumptions about what is morally acceptable or unacceptable and where the limits of our tolerance might lie. Our willingness to confront what is morally unacceptable might be said to lie at the heart of tragic drama, and therefore the act of exposing ourselves to what is shocking is intrinsic to the ethical activity of tragic witness. When Sarah Kane's first play, *Blasted*, was staged at the Royal Court in 1995, it raised many questions about this problematic relationship between shocking sensationalism and tragedy. Critics savaged it for what they claimed was its gratuitous violence and 'unadulterated brutalism'. 'Repeatedly firing a gun at the audience can only lead to diminishing returns', wrote Jane Edwardes in London's *Time Out* magazine, arguing that the representation of excessive physical violence can actually lead to fatigue and indifference rather than moral reflection. Even Aleks Sierz, a fan of Kane's work, noted after seeing the first performance that 'Kane's play makes you feel but it doesn't make you think'.[138] Artaud, of course, advocated just this visceral rather than cerebral response to theatre. But it does raise the question of the efficacy of shock. Does tragedy require one to *think* as well as to feel? In our 'self-destroying society', which, according to John Peter of the *Sunday Times*, Kane sees as 'aimless, brutish, barren, cannibalistic, prurient, diseased and terror-stricken', can we provide any transcendent moral vision, any coherent dramatic answer?[139] Should we?

The violence in Kane's plays, it can be argued, is an appropriately incoherent response to a world ruptured by atrocity. The physical walls of the hotel room in *Blasted* are literally exploded by a mortar bomb at the start of scene 3, and thus, by implication, the safe structure of the play is ripped apart by the shocking violence of war which it cannot ignore.[140] As the play progresses, the action becomes more and more grotesque and less realistic, from Ian and

Cate's rough oral sex to the soldier's graphic account of stabbing a woman to death to the soldier sucking out Ian's eyes to Ian eating the dead body of the baby. In each case, the violence is not gratuitous but an attempt to re-enact the horrors of war, to bring what has happened elsewhere into the personal, domestic consciousness. As the soldier says to Ian, the terrible brutality of war, in which rape, torture and cannibalism take place on a regular basis, must be acknowledged and described. 'Some journalist, that's your job', he tells Ian. 'Proving it happened. . . You should be telling people' (scene 3, p. 47). He goes on to rape Ian in an apparent attempt to bring home to him exactly what happened to his girlfriend and to try to understand it himself:

> *When the* **Soldier** *has finished he pulls up his trousers and pushes the revolver up* **Ian's** *anus.*
> SOLDIER Bastard pulled the trigger on Col. What's it like?
> IAN (*Tries to answer. He can't*) (scene 3, p. 49)

Ian's stunned silence in this situation is testimony to the morally appropriate inability to fully comprehend atrocity. Neither he nor the soldier can say 'what's it like', because the horror is unutterable and can only be blindly imitated in surreal or hyper-real fashion.

But Kane's plays also explore what survives this violence. Although almost our last vision of Ian is of his blinded head sticking out of a hole in the floor, dying after eating the remains of the baby, the final image of the play itself is arguably tender. Cate returns, blood seeping between her legs, and feeds Ian (now dead and apparently in limbo) with sausage and bread she has scavenged. His response is to thank her; the last words of the play thus express gratitude. Similarly, Kane's third play, *Cleansed*, stages couples caring for each other even in the worst situations of torture, abuse and mutilation, presided over by the mysterious doctor, Tinker. Carl and Rod's lovemaking, even when Carl has no tongue, hands or feet, or the final image of Grace holding Carl's stump of an arm after their amateur hacked-off sex change, are testimony to a basic human capacity to love one another, even under the most de-humanising conditions.[141] Indeed, even Tinker's brutal acts of dismemberment – cutting out Carl's tongue, after Carl has promised never to betray or lie to his lover, and cutting off Grace's breasts after she has expressed a wish to look like her brother – constitute a series of strictly logical responses to characters' declared intentions or desires which can be interpreted as acts of love. Like the scientists in Büchner's *Woyzeck*, Tinker subjects these characters to a cold, experimental gaze, testing their endurance and humanity. And thus the play also tests its audience, carefully balancing amorality and morality, violence and redemption, with a logical clarity of vision in a chaotic universe.[142]

The playwright Howard Barker observed that 'the most appropriate art for a culture on the edge of extinction is one that stimulates pain' and that the spectacle of this pain is both complex and beautiful in its resistance to common platitudes and traditional consolation.[143] Kane's interrogation of common platitudes through her searing images of physical mutilation and desperate tenderness between characters draws on a long tradition of moral scepticism, bodily degradation and tragic performance. They recall Beckett's repeated pairings – of the blind Pozzo and Lucky, or the blind and disabled Hamm and Clov – which themselves echo mad Lear and blinded Gloucester's reunion on the heath. In each case in these plays, the nihilistic absence of pity is matched by a redemptive recognition of the inter-dependency of all humans, even if – or especially if – that inter-dependency is based on nothing more than a shared human body, a common capacity to eat, weep, shit and sleep. 'Can't get tragic about your arse' (scene 3, p. 50), the soldier says to Ian after raping him in *Blasted*. But *Lear*, Beckett, Webster and indeed Kane counter that observation by locating the tragic sense precisely in the human body, in its fragmentation, its pain and its endurance.

Case studies 2: Language

Tragedy's relationship to language is ambiguous. It depends on whether one locates the tragic in the traumatic or horrific experience itself or whether it is to be found in the attempt to describe, confront or understand that experience. For pain itself, according to Elaine Scarry, resists language; indeed it 'actively destroys it, bringing about an immediate reversion to a state anterior to language, to the sounds and cries a human being makes before language is learned'.[144] It is therefore impossible for the person in pain to put his overwhelming agony into words, though the pain is 'incontestably . . . present'. It is equally impossible for the person witnessing another's pain truly to understand his feeling and therefore to describe the suffering accurately. To have pain is to 'have certainty', writes Scarry; to witness another's pain is 'to have doubt'.

But the doubt which might render the witness speechless is regularly compensated for by therapeutic or forensic discourse, which attempts to control and mitigate the pain through words. These attempts, as Scarry puts it, to 'reverse the de-objectifying work of pain by forcing *pain itself* into avenues of objectification', involve inventing languages to tell the story of hurt, be it medical histories elicited by doctors or personal injury trials mounted by lawyers.[145] In this case, tragedy could be described as a process of 'objectification', since it transforms the unsayable into the sayable through performance. If physical pain destroys language and therefore 'unmakes' the world while others 'create' that world again through linguistic inventiveness, then the aesthetic form of tragic drama might be said to be axiomatic in its linguistic remaking.

The tragic act of describing suffering is performed most self-consciously in the Greek dramatic convention of the messenger speech. Here we see, in microcosm, one of the quintessential functions of tragedy, to tell the story of pain, always presaged by the chorus' demand to hear the tale. The messenger does not hold back in his description, but gives us the full graphic details, whether they be of Hippolytus torn apart by the monster from the sea or Pentheus destroyed by his mother and the other frenzied maenads.[146] One of the most arresting speeches is the account, in *Medea*, of the princess Creusa's death. She is killed by the poisonous robe which Medea has sent her as a gift and which, catching fire, burns into her flesh. The messenger tells us how her father put his arms about her in a final embrace and then found that he was hideously stuck to the body, 'as ivy clings to the shoots of the bay tree – and a terrible struggle ensued, for he wanted to lift his knee while she kept clinging to him' (1213–16; Morwood translation). It is a memorable image, of father and daughter glued together in death, for it figures our problematic relationship to tragic language. Like the father to his daughter, the chorus is irresistibly drawn to the messenger's words. Like both the father and the chorus, we are pulled into the horror of tragedy.

The messenger's speech, then, marks the first ambivalent stage in Scarry's 're-making' of the world after its painful rupture. The speech appears to go some way towards healing the pain, through voicing it, but at the same time it forces the listener to hear and participate in the horror, breaking down his defences. More disturbingly, the messenger speech can be duplicitous and lead to further tragic consequences, rather than constitute the first step on the way to healing as we expect. The messenger's speech at the beginning of the *Agamemnon* announces the fall of Troy, indicated by the signal of the beacon's flame. Clytemnestra amplifies this speech for the chorus, explaining first the way in which the chain of beacons, from Troy to Argos, spreads the news and then, in a second speech, describing graphically the sack of the city. The irony is that these are details which Clytemnestra, at home in the palace in Argos, cannot possibly have known, relying solely on the simple message of the beacon signal, and yet the chorus of old men is more satisfied with her improvised fiction of the fall of Troy than with the technicalities of the beacon. As Simon Goldhill points out, 'the fact that the message Clytemnestra provides for the light is so markedly a fictitious, imaginative weaving of words emphasizes the arbitrary connection of signifier and signified in the process of message sending and receiving'.[147]

The *Oresteia* reveals the extent to which language, rather than being the first stage in healing suffering, becomes the source of suffering itself, becomes, indeed, the destabilising force of tragedy. The trilogy examines the deceptive power of language to persuade, from Clytemnestra's powerful speech which persuades Agamemnon to walk on the carpet up to the palace, with fatal consequences, right up until Athene's successful advocacy of Orestes' cause in the court case staged at the end of the *Eumenides*. In fifth-century Athens, rhetoric was the key to power, persuading the democratic assembly to vote for a particular position or pushing the jury in the law courts into convicting or acquitting the accused. It formed a central part of a young man's education, since a facility in persuasion was essential for success. Thus it is understandable that language came under 'tragic critique', in Goldhill's words, with inevitable consequences for the broader uncertainties about politics, justice or ethics.[148]

Euripides highlighted this 'tragic critique' of rhetoric with his repeated use of the convention of the *agon* in his plays. At some stage in each play, two characters debate a question, almost as if they were no longer deeply implicated in the tragic action but rather were students of rhetoric, debating some academic point. So, for example, in *The Trojan Women* Hecuba and Helen debate whether Helen is guilty of betraying her husband and eloping with Paris, and Medea and Jason debate whether Jason is justified in abandoning Medea and marrying his new bride. In each case the characters draw attention to the rhetorical context of their words or *logos*. 'May I plead in answer [*ameipsasthai logō*]' (903), says Helen, and Hecuba replies, appealing to Menelaus who has been nominated as judge of the debate: 'Hear her, Menelaus, that she may not die without this allowance and let me plead against her [*tous enantious logous*]' (906–7). The dramatic irony is that this debate is being held, not in a debating school in Athens, but in the midst of the carnage and devastation following the sack of Troy. Euripides thus exposes the inappropriateness of forensic or rational language under these conditions. Far from giving voice to pain and thus healing it, this language jars with the suffering before us. There is something grotesque about the staging of an *agon* when everything around it has become irrational *agonia*.

Timothy Reiss has argued, in *Tragedy and Truth*, that tragedy works retrospectively. Tragedy makes sense of and invents a discourse for suffering: 'Tragedy appears ultimately as the discourse that grasps and encloses a certain "absence of significance" that may well be common to all discursive acts at the "inception" of the discourse making such acts possible, and that renders impossible, before such particular ordering, the meaningfulness of any such discourse', he writes.[149] But Reiss' argument posits a very rational and efficient interpretation of language, in suggesting that it can make sense of or 'order' suffering before the tragedy can be staged. It seems instead, from all I have discussed so far, that tragedies perform the moments of suffering's successful or unsuccessful translation into language with problematic consequences. In drama, we see the ambiguous transmutation in *process*, rather than its successful *results*.

If tragedy is thought to involve the ongoing *process* of translation, then the moments of silence and miscommunication in tragic drama become central to performance. In the midst of the riddling, deceptive language of the *Oresteia*, Cassandra's silence (for what amounted to about fifteen minutes in Peter Hall's 1980 National Theatre production) acquires a telling power. When she does finally break her silence, it is to utter fragmentary prophetic exclamations which leave the chorus baffled. Yet despite the fact that she can foresee her death at the hands of Clytemnestra clearly, she submits to her fate and enters the palace. 'The luckiest hours like scribbles in chalk on a slate in a classroom . . . Everything's wiped out', she wrote in chalk on the floor, for an agonisingly long five minutes in Katie Mitchell's 1998 National Theatre production, before going into the palace. No words were spoken. Hermione, another victim of men's plots in *The Winter's Tale*, similarly cannot enter back into the familiar world of speech after she is miraculously restored to life. 'That she is living, / Were it but told you, should be hooted at / Like an old tale; but it appears she lives, / Though yet she speaks not' (V.iii.116–19), says Paulina, when Leontes urges his wife to speak. Her silence registers a certain resistance to the easy reintegration of tragedy back to comedy. There will be no superficial 'hooting' or vernal glossing over her sacrifice, after all that she has suffered for sixteen years.

Silence can be powerful. But even silence can be misinterpreted or mistranslated. Phaedra's silent, dead body, for example, appears to corroborate her words of outraged shame scrawled on the tablet hanging around her neck. But her words turn out to be a wicked lie, which inadvertently cause the death of the man she wrongly accuses of raping her. Here then, we witness the fatal misinterpretation of language by Theseus, apparently validated by the silence of his wife's body. The translation of trauma into language is itself the source of further tragic bewilderment. A second example of the misinterpretation of silence can be found at the beginning of *King Lear*. 'Unhappy that I am, I cannot heave my heart into my mouth' (I.i.90–1), says Cordelia when compelled to declare her love for her father in order to win a third of the kingdom. Her solution is to 'love and be silent', in the hope that her lack of words will appear more sincere than the elaborate, rhetorical declarations of her sisters. But in fact her father misinterprets her reply of 'nothing', apparently believing it reveals a lack of gratitude and tenderness, and banishes her, with disastrous consequences for himself and for the kingdom. Thus Cordelia's 'Nothing' turns out to be pregnant with unintended, tragic meaning.

In more recent drama, which has become 'a theatre of language where man's words are held up to us as a spectacle', according to Jean Vannier, silence becomes positively eloquent.[150] Harold Pinter's plays explore the fight for dominance and underlying vulnerability in human relationships through the medium of language. In this battle, apparently innocuous and inconsequential casual conversation carries underlying meanings, and the pauses between remarks are further aggressive tools in the psychological struggle. The language appears colloquial or even clichéd, but, in Pinter's words, 'under what is said another thing is being said'.[151] In this context, silence is potentially both a weapon and a fearful moment of self-revelation, when the main object is to survive through secrecy and defensive obfuscation. 'I think that we communicate only too well, in our silence, in what is unsaid, and that what takes place is a continual evasion, desperate rearguard attempts to keep ourselves to ourselves' (p. xiii), Pinter said. *The Caretaker*, among the most Beckettian of Pinter's plays, depicts this need for three men, Davies, Mick and Aston, 'to keep ourselves to ourselves', in the cramped confines of one room. In particular Davies, the tramp figure, attempts to evade categorisation of his origins or identity by stumbling over his replies, diverting the conversation or holding out the false hope that his 'papers', which hold the key to his identity, might be collected in Sidcup. But these gambits are challenged by Mick's alternating attack of violent verbal interrogation and threatening pauses:

> DAVIES I was brought here!
> *Pause*
> MICK Pardon?
> DAVIES I was brought here! I was brought here!
> MICK Brought here? Who brought you here?
> DAVIES Man who lives here. . . . he. . . .
> *Pause*
> MICK Fibber.   (Act II, p. 32)

Like Beckett's *Waiting for Godot*, Pinter's play hovers between tragedy and comedy, drawing upon music hall routines for easy laughs while suggesting an underlying hopeless melancholia But the end of *The Caretaker*, in which the old man Davies is expelled from the room by the two younger men, ensures that this play moves beyond where, according to Ronald Knowles, 'the "point" of laughter and silence both begins and ends',[152] to a bleak prospect of inhumanity and the 'menacingly tragic absence of social recognition'.[153] In performance, Aston's silence at the window, his back to Davies, as the old man struggles in his bewildered isolation, encapsulates this nihilistic lack of response between characters:

ASTON You make too much noise.
DAVIES But . . . but . . . look . . . listen . . . listen here . . . I mean . . .
Aston turns back to the window.
What am I going to do?
Pause
What shall I do?
Pause.
Where am I going to go? (Act III, pp. 75–6)

For Pinter, silence sums up all the loneliness prevalent in post-war, impoverished Britain, as well as a strictly theatrical, linguistic conflict. For other recent dramatists, especially Beckett, silence takes on a more metaphysical significance. Silence, under this dispensation, must be associated not with pain, as Scarry argues, or Pinter's inhumanity, but with non-existence. The battle between life and death is exemplified by the struggle over language. On the one hand, characters in Beckett use language as their last bulwark against extinction. They might be said to 'rage against the dying of the light', to coin Dylan Thomas' phrase, and thus the tragic sense in Beckett might be said to be located in the continuing urge to speak and assert one's vitality, right up until the moment of extinction. But on the other hand, characters also long for death and silence, and to surmount the 'inferiority of words'.[154] So they find themselves in the double bind between 'the inability to speak and the inability to be silent'.[155]

The tortuous dilemma between language and silence – or, by extension, between life and death – is dramatised most sharply in Sarah Kane's last play, *4:48 Psychosis*, in which there are no longer designated characters, as such, but just voices, unassigned to particular actors in the play-text, speaking the most poetic language through the trauma of mental breakdown. After rehearsing the reasons for and against committing suicide and the agony of mental illness, the play builds to a great crescendo:

Speak
Speak
Speak . . . . .
No one speaks

Validate me
Witness me
See me
Love me
(p. 243)

In the original Royal Court production, these words were projected onto a mirror hanging above the heads of the three actors, fetishised as objects and spoken with increasing vehemence. One could feel the urgency behind their articulation; the finale amounted to a vibrant, creative flourish, 'strangely uplifting', according to one critic.[156] The very different version by Tangram Theatre, directed by Daniel Goldman, expanded the Royal Court's three actors to a seven-woman chorus, focusing upon the group choreography. The chorus huddled together before dispersing to utter the last words – 'watch me' – each in isolation, punctuated by long intervals of silence. These two very different methods of staging the ending of Kane's play – one loud, the other quiet – explore the subtle connections between language as a lifeline, 'validating' the speaker, and language as a further form of suffering, buffeting its victims. Tangram Theatre's final, silent, staged suicide without a body (simply a noose and falling chair) captured beautifully Kane's self-aware, performative final note, ironically speaking her own annihilation: 'watch me vanish . . . . . . please open the curtains'.[157]

Chapter 3

Tragic theory

3.1 Aristotle

Nearly all writing on tragedy returns to Aristotle. He first considered drama in general – and tragedy in particular – as worthy of analysis. Indeed he established the term 'drama' for theatre performance: 'dramas are so called because they represent people in action'.[1] While the great period of tragic playwriting in Athens had finished with the death of Euripides in 406 BC, some seventy years earlier, Aristotle was the first writer to take the cultural phenomenon of the Greek dramatic festivals seriously. As a result of his examination of the generic definition, the aesthetic form and the social effectiveness of tragic plays, the notion of tragic theory, or the philosophy of tragedy, was born. It could be said that most of the questions about tragedy which continue to vex us today were first formulated by Aristotle.

Aristotle importantly considered the function of tragedy within society. A generation earlier Plato had wished to ban poets from his ideal republic because of their disturbing effect upon the emotions:

> When we listen to some hero in Homer or on the tragic stage moaning over his sorrows in a long tirade, or to a chorus beating their breasts as they chant a lament, you know how the best of us enjoy giving ourselves up to follow the performance with eager sympathy . . . To enter into another's feelings must have an effect on our own: the emotions of pity our sympathy has strengthened will not be easy to restrain when we are suffering ourselves.[2]

But Aristotle, the political pragmatist, was prepared to integrate tragedy within his wider scheme of things. Tragic drama was an established institution within the city of Athens. The emotions, moreover, were an unavoidable component of human nature. So Aristotle sought to understand them, rather than to wish them away. How was one to account for tragedy? What purpose did it serve? How did it succeed in channelling the emotions?

117

Aristotle's answer to these questions offers both a formal and a functional definition of tragedy. In other words, he maintains, in the *Poetics*, that the essence of tragedy is to be found both in the components of the tragic drama itself and also in the effect it has upon the audience.[3] The question of emphasis – is Aristotle more interested in the aesthetic structure of plays or in the audience response? – continues to intrigue literary critics and debates rage about the precise relation between events viewed on stage and the emotions felt or purged in the audience.[4]

Central to Aristotle's account of tragedy is the claim that tragedy involves a plot. The tragic sense, in other words, depends upon action rather than upon a situation or the timeless condition of the world. This becomes an important point of contrast with the post-Romantic understanding of tragedy, as I will show later.

> We have stipulated that tragedy is mimesis of an action that is complete, whole and of magnitude . . . A whole is that which has a beginning, middle and end. A beginning is that which does not itself follow necessarily from something else, but after which a further event or process naturally occurs. An end, by contrast, is that which itself naturally occurs . . . but need not be followed by anything else. A middle is that which both follows a preceding event and has further consequences. Well-constructed plots, therefore, should neither begin nor end at an arbitrary point, but should make use of the patterns stated.   (1450b23–34)

Aristotle is interested here in a formalist account of tragedy, in the 'well-constructed plot'. According to this argument, it is important for tragedy to have a distinct shape which unfolds logically and which comes to a satisfying close: 'An end is that which itself naturally occurs but need not be followed by anything else'. Yet the tragic narrative also involves change and historical process, as events arise as a consequence of others. Tragedy, for Aristotle, happens within the familiar unfolding of history.

Since Aristotle viewed tragedy as a process rather than as a static situation, he placed particular emphasis upon the choices and decisions which the individual hero makes. The crucial shift from the 'beginning' to the 'middle' of the plot is dependant upon a wrong decision taken or a wrong course of action pursued: 'a change not to prosperity from adversity, but on the contrary from prosperity to adversity, caused not by depravity but by a great error [*hamartia*] of a character' (1453a13–16). The word which Aristotle uses here – '*hamartia*' – is sometimes translated as 'flaw'. This translation implies that Aristotle is talking about some moral flaw in the hero's character. But 'hamartia' is less about a character defect than about an error in judgement which led to a wrong decision or a wrong course of action.[5] The emphasis, in other words, is upon action rather than upon character.

Every tragic theorist has a play which best exemplifies his particular philosophy. In Aristotle's case, this is *Oedipus the King*. In *Oedipus*, one can supposedly see the different stages of the plot. He is a man of reasonable fortune, the leader of his city. He makes a wrong decision; he suffers a reversal of fortune (a *peripeteia* as Aristotle calls it); he comes to recognise his terrible change of fortune (*anagnorisis*); and he is left at the end in utter abjection, from which no more results can follow. Indeed Aristotle says that *Oedipus* is the ideal tragedy because the 'reversal' coincides with the 'recognition'. Then it produces the greatest emotional impact because it is 'most integral to the plot' (1452a36–7). But even *Oedipus*, Aristotle's quintessential tragedy, proves to be more complex than his analysis of a linear narrative suggests. For when does Oedipus make the wrong decision (*hamartia*)? At the moment of leaving Corinth to escape his adopted parents? When he meets his father at the crossroads? When he solves the riddle of the sphinx? When he sends to the oracle a second time, at the beginning of Sophocles' play? The multiple narratives and time frames, which cohere dreadfully in the final moment of recognition in Sophocles' play – 'I am on the verge of hearing something terrible, but hear it I must' (1170) – belie the simplicity of Aristotle's account.

Ultimately, however, Aristotle is interested in these plot structures because of the effect they have upon the audience, for 'such a joint recognition and reversal will yield either pity or fear'. These emotions are strangely intellectual rather than instinctive. They are less dependant upon the visual spectacle or even the power of a particular performance than upon the formal qualities of the plot. Aristotle talks of the reader being able to be 'aroused by the actual arrangement of the incidents', without seeing them dramatised on stage.

> The plot should be so structured that, even without seeing it performed, the person who hears the events that occur experiences horror and pity at what comes about. (1453b3–6)

What follows has proved to be the most controversial part of Aristotle's argument. He claims that the arousal of the emotions leads inevitably to the calming of them. In other words, the very fact of pity and fear being stirred up in the theatre ultimately eliminates, moderates or exhausts them so that they are no longer troubling in the world outside: '. . . through pity and fear accomplishing the catharsis of such emotions' (1449b27–28).[6] The word *catharsis* literally means washing, purifying or purging. The source of the controversy lies mainly in the ambiguity of the Greek at this point (*pathēmaton katharsin*) since, grammatically, it is not clear what is the connection between the emotions (*pathēmaton*) and the washing (*katharsin*). Is the subject washed free of the emotions? Or is it a washing of the emotions, a purification of the feelings of fear and pity already felt?

There are many different interpretations.[7] But what seems important to me is the fact that, in this simple phrase, Aristotle raises the question of the relationship between pain and relief or, in other words, the connection between suffering disturbing emotions and finding pleasure in witnessing them. In this elliptical comment about catharsis, he confronts the mystery of why audiences are drawn to tragedy and why they apparently enjoy watching people suffering on stage. It might be that the ambiguity of the Greek reflects the intractability of the problem; in other words, that the difficulty of understanding Aristotle's phrase here is no coincidence but rather it rises out of the necessarily tangled, complicated nature of Aristotle's thinking about this issue. Certainly the relationship between pain and pleasure depends upon the degree of identification between the sufferer and the spectator. In his description of pity and fear in his book on *Rhetoric*, Aristotle is alert to the dangers of identifying with the object of these emotions too much: '[fear] is a pain or disturbance arising from a mental image of impending evil of a destructive or painful sort'; '[pity] is a sense of pain at what we take to be an evil of a destructive or painful kind, which befalls one who does not deserve it, which we think we ourselves or someone allied to us might likewise suffer and when this possibility seems near at hand'.[8]

The chorus in *Oedipus* reacts to the vision of him blinded thus:

> ... godforsaken, cursed by the gods!
> I pity you but I can't bear to look.
> I've much to ask, so much to learn,
> So much fascinates my eyes,
> But you ... I shudder at the sight.
> (1438–42; Fagles translation)

In the chorus' ambivalence about the activity of looking at Oedipus, we can see Aristotle's '*pathēmaton katharsin*' dramatised. Members of the chorus identify with their king, now 'godforsaken', to the extent that they cannot bear to look at him. But they also can achieve enough distance to be able to 'learn' from him ('We enjoy looking at accurate likenesses of things which are themselves painful because ... as we look, we learn and infer what each is' (1448b10, 16–17), as Aristotle writes in *Poetics*). So the chorus twists and turns, demonstrating physically the contortions of *catharsis* and the fascinating problem of why tragedy gives pleasure.

3.2 Hegel

While Aristotle acknowledged the presence of both intellectual engagement and raw emotion in our response to tragedy, Hegel focused upon the mind. He believed that 'Reason is the law of the world and that, therefore, in world history things have come about rationally'.[9] Tragedy was just one aspect of this rational process. That is to say, tragedy occurred as a result of a logical and historical sequence of events and consequences which could be analysed rationally and clearly understood. If particular cases from the past were anatomised correctly, this clarity of comprehension could be achieved empirically, arising from historical examples. But it could also be understood theoretically, because the same principles seemed to apply in each event. Hegel's sense of the universality of history, the feeling that certain incidents always produced the same consequences, was crucial for his belief that one could actually learn principles from the past in order to apply them in the future. Tragedy – and by extension history – fulfilled a didactic role which, if accepted in the right spirit, could lead to social progress in the future.[10]

It is difficult to understand Hegel's comments on tragedy without having some appreciation of his wider theory of history. For he presented tragedy as arguably the dramatisation of historical forces and their casualties. History was teleological, in the sense that it was always progressing forward to the future, and ultimately it would lead to the goal of the universal state of freedom. But in the meantime, individuals, states and even whole cultures or ages of civilisation, must go through a series of conflicts in order that freedom could finally prevail. One belief system would clash with the next and be crushed or subsumed in the onward march of time. History was a continual dialectical process of development through conflict in which one learnt from one's opponent even as one was biting the dust.[11]

There is actually a great debate among scholars of Hegel as to how far he considered history an abstract principle rather than the sum of events in the material world. Was there a 'spirit' of history which imposed a teleological purpose upon the world and ensured that everything was driven forward to the future? Or did events just happen in the real world and yet somehow the seeds of their future purpose were embedded within them? Was there a transcendental or even divine system or did the continual process of dialectical collision with other external circumstances produce the desired end result? Whichever interpretation of Hegel one veers towards, what is important for our understanding of tragedy is that ultimately, in his vision of history, he was prepared to sacrifice individuals and particular things in the name of the general movement of mankind towards freedom. The historical process, he famously wrote, is 'the slaughter-bench on which the happiness of peoples, the wisdom of states, and the virtues of individuals have been sacrificed'.[12]

Tragedy raises precisely those questions of the sacrifices of history and the relation between the individual and larger, impersonal forces. According to Hegel, tragedy dramatises the moment of collision between two states of belief or what he terms 'equally justified powers':

> An individual's decision, justified by the object he aims at, is carried out in a one-sided and particular way, and therefore in specific circumstances, which already carry within themselves the real possibility of conflicts, he injures another and equally moral sphere of the human will. To this sphere another person clings as his own actual 'pathos' and in carrying out his aim opposes and reacts against the former individual. In this way the collision of equally justified powers and individuals is completely set afoot.[13]

Rather than arguing with Aristotle about the 'hamartia' of the individual action, Hegel maintained that both individuals in the conflict are right. As Walter Kaufmann puts it so succinctly, the 'conflict is not between good and evil but between one-sided positions, each of which embodies some good'.[14] So Orestes prays, in Aeschylus' *Libation Bearers*, before going to kill his mother – 'War-god shall encounter War-god, Right shall encounter Right' – even if Electra immediately questions the perfect balance of this statement: 'O ye gods, decide aright the plea of right'.[15]

According to Hegel, the tragedy which best exemplifies his vision of the tragic collision of two forces is Sophocles' *Antigone*. In this play, the two main characters, Antigone and Creon, represent different spheres of values or beliefs, which are equally valid and which will inevitably come into conflict. Antigone honours the principle of family relationships and the gods of the underworld; Creon recognises only Zeus and the values of the city which he upholds. Their decision to act in accordance with these belief systems is not made according to individual whim or casual character trait but because of the principles which they are determined to represent and uphold, the 'ethical right', as Hegel says, 'to a definite course of action'. Both are committed to making their particular sphere of concern paramount; both are justified in their beliefs; both carry out their actions in the name of those beliefs to the exclusion of all other arguments. The inevitable conflict between them dramatises not just the collision of these individuals but the intractable debate between different moral priorities in political life. Living in a polis will always involve negotiating the competing demands of family and city.[16]

Antigone is Hegel's prime illustration of his theory, but one could also imagine some of Shakespeare's plays fitting this account of the collision of two equally justified powers. Think, for example, of *Richard II*, in which Richard's divinely ordained but practically incompetent kingship is contrasted with the skilful leadership of the usurping Bolingbroke. Both have some moral claim on the path they are pursuing and, in the inevitable conflict between them, we see the notion of kingship itself being questioned. Richard's divine interpretation of kingship – 'for every man that Bolingbroke hath pressed / To lift shrewd steel against our golden crown, / God for his Richard hath in heavenly pay / A glorious angel' (III.ii.54–7) – is undermined by Bolingbroke's more meritocratic definition. When Richard is no longer king, he wonders whether he is any longer himself; the result is a form of existential nihilism:

> Then am I kinged again, and by and by
> Think that I am unkinged by Bolingbroke,
> And straight am nothing.   (V.v.36–8)

In this Hegelian interpretation of the tragic within Shakespeare's history plays, we can arguably see a political interpretation of tragedy which was to have an important influence on Brecht's epic theatre later.[17] Tragedy becomes not about the individual hero, in the Aristotelian or Romantic sense, but rather about the collision of powers, involving the whole of society, in which no one is at fault but all suffer.

But most controversial is Hegel's analysis of tragic resolution. According to him, the conflict is brought to an end through a more general or higher reconciliation, at the expense of the individuals concerned.

> Above mere fear and tragic sympathy there therefore stands that sense of reconciliation, which the tragedy affords by the glimpse of eternal justice.[18]

The tragic protagonists destroy themselves in the conflict but harmony is restored because the transcendent principle of justice prevails. This troubles us as a theory for two reasons. Firstly, it assumes that our emotional response to tragedy – Hegel's 'mere fear and tragic sympathy' – can be mitigated or chastened by a rationalisation of it. Stop feeling pointless sympathy for the hero, is the message, and start appreciating intellectually the elegance of the narrative thread of history. Hegel explains:

> The true development of action consists solely in the cancellation of conflicts as conflicts, in the reconciliation of the powers animating action which struggled to destroy one another in their mutual conflict.

Only in that case does finality lie not in misfortune and suffering but in the satisfaction of the spirit, because only with such a conclusion can the necessity of what happens to the individuals appear as absolute rationality, and only then can our hearts be morally at peace: shattered by the fate of the heroes but reconciled fundamentally.[19]

Satisfied when Antigone has hanged herself? *Morally at peace* when Creon, bereft of all his family, is hounded from the city into exile? We might, at this point, want to side with Aristotle and reply that human passions are unavoidable and intractable, not to be schooled out of us by the calm Hegelian voice of reason.

The second reason that Hegel's theory of tragic resolution is problematic is that it depends upon a notion of 'eternal justice' which we perhaps find hard to endorse. It assumes that there is some governing principle of moral good or some teleological purpose over and above the petty collisions and struggles of individuals, which ensures that everything ultimately is for the best. But many of Euripides' plays challenge this assumption by questioning the existence of justice or the gods, and Aeschylus' *Oresteia*, which has been governed by appeals to Justice (or *dikē*), ends with the uncertainty over whether justice has prevailed or whether the resolution has been reached through Athene's superior powers of rhetoric. Even Antigone questions whether divine justice exists, given her experience: 'What ordinance of the gods have I transgressed? Why should I look to Heaven any more for help, or seek an ally among men?' (921–3, Kitto translation). These tragedies raise the possibility that 'eternal justice' might be a mirage, the smokescreen of autonomous capricious gods or the projection of human wishes.

3.3 Nietzsche

Nietzsche reacted against Hegel's rational account of Greek tragedy. For Nietzsche, the ancient Greek world was not a place of calm reflection and logical order, but was driven by primitive forces of desire, violence and fear, exemplified by the chaotic ritual worship of Dionysus. Instead of the statuesque, white-marbled image of antiquity promoted by some of the Romantic writers a century earlier, Nietzsche made an important breakthrough in offering a disordered, irrational and internally riven picture of ancient Greece. But he actually found a strange pleasure in this picture. Indeed, he believed that tragic drama offered a way of confronting the implications of nihilism and he called for the ancient tradition of the art form to be revived.[20]

Nietzsche's vision of the world as without meaning or divine purpose was derived from the earlier German philosopher Schopenhauer. According to

Schopenhauer, the world is polarised between the 'will' and 'representation'. As 'representation', it exists only for us to be able to perceive it and understand it and, as such, it is no more than a projection of our intellect. We impose purpose and causality upon it through our intelligence. But underlying this illusion, it exists as 'will', as the instinctive forces of nature, such as pain or pleasure or what Schopenhauer calls 'blind urges'. This essential condition of the world has no reason or motivation, no purpose and no final teleology. Whenever we try to control it, we simply manifest the will unconsciously; it is present in every human desire, including the desire to maintain order. Indeed Schopenhauer suggests that existence is a continual oscillation between the hope for purpose or fulfilment and the realisation that this yearning can never be satisfied:

> Eternal becoming, endless flux, belong to the revelation of the essential nature of the will. Finally, the same thing is also seen in human endeavours and desires that buoy us up with the vain hope that their fulfilment is always the final goal of willing. But as soon as they are attained, they no longer look the same, and so are soon forgotten, become antiquated, and are really, although not admittedly, always laid aside as vanished illusions. It is fortunate enough when something to desire and to strive for still remains, so that the game may be kept up of the constant transition from desire to satisfaction . . .[21]

In *The Birth of Tragedy*, Nietzsche reiterates Schopenhauer's distinction between 'representation' and 'will' with the analogies of two Greek gods, Apollo and Dionysus. The Apollonian drive in the world amounts to the principles of order, individuality, reason, art, creativity and the 'beautiful illusion of the inner fantasy world'.[22] The Dionysiac drive, in contrast, represents the forces of intoxication, annihilation, irrationality and what Nietzsche calls 'primal One-ness' (p. 25). We attempt to live necessarily in the world of Apollo – by making representations to ourselves of the world, the gods, justice, reason and so on – but we discover that our 'Apolline consciousness alone, like a veil, hid that Dionysiac world from [our] view' (p. 21). However, while for Schopenhauer our realisation of the reality of the 'will' is a cause of deep pessimism or a 'dead-ening languor', for Nietzsche this discovery becomes strangely the source of joy. He relishes the tearing down of individualism back to the 'primordial one-ness' because it involves a degree of self-abandonment and release. After all, as Nietzsche says, the 'entire existence' of the Apolline Greeks, 'with all its beauty and moderation, was based on a veiled substratum of suffering' (p. 26) and when the individual abandoned himself to the self-oblivion of the Dionysiac, 'excess was revealed as truth, contradiction; the bliss born of pain, spoke from the heart of nature' (p. 27). Pain and bliss are intimately intertwined in Niet-zsche's contradictory view of tragedy.

Nietzsche differs from Schopenhauer too because he imagines the destruction of illusion as happening at a particular moment in tragic drama, at a specific temporal point in the tragic narrative. Schopenhauer posits tragedy as a static condition of existence. 'The true sense of tragedy', he writes 'is the deeper insight that what the hero atones for is not his own particular sins, but original sin, in other words, the guilt of existence itself'.[23] But Nietzsche is interested in the temporal structure of tragic drama. According to him, Greek tragedies begin with the duality of a Dionysiac chorus and an Apollonian dialogue between individual characters staged before it. During the course of the drama, the hero realises the deceptive nature or fragility of his distinct identity, and allows himself to be drawn back into the Dionysiac. Aristotle's 'peripeteia' becomes Nietzsche's 'negation' of the hero or the 'fragmentation of the *principium individuationis*' (p. 17). So we see, for example, Oedipus brought back to the Dionysiac nature he had sought to escape, when he is stripped of his heroic identity and ends up an abject outcast: 'what the myth seems to whisper to us is that wisdom, and Dionysiac wisdom in particular, is an abominable crime against nature; that anyone who, through his knowledge, casts nature into the abyss of destruction, must himself experience the dissolution of nature'.[24]

One of Nietzsche's main contributions to the development of tragic theory is to give serious consideration to the pleasure which tragic drama gives. He addresses the question of why the ancient Greeks were committed to the institution of tragic performance and why tragic drama is still crucial to culture today. The answer to this is partly because of the relief or even ecstasy of the Dionysiac self-abandonment which the tragic dissolution of the Apollonian involves. He writes of the 'blissful ecstasy which rises up from man's innermost core' (p. 17) at the moment when he loses his distinct identity and is sucked back into the crowd. And the answer lies also partly in the fact that tragic performance, and art more generally, transfigures the Dionysiac horror into something beautiful and bearable:

> Aware of the truth from a single glimpse of it, all man can see now is the horror and absurdity of existence . . . Here, in this supreme menace to the will, there approaches a redeeming, healing enchantress – *art*. She alone can turn these thoughts of repulsion at the horror and absurdity of existence into ideas compatible with life.[25]

When we might be faced with the prospect of Schopenhauer's pessimism, seeing cynically into the 'game' or the pointlessness of things, Nietzsche's art, moving between the energy of the Dionysiac and the beauty of the Apollonian, can reawaken our curiosity and enthusiasm for more life and more experience.

Life, as Nietzsche says, is 'indestructibly mighty and pleasurable'. Contrary to Hegel, it cannot be intellectualised. Contradictory, dissonant and fragmentary, Nietzsche's tragedy is modernist in its mode, modern in its appeal.

Most importantly, Nietzsche's tragic vision is aesthetic. The dissonance between the Apollonian and Dionysiac principles is based not upon morality or modes of thought but upon types of creativity. Apollo offers the allure of art, sculpture and literary endeavour; Dionysus, like Schopenhauer's life force or 'will', is 'eternally creative, eternally destructive'. The battle between the two restores a balance between these two types of creative urges. So 'only as an aesthetic phenomenon is the world justified', notes Nietzsche. Tragedy teaches us to see the whole – Dionysiac and Apollonian – as an organic work of art and not care about the moral fate of individuals. Greek tragedy provided a forum or a structure for an endlessly repeated aesthetic justification of creation and destruction.

But even while Nietzsche reveals some awareness of the place of Greek tragedy in Athenian culture, he is not interested at all in the political or social function of Greek tragedy. The chorus, for him, represents the ritualistic groups of Dionysiac worship, not the people of the polis. The origins of tragedy lay in religion, he argues, and not in the democratic assemblies. As a result Nietzsche is not interested in the aspects of tragic drama which bear comparison with practices in the assembly or the law-courts. He is not concerned with dialogue, the place of rhetoric, the focus in the plays upon language and the dangerous power of persuasion. Motivation comes from irrational, atavistic compulsions, and not from the careful, if erroneous, rational weighing of cause and effect. This is the reason why Nietzsche becomes so critical of Euripides and so adamant that Greek tragedy degenerated from its original roots in Dionysiac ritual. The logic of Euripides and his grimly ironic parody of the language of fifth-century Athens does not fit Nietzsche's sense of the irrational, mysterious force of tragedy.

Nietzsche's silence about tragedy's roots in Athenian political culture matters because it leads to a blindness in his thinking about tragedy as performance or even in locating precisely the tragic sense, both tasks which initially seem to be at the heart of the Nietzschean project. Nietzsche blurs the distinction between the spectator and the chorus, so that both participate in the Dionysiac intoxication. He explains this by arguing that under the influence of Dionysus, all boundaries and divisions give way 'to an overwhelming feeling of unity'. Therefore the implication is that the emotions of ecstatic pleasure and pain are experienced by the characters on stage, rather than simply and entirely by the spectators watching the performance. The watchword for tragedy according to Nietzsche is participation, not spectatorship. 'What kind of artistic genre would be one derived from the concept of the spectator?', he asks rhetorically. Drama becomes, then, a ritual enacted by those on stage; it is not a performance designed to evoke a reaction in an audience in the heart of a city.[26]

3.4 Kierkegaard

Hegel's optimistic belief in a transcendent principle of justice also proved the starting point for Kierkegaard's very different thinking. In contrast to Hegel's confident rationality, Kierkegaard's tragic vision was irrational, unpredictable, inexplicable and despairing at times. And while Hegel developed his theory of the progress of history in logical, dialectical steps, Kierkegaard wrote in a fragmentary, mystical style, offering his readers not a coherent nor arguably even an authentic voice.

Literary critics who attempt to draw upon Kierkegaard's writing in order to develop what they consider to be his theory of tragedy often give the impression that he wrote in a straightforward, organised and philosophical way with a clear-cut set of beliefs. They take his words at face value. But in fact, his main books which have implications for tragedy are written in the voices of different personae – 'A' and 'B' edited by Victor Eremita in the case of *Either/Or*, Johannes de Silentio in the case of *Fear and Trembling* – and so are infused with the uncertainty of Romantic ambiguity. They are a mixed collection of writings too. The papers of the aesthete 'A', which comprise the first volume of *Either/Or*, include not only the essay 'The Ancient Tragical Motif as Reflected in the Modern' but also, among other things, the despairing ramblings of 'Diapsalmata' and the concluding 'Diary of the Seducer'. Indeed, *Fear and Trembling* and *Either/Or*, which are most often cited by subsequent writers on tragedy, are not really about tragedy as such, and the few specific references to tragedies, which Kierkegaard does make in them, are quite conventional and unoriginal. But what Kierkegaard does write about – guilt, sacrifice, belief, isolation – has profound implications for our sense of the tragic and this is why his influence on later writers, especially existentialists such as Camus and Sartre, has been so important. His work brings together faith and despair in a paradoxical combination which seems to chime increasingly with the concerns of postmodernity.[27]

Central to Kierkegaard's vision, if it can be called that, is the impact upon faith of the modern state of solitary individualism. In modern life, there are none of what Kierkegaard (picking up Hegel's terms) calls the 'substantial categories' which supported the individual in ancient times, such as the family or the state. Instead the individual is left 'entirely to himself'.[28] He takes upon himself the responsibility for his actions and consequently he internalises the guilt too for his misdeeds. While, in the past, the hero's actions might be seen in the context of fate, of a universal system of ethics and a shared understanding, now in atomised modernity they are unique to him, incommunicable. This could lead to despair; it could also lead to comedy:

> When the age loses the tragic, it gains despair. There lies a sadness and a healing power in the tragic, which one truly should not despise, and when a man, in the preternatural manner our age affects, would gain himself, he loses himself and becomes comical.[29]

According to 'A', the supposed author of the essay on the 'Ancient Tragical Motif', it would be tragic if the hero set his 'hamartia' in the context of objective fate and transcendent forces but sadly comic if he suggested that his 'accidental individuality' took priority over the general development of the world (p. 140). Compassion is essential for tragedy but compassion would be impossible to extend to such a private individual.

However *Fear and Trembling* is devoted to contemplating precisely this scenario, the individual who maintains that subjective belief has a higher claim than universal ethics. The book revolves around the story of Abraham's sacrifice of Isaac. Abraham is told by God to sacrifice his son and he obeys without question, despite the fact that his son is infinitely precious to him. At the last minute, God replaces Isaac with a ram. Why, the narrator of *Fear and Trembling* asks, is Abraham admired and not condemned as a would-be murderer? Why is God revered and not reviled as a torturous tease? The answer Kierkegaard gives is that, in terms of human ethics, Abraham *is* a murderer since he fully intended, right to the last moment, to kill Isaac. But in terms of religious belief, he is uniquely devout because he put faith in God's injunction above all other considerations – reason, love, nature, morality – or, as Kierkegaard puts it, he 'suspends the ethical for the teleological'.[30] Kierkegaard deduces from Abraham's story that belief is not dependent on reason or the normal world of ethics but must be based on subjective intuition. It runs counter to all conventional expectations and therefore, he says, it is absurd. Kierkegaard – or rather the narrator, Johannes de Silentio – rehearses various rational explanations for the Abraham story, which read like tragic narratives: at the moment of sacrifice, Isaac prayed to God to rescue him, little knowing it was God's injunction that his father was obeying, and Abraham deliberately kept him under that illusion, so that his faith in God remained unwavering while his trust in his father was shaken utterly; or Isaac saw the fear in Abraham's eyes as he raised the knife and he lost his faith at that point, the world becoming dark for him henceforth. But ultimately these stories have to be rejected, because it did not happen like that and there were no extenuating circumstances. The story remains an enigma, beyond our rational understanding, and that demonstrates its realm in the mystery of faith.

In the course of the discussion, Silentio/Kierkegaard contrasts Abraham with another great mythical child murderer, Agamemnon, who sacrificed his daughter Iphigenia. The comparison for Kierkegaard highlights the difference between the tragic hero and the man of faith:

> The difference between the tragic hero and Abraham is obvious enough. The tragic hero stays within the ethical. He lets an expression of the ethical have its *telos* in a higher expression of the ethical . . . With Abraham it is different. In his action he overstepped the ethical altogether, and had a higher *telos* outside it, in relation to which he suspended it . . . It is not to save a nation, not to uphold the idea of the State, that Abraham did it . . . He does it for the sake of God because God demands this proof of his faith; he does it for his own sake in order to be able to produce the proof.[31]

According to this argument, Agamemnon's action is understandable because it is committed in the name of various identifiable groups: the army, the state, the angry gods. Abraham's act, however, is not done for any *reason*; it is dependent purely on private belief which is its own end.

Kierkegaard's distinction between the tragic hero and the man of faith is clear-cut. However it depends partly on maintaining the Hegelian sense that the principle of justice and ethics in Greek tragedy remains unproblematic and that the purpose for which Agamemnon sacrificed Iphigenia is not questioned by Euripides as a mirage. ('How do I know that this is not merely just a fiction?' (1617), asks Clytemnestra, on being told of the miracle at the sacrifice). And the distinction depends too on an unshaken religious belief, which can contemplate 'the suspension of the ethical' for the sake of God. But what would happen if, as Kant suggests, Abraham were simply wrong?[32] The danger of Kierkegaard's theory is that there are no safety checks upon belief, no way of testing faith by commonly shared notions of proof, reason or morality. It paves the way to solipsism, alienation, madness.

So although Kierkegaard himself writes with the certainty and zeal of religious belief, nevertheless when his work is read against the grain by subsequent followers, particularly the existentialists, the tragic implications of its openness to doubt become apparent. The isolation of the individual, who is left at the mercy of an absurd universe and who can only intuit subjectively God's commands without the consolation of community and without rational proof that God actually exists, is a matter for despair. Liberated from ethical constraints and external regulation, this alienated individual must take on his own sense of sin and guilt. Adam, Kierkegaard writes in *The Concept of Anxiety*, had a premonition of guilt in the Garden of Eden, even before he ate the apple, because of God's injunction not to do so.[33] His mind was darkened by the prospect of sin, and the moral dilemma of whether or not to commit it, even while he was still supposedly free and innocent. So, by extension, we are burdened by doubt and guilt at the very prospect of making decisions in life, of choosing our course of life. The act of living as individuals, in other words, fills us with agony or *angst*. For Kierkegaard, that agony is the prerequisite of faith; for the reader who cannot make the leap to belief in God, that agony is the terrifying realisation of modern individualism, and its consequential nihilistic loneliness.[34]

3.5 Camus

The French writers Albert Camus and Jean Paul Sartre developed some of the ideas in Kierkegaard's and Nietzsche's philosophy to formulate an existential vision of life with tragic overtones. From Kierkegaard, they took the concepts of absurdity and anxiety (originally *angst* in Kierkegaard; *angoisse* in Sartre). Kierkegaard's absurdity described a world ultimately determined not by reason but by the inexplicable and unpredictable, by the enigmatic event born of faith. Contemplating the absurd left one dizzy but at least one was supported by an unknowable God. From Nietzsche, however, Camus and Sartre inherited the notion that there is no God and that morality or divine purpose is derived from the human imagination. This is vividly summed up by Nietzsche, in 'The Gay Science', in the words of a madman, who runs out prophetically into the marketplace to harangue the sceptical men gathered there:

> Where is God? I'll tell you! We have killed him – you and I! We are all his murderers. But how did we do this? How were we able to drink up the sea? Who gave us the sponge to wipe away the entire horizon?[35]

When Kierkegaard's absurdity is stripped of God's reassurance, the world becomes frighteningly empty, meaningless, nihilistic. It was this world, with all its potential for tragedy, which Camus and Sartre confronted.

Sartre actually maintained that his philosophy was optimistic. 'Existentialism is nothing else but an attempt to draw the full conclusions from a consistently atheistic position. Its intention is not in the least that of plunging men into despair', he wrote in 1946, defending himself against some vicious attacks.[36] But the trajectory of his theories seemed to tend towards the tragic. At the heart of his project was the logical consequences of a world without God. If there is no God, then any purpose or consciousness which exists depends upon a radical subjectivity in humankind. 'I think therefore I am', Descartes had written, and Sartre developed this idea into an argument that thinking or consciousness were the basis for existence. 'Man is nothing else but that which he makes of himself . . . man will only attain existence when he is what he purposes to be'. What becomes tragic is that Sartre sees this need to think about one's existence and to make choices about what kind of person one wants to be as deeply burdensome. He speaks of the 'anguish' of this responsibility, rather as Kierkegaard wrote of the 'angst' of ethical choice. If somebody experiences no anguish, Sartre believes, then that person is simply deceiving himself or suffering 'bad faith'. Thus the freedom of being liberated from God or any regulation could equally be described in terms of 'abandonment'. God is not going to suddenly help man but he is alone in the world, lost in the pressure to make the correct decision. 'Man', Sartre puts it strikingly, 'is condemned to be free'.[37]

Sartre's claim is given dramatic form in his play, *Huis Clos* (*No Exit*), in which three people find themselves after death waiting together in a small, confined room. They anticipate the conventional torments and tortures of hell: the fire, the whips and chains. But as they wait, they fill in the time chatting. As they talk, they discover exactly how each can disturb or hurt the other in conversation. By the end of the play, they realise that they are never going to move to the conventional hell but that they are condemned to talk with the others for eternity. It is a cruel depiction of human nature and a harsh conclusion about freedom. 'Hell', says one of the characters, Garcin, 'is other people'.[38]

While Sartre placed more emphasis upon action and upon interpersonal communication as ways of confronting the anguish of existence, Camus focused upon the consciousness. Sartre's good or bad faith depends arguably upon making the right decisions about one's actions regarding other people; Camus's depended upon rising above one's own situation with 'scorn'. Like Sartre, Camus saw contemporary life as conducted largely without reflection and as fundamentally meaningless. People lead unauthentic lives, in the sense that they have not made conscious decisions about their daily routines and identity. Camus imagines a moment when a man might suddenly realise his inauthenticity or pointlessness:

> It happens that the stage-sets collapse. Rising, streetcar, four hours in the office or the factory, meal, streetcar, four hours of work, meal, sleep, and Monday Tuesday Wednesday Thursday Friday and Saturday according to the same rhythm – this path is easily followed most of the time. But one day the 'why' arises and everything begins in that weariness tinged with amazement.[39]

At this point, this newly conscious person becomes aware of the 'absurdity' of existence, or, in other words, the self-deception of continuing as if there were some defining significance in the world when in fact there is none. But even while he becomes aware of the absurdity, he must confront it. Suicide is a cowardly option, Camus concludes, because it is to yield precisely to the logic of the absurd, that there is no point in existence. Instead, one must resist by simply 'living the absurdity'.

Camus illustrates these arguments with a story: the myth of Sisyphus. In ancient Greek mythology, Sisyphus was condemned to spend eternity in the underworld pushing a rock up to the top of a hill, only to watch it roll back down to the bottom again for him to repeat his task. The endless repetition of Sisyphus' action without reason or goal illustrates the tedious emptiness of contemporary life with its banal daily routine and invented fiction of purpose. But in the retelling of the story, Camus becomes interested in the moment when Sisyphus has to turn around and go back down the hill to collect the rock again.

> I see that man going back down with a heavy yet measured step toward the torment of which he will never know the end. That hour like a breathing-space which returns as surely as his suffering, that is the hour of consciousness. At each of those moments when he leaves the heights and gradually sinks towards the lairs of the gods, he is superior to his fate. He is stronger than his rock.   (pp. 108–9)

In the brief period when Sisyphus is not performing his task – pushing the rock uphill – he can gain a mental perspective upon it. This allows him to see the absurdity of what he is doing and therefore immediately to rise above it, because he has made a conscious decision to think and not simply to participate and push.

Camus transforms the bleakness of Sisyphus' situation into something unexpectedly positive. The language he uses to describe Sisyphus' state of mind as he walks back down to collect his rock is all about superiority and transcendence:

> Sisyphus, proletarian of the gods, powerless and rebellious, knows the whole extent of his wretched condition: it is what he thinks of during his descent. The lucidity that was to constitute his torture at the same time crowns his victory. There is no fate that cannot be surmounted by scorn.   (p. 109)

Lucidity, victory, scorn: Sisyphus rises above his situation through his heightened awareness of his situation. He gains mastery over the pointlessness of his task, not through any physical resistance or rebellion, but through his own understanding of its meaninglessness. So Camus suggests that, by idealising the individual consciousness at the expense of the environment, one can surmount despair and make the viewing of tragedy possible and bearable.

The emphasis which Camus places upon consciousness means that his approach to tragedy is fundamentally aesthetic rather than ethical, as it is for Hegel. The tragic hero does not play a role in changing society either politically or morally, but merely gains a perspective upon it. And therefore perspective – the way we see things – becomes crucial. Sartre's sudden tragic realisation of absurdity left him feeling sick, rather like Kierkegaard's dizziness:

> I recall better what I felt the other day at the seashore when I held the pebble. It was a sort of sweetish sickness. How unpleasant it was! It came from the stone, I'm sure of it, it passed from the stone to my hand Yes, that's it, that's just it – a sort of nausea in the hands.[40]

In contrast, at the end of Camus' 'The Outsider', Meursault, waiting for his execution, is infused with wonder at the sensuous, albeit 'indifferent', beauty of the world:

> I woke up with stars shining on my face. Sounds of the countryside were wafting in. The night air was cooling my temples with the smell of earth and salt. The wondrous peace of this sleeping summer flooded into me . . . I looked up at the mass of signs and stars in the night sky and laid myself open for the first time to the benign indifference of the world. And finding it so much like myself, in fact so fraternal, I realized that I'd been happy, and that I was still happy.[41]

Like Sisyphus' 'scorn', Meursault's happiness and sense of beauty offers him a vantage point from which to view the tragedy of his situation. The individual consciousness, elevated and detached from events here to an alarming degree, offers a form of redemption which, for some critics, mitigates the tragedy.[42]

3.6 Girard

It is possible to detect, by the middle of the twentieth century, a growing belief that tragedy was more amenable to the insights of anthropology than to philosophy. Of course, anthropologists had been interested in Greek tragedy, and more generally Greek mythology, before. In the wake of Nietzsche's *Birth of Tragedy*, the 'Cambridge ritualists' such as Jane Harrison and James Frazer became fascinated by the stories of sacrifice, death, descent to the underworld and rebirth which seemed to permeate the ancient Greek imagination. These narratives symbolised for them the universal story of death and rebirth which they believed lay at the heart of all religions.[43]

But by the middle of the twentieth century, there were two major intellectual developments. The first lay in the recognition that ancient Greek culture was very different from modern Western culture and therefore the study of it should be more akin to the ethnographical study of other cultures conducted by anthropologists than to historical approaches which assumed lines of continuity between the past and the present. The consequence of this recognition was that tragedy, as an art form, owed its origin to a society whose values and practices were somewhat mysterious and were to be understood only with difficulty and after detailed, anthropological study.

But the second development made that work of understanding the Greeks much easier. The structuralist approach to mythology and primitive societies pioneered by Claude Levi-Strauss was premised on the idea that culture was organised within a system which was logically coherent and which could therefore be interpreted. Levi-Strauss, for example, analysed the distinctions people made between sacred and taboo places, between practices which were acceptable and those which were forbidden, in order to understand, by these structures, the underlying values of the people.[44] So by extension, ancient Greek culture, its myths, religion, ritual and drama, could be analysed according to its structures and distinctions within a self-contained semiotic system.[45] While the culture might not be analysed according to Western, philosophical logic, therefore, it nevertheless obeyed its own internal rules which made interpretation and explanation possible.

According to anthropologist René Girard, central to understanding the dynamics of ancient Greek society was the practice of sacrifice. This practice formed the crucial part in religious ritual and its ramifications could be detected far wider, in the political, social and dramatic life of the community. Girard maintained that primitive societies were prey to a level of rivalry and violence, endemic to group living, which had to be channelled and controlled. The best way to control the violence was to focus attention upon one supposed source of it and to sacrifice that source. As a result, the practice developed of finding a 'scapegoat', or substitute victim, which could take on all the blame for the ills of the society. This victim, usually literally a goat, would either be killed as part of a religious ritual or else driven out of the city into the wilderness, taking all the anger and violence with it. The sacrificial victim was therefore both hated and yet also worshipped for its role in purging the community of its troubles. It was an object of fear and reverence, of ill and good, the ambiguous *pharmakos* (which means both 'poison' and 'cure' in Greek).[46]

The dynamics of ritual sacrifice can also be extended to Greek tragedy. For most important to Girard's argument about the scapegoat is the notion that it represents the community; therefore figures other than goats – or indeed animals – can be selected for sacrifice. Girard goes on to argue that in fact a king is the ideal choice for a sacrifice, because, as the leader, he represents the community better than anyone within it. As king, he also stands outside the community and consequently does not disturb the city's equilibrium by undue sympathetic tugs upon the heart. Remember Oedipus' careful delineation of his relation to the polis when comparing his grief with that of the citizens of Thebes: 'Your sorrow touches each one of you alone and nobody else but my spirit is grieved both for the city and for me and for you' (62–4). He acts both as the city's representative here – grieving for the city – and yet also is set apart from the city, because he feels its troubles in a different way, indeed more intensely, than do its citizens.

The ideal result of the Girardian sacrifice is to restore the equilibrium of the community. If the city's anxiety and violence is met by a corresponding victim or scapegoat, then the violence can be effectively purged and the city will be calmed. But if there is a failure to find an exact correspondence, or if the scapegoat is deemed either too removed from the community or too close to it, then there arises what Girard terms a 'sacrificial crisis': 'The hidden violence of the sacrificial crisis eventually succeeds in destroying distinctions, and this destruction in turn fuels the renewed violence' (p. 49). Now the pure violence of sacrifice might be tainted with impure or misdirected violence. Or the careful structure of correspondence and distinctions might become confused and therefore the sacrifice will lose its clear-cut effect of catharsis. Girard cites Heracles' sacrifice of his children in Euripides' play and Deianira's 'sacrifice' of her husband Heracles in Sophocles' play *Women of Trachis* as examples of impure violence, when the expected ritual sacrifice is perverted by the tragic imbalance of the community and the loss of distinctions.

So tragedy, according to Girard, dramatises both the ritual dynamics of sacrifice, which relies upon correspondences and distinctions, and also the perversion of that sacrifice, when distinctions and order break down. The two types of sacrifice may become blurred. 'The difference between sacrificial and non-sacrificial violence is anything but exact', observes Girard, and indeed the violence of the ritual sacrifice can spill over into the chaotic violence of the sacrificial crisis. But as one act of violence invites the next, it is possible to imagine the state of disorder eventually ending in one final sacrifice which purges everything before it. So in revenge tragedy, the loss of definitions results in a succession of murders. De Flores' murder of Alonzo de Piracquo in 'service' to Beatrice changes – and is a result of a change in – the moral and social hierarchy of Middleton's *The Changeling*: 'Here's beauty changed / To ugly whoredom; here, servant obedience / To a master sin, imperious murder'(V.iii.197–9). In Tourneur's *The Revenger's Tragedy*, Vindice believes erroneously that he can intrigue to murder members of the corrupt court, without getting corrupted himself. But he loses the distance and distinction between his moral position and those he aims to punish: 'Tis time to die when we are ourselves our foes' (V.iii.118). Eventually, in these plays, however, order of some sort is re-established and the corruption and violence is purged. 'Justice hath so right / The guilty hit, that innocence is quit / By proclamation, and may joy again', observes Alsemero at the close of *The Changeling* (V.iii.185–7).

Girard's account of tragedy as sacrifice is useful because it sheds light upon Aristotle's notion of *catharsis* and the question of how tragedy 'effects relief' or indeed gives pleasure. In the ambiguous figure of the *pharmakos*, we can see the double meaning of tragedy as the source both of benefit and of harm, of enjoyment and of disturbance. And in Girard's careful analysis of types of violence, we can learn something about the intimate relation between order and disorder in tragedy. But ultimately Girard's account of sacrifice might appear too formulaic and removed both from the details of the text and from history to be anything more than provocative food-for-thought. After all, how can one realistically analyse Tourneur or Middleton in the light of Athenian religious sacrificial practice two thousand years earlier? It is when Girard's theories are combined with a serious historical sense, as they are by Jean-Pierre Vernant and Paul Vidal-Naquet, that they become most powerful and engaging.

Case studies 1: Fate

Playwrights and philosophers have always assumed that tragedy is bound up with questions of fate. Fate offers the tragic event a cause and an explanation. It lends the action a gravity by linking it to larger, metaphysical forces. To suggest otherwise, namely that tragedy is unaffected by fate, is either, as Kierkegaard points out, to leave the tragic character frighteningly alone and guided only by his own judgement,[47] or to abandon him to the mercy of the purely arbitrary and accidental.

However, despite this assumption that, as Terry Eagleton puts it, 'tragedy and fate walk hand in hand', philosophers have not come up with a working definition of the concept and there has been very little sustained writing on the topic.[48] This lack of guidance is perhaps due to the fact that the notion of fate depends on three distinct but overlapping fields: philosophy, literature, and the anthropological study of religious and cultural practice. In other words, we can think of fate either as the metaphysical or theological account of the cause of things (philosophy); or as the formal narrative which shapes the plot and reveals the necessary consequences of the hero's actions (literature); or as the common cultural beliefs in fates, oracles and prophecy (anthropology).[49] Tragedy draws upon all three definitions in complicated combinations in its attempt to explain the necessary causes of certain terrible events and to set human misery within some scheme of transcendental or aesthetic justice.

Ancient Greek mythology accounted for different fatalistic forces, which at various times might be in conflict with one another. The Fates or *Moirai*, represented in Homer and Hesiod as old women spinning, decided the length of any human life; Zeus, the chief Olympian god, presided over human affairs and might be appealed to by mortals or by other immortals in order to bring certain events into being; the oracle of Apollo could be consulted at Delphi for enigmatic predictions about the future; meanwhile, the scales of Fate might tip mechanistically in order to decide anyone's fortune. Sometimes the gods and fate work in tandem; at other times they appear to be independent of each other. These different narratives of determinism actually testify to a radical uncertainty, in the ancient Greek mind, about divine agency, or at least a sense of its fluidity and ambivalence. Homer's *Iliad*, which formed the bedrock of ancient Greek religious knowledge and practice, reveals, at its core, conflicted providential forces. Achilles already has his *moira*, a tragically short allotted span of life; Hector is 'doomed by fate' to be killed by Achilles. But in Book 22, in the middle of their protracted battle, Zeus holds up his golden scales to decide which of the two heroes will lose: 'In the pans he put two fates of death's long sorrow, one for Achilleus and one for Hektor the tamer of horses, and he took the scales in the middle and lifted them up: and Hektor's day of doom sank down, away into Hades, and Phoibus Apollo left him' (Bk 22.209–13: Hammond translation). It is possible to identify a similar sense of many different gods and fates causing (or over-determining) events in Aeschylus' *Oresteia*, where Clytemnestra's murder of Agamemnon, for example, is ascribed to various divine forces: Justice, Ate (mad anger), the Avenging Fury, the spirit of Helen, the curse or *daimon* on the house of Atreus.

In contrast, Aristotle's account of tragedy contains no reference to the gods or fate. Instead, according to his *Poetics*, plots with causes and effects determine action. One might say that Aristotle offers a formal, aesthetic account of fate, in the sense that the shape of the drama, with its *peripeteia* and *telos*, dictates the rise and fall of the individual. Crucial to his analysis of causation is the process of decision-making or its failure: in other words, the *hamartia*. Unlike Plato, who believed that mistakes were only made through ignorance and that simply to know virtue was to pursue it, Aristotle was well able to contemplate the rational making of mistakes. In his *Nicomachean Ethics*, he argued that any action of an individual made not under external physical duress must be considered voluntary and carries responsibility. But he distinguished between 'voluntary' action (*hekon*) and 'counter-voluntary' action (*akon*). Counter-voluntary action is conducted not in complete ignorance nor because of base desires, but because one of the crucial areas of knowledge needed for rational decision making was absent:

> For both pity and sympathy depend on particulars; it is the person who is in ignorance of one of these that acts counter-voluntarily . . . There is the matter of who is acting, what he is doing, in relation to what or affecting what, sometimes also with what (as for example with a tool), what the action is for (e.g. saving someone) and how it is done (e.g. gently or vigorously) . . . In the case, then, of what is said to be counter-voluntary on the basis of this sort of ignorance, the action must in addition cause distress to the agent and involve regret.[50]

Thus while the tragic plot was pre-set and was, of course, mostly drawn from existing mythological narratives whose outcomes were well known, the hero's freedom to make the right or wrong decision was, according to Aristotle, dependent upon his capacity to know and gather together all the pieces of information necessary for wise deliberation. To let one of these jigsaw pieces slip was to go down the inevitable and tragic path of 'distress' and 'regret'.

We can see this 'counter-voluntary' decision-making enacted in Aeschylus' play, *Seven Against Thebes*. Eteocles appears to be in control of military strategy, appointing captains to oppose the enemies at the seven gates of Thebes. He decides who is the most appropriate opponent for each foe, based on the description of each warrior, his character and the blazon on his shield. But eventually he discovers that the 'most just' opponent of his brother is himself and at that point he realises the fulfilment of his father's curse, that brother will kill brother. So the exercise of Eteocles' active will paradoxically brings about the outcome he most fears, based upon apparently rational ideas of justice. For, as Pierre Vidal-Naquet points out, 'it is his own destiny that Eteocles repeatedly announces', as he organises the earlier duelling opponents.[51] Eteocles' language is riven with dramatic irony. He refers, for example, to the violent icons on the enemies' shields which foreshadow self-reflexively the violence to be inflicted upon them but this irony in fact only replicates unconsciously the ultimate ironic doubling in the play, namely the deadly encounter between the two brothers. 'The bearer of this arrogant device will see the symbol fully justified: it does foretell violence – to himself', Eteocles says of Tydeus (l. 404) but the ironic implication is that every sign and symbol Eteocles supposedly interprets and controls ultimately 'foretells violence to himself'. The riddling language, which Eteocles freely uses, turns out to have meanings that he does not fully understand at the time and which become clarified in a terrible moment of recognition:

> Alas, maddened by god and god-abhorred,
> All-wretched is mine and Oedipus' race!
> Ah me, now my father's curse is fulfilled![52]

Riddling language is crucial to the fulfilment of fate in *Macbeth* too. The play turns on the subtle distinction between prediction and predetermination. Predictions about the future offer a vision of narrative patterns rather than a predestined *fait accompli*. In other words, oracles and fortune-tellers see into future and identify the shape of events to come but they do not make those events happen. In *Macbeth*, the witches prophesise Macbeth's rise and fall, but they do not determine it. Central to the play is the notion of 'equivocation': in other words, the use of ambiguous and misleading language, often drawing on terms which have two different meanings. As Aristotle suggested, nobody would choose to commit an evil action unless there was some failure in logic in the process of decision-making. So, in the seventeenth century, it was believed that somebody would only choose to commit an evil act if the devil equivocated with him, ambiguously making evil appear good. The witches thus tempt Macbeth to evil by their equivocal language, making him believe that his desire is already tantamount to its fulfilment, that their prediction is already destiny: 'All hail, Macbeth, that shalt be King hereafter!' (I.iii.48). Banquo is alert to the danger:

> Oftentimes, to win us to our harm,
> The instruments of darkness tell us truths,
> Win us with honest trifles to betray's
> In deepest consequence.   (I.iii.121–4)

But Macbeth immediately starts trying to hasten the future, speeding up time, feeling (in his wife's words) 'the future in the instant' (I.v.56) and compressing the analysis of his motivation in his effort swiftly to do 'the deed'. The internal evil in his own mind becomes bound up with the external evil of the witches, until subjective and objective worlds become blurred and 'nothing is but what is not' (I.iii.140–1). The witches wind up 'the spell' at the beginning, apparently catching Macbeth as a victim, but since Macbeth echoes their words in his opening line – 'So fair and foul a day I have not seen' (I.iii.36) – and later apparently invites supernatural instruments of darkness – the dagger, Banquo's ghost – it seems that he is also able to conjure up imaginatively the fate that lures him to damnation. This gives him an illusion of supernatural power, a 'charmed life', which right to the last makes him believe that he can shape his own fortune. 'Come fate into the list / And champion me to th' utterance!' (III.i.72–3), he says as he remembers the witches' prophecy about Macduff and plans to murder him; 'Lay on, Macduff, / And damn'd be him that first cries, "Hold, enough!"' (V.x.33–4), is his final line.

In contrast, once Eteocles realises his doom, the attitude to fate in Aeschylus' play changes dramatically. Now fate is not a force to be resisted or controlled but instead it is actually embraced. The chorus talks of a 'evil passion' driving Eteocles to his death, while Eteocles appears generously fatalistic: 'Gods? By now, it seems, they've abandoned me; the gift of my death is what they'd admire. So why cringe any more before death's blow?' (702–4). Indeed the chorus tries to persuade Eteocles out of his decision to fight, still retaining an Aristotelian sense of the free nature of decision – 'destiny's mood may veer and just at the last moment alter, and perhaps come upon you with a kindlier breath' (705–8) – but Eteocles is adamant: 'When god gives evil, man cannot escape' (719). The force sweeping Eteocles along, rhythmic in its relentless power, is more like Nietzsche's notion of fate than Aristotle's. Unlike the careful doomed logic in Aristotle's account, fate for Nietzsche is a natural and irrational force, the inevitable conflict between the Apollonian and the Dionysiac drives, which sweeps over the hero and tears him back to primordial oneness. At that moment he feels both 'dread' and 'blissful ecstasy', a kind of 'intoxication', since he is being brought back to the state of nature and away from the struggle for individualism and control.

Nietzsche's notion, of 'the blissful ecstasy, which, prompted by the same fragmentation of the *principium individuationis*, rises up from man's innermost core', was to have a huge influence upon dramatic explorations of fate in the early twentieth century. Instead of the metaphysical dimension of the Greeks, which had lent decision-making an extra gravity, Nietzsche offered irrational forces which were larger than any individual. Inspired by this, Yeats wrote of tragedy as the 'drowner of dykes that separate man from man', the 'confounder of understanding' which moves us 'almost to the intensity of trance'.[53] In Synge's play, *Riders to the Sea*, these huge Nietzschean forces are figured as the waves and currents of the sea, which in time carry away and drown all of Maurya's sons. She strives to resist the relentless attrition of her family, but warned by ghostly omens of the futility of resistance and subsequently given the confirmation of her last son's death, she almost welcomes the passivity of submitting to fate. 'They're all gone now, and there isn't anything more the sea can do to me . . . I'll have no call now to be up crying and praying when the wind breaks from the south, and you can hear the surf is in the east.'[54] The women join together in a vocal lament, turning sorrow into a song of mournful unity: 'No man at all can be living for ever, and we must be satisfied'.

Nietzsche's interest in fate as the irresistible force which rises from 'man's innermost core' can be compared with Freud's exploration of the different drives which control the psyche. Psychoanalysis offers a description of the individual not fully in control of his actions, much less his thoughts. He is liable to be overwhelmed by desires and anxieties which were repressed by the conscious mind and thus given extra power and incomprehensibility by the prohibition. What was suppressed becomes more desirable, more terrible and more irresistible, because it has become so inextricably bound up within the very identity of the individual.[55]

This Freudian eroticised sense of fate is exemplified in the plays of Spanish playwright Lorca, in which the mysterious compulsions which drive characters are figured in naturalistic terms.[56] In *Blood Wedding*, the Bride longs to make a good marriage to the Groom, who is richer than her family and whose vineyards are prospering, but she is dragged down against her will by the atavistic pull of her old desire for Leonardo. Appropriately in the drylands of rural Spain, this fatalistic sexual drive is figured as a physical thirst: 'I was a woman consumed by fire, covered with open sores inside and out', she tells the Groom's mother after the fatal elopement with Leonardo during the wedding, 'and your son was a little bit of water from whom I hoped for children, land, health! But the other one [Leonardo] was a dark river filled with branches that brought close to me the whisper of its rushes and its murmuring song' (*Blood Wedding*, III.ii, pp. 61–2). The Mother feels that she should be taking her revenge on the Bride, for abandoning her son and indirectly causing his death (the implication is that Leonardo and the Groom have killed each other over their love for the Bride), but instead she finds herself inexplicably joining her in a lament for the dead.

Desire and fate are both mysterious in Lorca, erupting out of the unconscious and arguably with no object or purpose. In the next play in his rural trilogy, *Yerma*, the heroine is desperate for a child and prepared to go to supernatural lengths (visiting the conjuror at night or joining a pagan fertility ritual at a mountain shrine) in order to conceive a child. But in her childlessness, her desire becomes deeper and more diffuse until it is for more than simply a child. It becomes an insatiable desire for satisfaction from life itself. 'I'm like a parched field big enough to hold a thousand teams of oxen ploughing . . . Mine is pain that is no longer of my flesh' (Act III, p. 112), she says. Her husband recognises the fact that her desire appears to have lost a specific object: 'I can no longer put up with this constant grieving over obscure things, unreal things made of thin air' (p. 113). As the play progresses it seems as if, unlike *Blood Wedding*, desire and fate have opposing goals. Yerma's desire is to fulfil her purpose as a mother yet her fate, which the villagers beg her to accept, is to be childless and simply a good wife to her husband. But in the dramatic climax, it turns out that desire and fate are one. Overcome by the violence of her feelings, Yerma strangles her husband to death. 'Barren. Barren, but sure. Now I know it for certain. And alone' (p. 115). Her childless fate is now guaranteed by the death of the one person – her husband – who had the power to change it and to impregnate her. Instead of the uncertainty and lack of focus which racked her throughout the play, she now has certainty and closure. And like Maurya and the Mother, she is both exhausted and relieved by the submission to this force of fate: 'I will sleep without suddenly waking up to see if my blood is proclaiming other, new blood' (p. 115).

The implication of Freud's eroticised fate is that psychological acts of desire and repression, of substitution and memory, whether conscious or unconscious, determine an individual's actions. In other words, 'Character is Fate', as Thomas Hardy famously commented in *Mayor of Casterbridge*.[57] Nineteenth-century tragedians explored the Darwinian repercussions of this concept, from the case of Büchner's Woyzeck, whose limited diet of peas supposedly determined his character and subsequently his murderous action, to George Eliot's speculation about environmental pressures upon Maggie in *Mill on the Floss*:

> The tragedy of our lives is not created entirely from within. 'Character', says Novalis, in one of his questionable aphorisms – 'character is destiny'. But not the whole of our destiny. Hamlet, Prince of Denmark, was speculative and irresolute, and we have a great tragedy in consequence. But if his father had lived to a good old age, and his uncle had died an early death, we can conceive Hamlet's having married Ophelia, and got through life with a reputation of sanity, notwithstanding many soliloquies, and some moody sarcasms towards the fair daughter of Polonius . . .[58]

Indeed one can see novelists in the nineteenth century bringing classical ideas of fate into conflict with the more imminent new ideas about character and consciousness, in order to explore and test the new ideas. Hardy's *Mayor of Casterbridge* suggests for the first half of the novel that Henchard's fortunes are directly related to his hot-headed, ill-tempered and impulsive character. This irascibility led him to the fatal decision to sell his wife, in the opening scene, and to break the friendship with Donald Farfrae. Indeed Hardy compares his character to that of Faust, who courted his own downfall.[59] But in the second half, it appears that the world is against Henchard, whatever he does. Now fate is not related to character but to the impervious nature of the cosmos, which condemns Henchard to a life beyond redemption ('he cursed himself like a less scrupulous Job') and as a self-banished outcast, reminiscent of Cain: 'I – Cain – go alone as I deserve – an outcast and a vagabond. But my punishment is *not* greater than I can bear', says Henchard as he leaves Casterbridge in disgrace.[60] Unlike the biblical comparisons, Henchard does not even seek justification in himself or in God, but shoulders a burden of guilt which is disproportionate to divine punishment. The effect is to suggest a world of injustice, in which individuals struggle to impose their notion of fate (character traits, religious explanation) upon a much bleaker, non-human and incomprehensible set of forces.

Hardy's heavy-handed imposition of fate, therefore, which sees his characters as minuscule victims in the harsh landscape of Wessex, presided over by unfeeling gods, could ultimately be ironic. In Hardy's case, it might be that characters invent their own personal destiny which ends up fulfilling the unconscious demands of a more immanent and larger Fate or Will. But for other writers, it seems as if fate itself is invented as an explanation in order to avoid personal guilt. 'Law condemns, not to punishment but to guilt. Fate is the guilt context of the living', wrote Walter Benjamin. Characters externalise their own sense of guilt in the form of a fated narrative, which appears to tell an understandable story about their lives and their engagement with their environment. 'It is never man but only the life in him that [fate] strikes – the part involved in natural guilt and misfortune by virtue of illusion', he continues.[61] But the illusion is necessary because the alternative is unbearable. *King Lear* opens up the possibility that there is 'no cause' for the play's events and that violence can just spiral out of control, sparked by the accidental phrase or word. For example, the violence of the blinding of Gloucester gains a momentum of its own:

> GLOUCESTER   ... I shall see
> The winged vengeance overtake such children.
> CORNWALL   See't shalt thou never. Fellows, hold the chair,
> Upon these eyes of thine I'll set my foot.   (III.vii.66–9)

Lear is based upon a traditional fairy-tale plot – the father and his three daughters – which arguably counters the chaos with its narrative expectation. The medieval concept of the wheel of fortune also permeates the play. 'The lamentable change is from the best / The worst returns to laughter', says Edgar. But these consoling ideas of fate are challenged during the course of the play, until they appear to be merely comforting fictions. Similarly the Kiéslowski film *Blind Chance*, which follows three different hypothetical stories according to whether the protagonist misses or catches a train, plays with concepts of fated narrative. The film suggests that tragic plots are shaped by the managed certainty of a totalitarian communist regime, as the main character, Witek, finds himself working either for or against the system, according to his original 'luck' at the station platform. In both *Lear* and *Blind Chance*, the absence of fate can only be imagined ironically, by the weighing of one story against another, by the painful stripping away of illusion.

Case studies 2: Politics

One of the key questions which has exercised tragic theorists in recent decades has been whether tragedy can be reconciled with social progress and radical politics. In other words, can tragedy be radical and concerned with social equality or is it essentially a reactionary art form? This question arises partly because tragedy is felt to be a genre which appeals to the emotions while political activism relies upon reason and theory. A long-standing tradition has in fact persisted that 'theory', reason and social progress are intimately connected. Hegel's vision of the forward march of history depended upon a belief that reason guided events towards their utopian goal. Since theory – whether that be literary, cultural or political theory – is open and articulate about its critical rules, it is possible for anyone to follow those rules and reach the same level of understanding

In contrast to these accounts of theory and reason, tragedy is often assumed to be untheorisable and irrational. George Steiner, for example, maintains that it is 'irreparable', that the events in the story could never be altered according to circumstances or history. No amount of social or political improvement would change the trajectory of the classic tragic narrative because tragic plots are derived from the timeless moral dilemmas of the human condition. 'Tragic drama tells us that the spheres of reason, order, and justice are terribly limited and that no progress in our science or technical resources will enlarge their relevance', he writes in *The Death of Tragedy*.[62] Relinquishing responsibility for any atrocities, Steiner sees tragic events as the result of the 'otherness' of the world, rather than as the consequence of a linear, rational narrative of cause and effect: 'It waits for us in ambush at the crossroads. It mocks us and destroys us' (p. 9). Not only can we change nothing but we are even metaphysically rewarded for not trying to do so and for patiently accepting the injustices from which we are suffering. Man, he says, is 'ennobled by the vengeful spite or injustice of the gods' (p. 10). Thus, Jonathan Dollimore points out, the humanist view exemplified by Steiner 'mystifies suffering and invests man with a quasi-transcendent identity'.[63] Human nature becomes impervious to social change. As a result, tragedy might be said to reconfirm the status quo and the moral order of the universe, by encouraging political passivity and dramatising the fallacy of concerted revolution.

It is arguments like George Steiner's and others before him which have left some radical thinkers suspicious of tragedy as a genre or theatre art form. Brecht, for example, was concerned about the danger of bourgeois sympathy in the theatre and its implications for social action. The audience would expend all its energy in identifying with the troubles of the actor on stage, he believed, and then the people would leave the theatre satisfied and indifferent to injustice in the outside world.[64] Strindberg voiced similar reservations about tragic pity in the preface to *Miss Julie*, albeit with characteristic sarcasm: 'The time may come when we shall have become so developed, so enlightened that we shall be able to look with indifference at the brutal, cynical, heartless drama that life presents, when we shall have laid aside those inferior, unreliable instruments of thought called feelings, which will become superfluous and harmful once our organs of judgement have matured'.[65]

To counter the threat of bourgeois sympathy, Brecht developed his epic theatre which alienated its spectators from the characters and which invited the audience to think rationally about the events being dramatised. In *Mother Courage*, the central character is contradictory, drawing the audience into feeling sympathy for her and then alienating us by her apparent heartlessness when her children, like Swiss Cheese, are threatened. As our expectations are continually 'interrupted' while we are watching the play, we are supposedly forced to think rationally about courage, heroism and survival in times of war, not on a personal level but more generally.[66] However, it is an indication of how far Brecht's ideas were from the actual experience of watching tragedy that the moment in his play *Mother Courage* which audiences most respond to is the scene in which her mute daughter continues to beat her drum to warn the village of an imminent attack by soldiers at the cost eventually of her life (scene 11). This act of individual, tragic self-sacrifice pulls at the heart strings in a way that Brecht's theory about war and the history of human exploitation cannot. Although the play's business continues after Katrin's death and we see Mother Courage pulling her cart away at the end, to continue profiting from the war, emotionally the play ended with the death scene. We still think in terms of tragic closure, not epic's vast shapelessness, which eschews termination.

Another obstacle in the path to a politicised interpretation of tragedy can be found in the fact that political theorists today are becoming more sceptical about the possibility of decisive and effective action. Michel Foucault developed Jeremy Bentham's description of the panopticon prison as a metaphor for the regulation and oppression of contemporary society. Just as Bentham's prisoners imagine that a guard is watching them constantly and so behave themselves accordingly, so, Foucault argues, we internalise the rules that govern and constrain us.[67] The psychoanalytic critic Slavoj Žižek has extended this thesis by claiming that we even learn to love the hidden order which oppresses us and which dictates everything we do.[68] Both these thinkers maintain that since the system which governs us is internalised and that we cannot actually identify the rulers or the rules specifically, we cannot extricate ourselves from them. Change can only come about through a reversal in the structure of things, through an alteration in the power relations which lie behind the systems of dominance. But it cannot come about through individual action, inspired by some inner awareness of freedom and idealism. Revolution is therefore virtually impossible; the prevailing ideology seems to dictate everything, our actions, our thoughts and our very desires. Since decisive action and its consequences – or what Žižek calls 'the authentic act' – are generally considered crucial components of tragedy, this might seem to rule out tragedy that reflects contemporary politics.

In this respect, the only possible tragedy imaginable would be something like Büchner's *Woyzeck*, in which the hero (or arguably anti-hero) becomes so brutalised by the pressures of his environment that he loses his powers of judgement and murders his girlfriend in a fit of sexual jealousy. We witness his decline during the play, as both his mind and his body become subject to the surveillance of the elite scientists who are keeping him on a strict diet of peas and monitoring his reactions. By the time of the murder, it is hard to distinguish Woyzeck's individual agency from the expectations of society, based upon his class, gender and physiological condition. 'You see, us common folk, we don't have no virtue, all we got is our nature; but if I was a gent with an "at and a watch and a nice smart coat and could talk all posh, I'd be virtuous alright" '.[69] It is perhaps appropriate that this drama about the disintegration of the impoverished self in the Petri dish of elite science is fragmentary in form, since it is both modern in its apprehension of coercive ideology and deeply questioning of the conventions of tragedy.[70]

So can tragedy in fact be reconciled with social progress? Is radical tragedy possible? It can be, if the definition of tragedy is allowed to change over time. When a timeless notion of 'order' or 'belief' is extrapolated supposedly from Greek tragedy and used to analyse later tragedies, as Steiner does, then much modern drama fails to meet the definition and tragedy might seem to be an outmoded art form. But if, as Raymond Williams argues, the particular aspects of tragedy are allowed to change according to the historical period, then it is possible to imagine new tragedies being written and performed on the modern stage which are directly relevant to contemporary concerns. The only definition of tragedy in that case, according to Williams, is 'the dramatisation of a particular and grievous disorder and its resolution'.[71]

Moreover, to suggest that there is a stable order in the world in which tragic man finds himself 'an unwelcome guest', as Steiner does, is to abstract a notion of cosmic order which is far removed from the metaphysical conflicts inherent in many tragedies. Aeschylus' *Prometheus Bound*, for example, reveals the power structure among the gods to be radically unstable. Prometheus first helped Zeus in his struggle against the older gods, since, as he says, 'it is some sort of disease in tyrants not to trust their friends' (226–7). The hallmark of friendship is trust; the hallmark of tyranny is distrust. Zeus goes on to betray Prometheus, thus revealing the totalitarian aspirations which govern his harsh treatment of Prometheus in the play. However it emerges that Prometheus still retains power over Zeus, because he knows the name of the person who will eventually overthrow Zeus, a name which remains still a secret. He can choose whether or not to reveal this name to Zeus and thus to change the course of history:

> Yet the day will come when the lord of the blessed gods will have need of me, though I am tortured in harsh fetters, that I might reveal the new plan by which he is to be stripped of his sceptre and honours.   (168–72)

As a result, the balance of power in the universe might be said to be dependent upon the future negotiation between Zeus and Prometheus. The order of the gods is neither stable nor reliable. Indeed fate, belief, history, the future are all contingent upon the gods' changing willingness to dominate or liberate each other.[72]

The 'resolution' of disorder, then, which Raymond Williams describes at the end of tragedy, can sometimes mean the development of a new, ideal constitution rather than the imposition of the old order, if order and history are seen as fluid and flexible. Williams admits that revolution and tragedy are conventionally seen as mutually exclusive, and that revolution tends to produce epic rather than tragedy.[73] After a revolution is over, people tend to remember the overall triumph and forget individual struggles and deaths. Nevertheless it is possible to imagine 'the tragedy of revolution'. This would involve recognising the casualties of revolution and focusing upon the victims of the inevitable violence and sacrifices. Brecht's play *Galileo* draws attention to the difficulty of sticking to the theoretical ideals which inspire revolution when one's personal safety is at risk. When threatened by the inquisition with the instruments of torture, Galileo recants his belief that the earth goes around the sun. His retraction, in the face of the all-powerful and conservative Catholic Church, devastates his followers, who find their belief in him and all the principles he seems to represent shattered by this betrayal. Brecht portrays Galileo under house arrest, weakly enjoying his food in compliance with the regime, rather than martyred for his rational theory. But it emerges at the end of the play that, while Galileo himself is now effectively silenced, his ideas are still being transmitted in the form of papers, smuggled over the border. The message of the play is that the scientific revolution will continue and will eventually succeed, as ideas cannot be stopped, but that Galileo himself will end his days in cowardly and shameful isolation, unrecognised by the wider world. Revolutions have their individual victims and Galileo is one of them, his contribution to the struggle only useful for a time and then discarded.

Brecht did not intend the audience to sympathise with Galileo. He tries to distance us from the character by exposing his moments of weakness, and his willingness to betray his friends if necessary. We are expected only to engage intellectually with the question of Galileo's choice. And we should respond too to the dramatisation of its consequences, to the shame of Galileo, the reinvigoration of the Catholic Church as the most powerful institution in the country and the secret smuggling of scientific heresy which will finally change history. This is a play which asks its audience to rethink revolution in terms of large historical forces rather than individuals, as Hegel might have appreciated. 'Unhappy the land that has no heroes', says Andrea, to which Galileo tellingly replies, 'No. Unhappy the land where heroes are needed' (scene 14, p. 98).

But in contrast to Brecht, Raymond Williams offers a theory of radical tragedy which accommodates our 'need for heroes' and our tendency to feel emotional sympathy for individuals. If we identify with the main character in a tragic drama, this need not be interpreted as the bourgeois sympathy anatomised by Brecht, but rather the acknowledgement of our shared physical nature which ensures that we can actually progress as sensitive and radicalised human beings. 'We have to see the evil and the suffering, in the factual disorder that makes revolution necessary, and in the disordered struggle against the disorder', Williams explains. 'We make the connections, because that is the action of tragedy, and what we learn in suffering is again revolution, because we acknowledge others as men.' So, when Kratos and Hephaestus are binding Prometheus to the rock, Hephaestus finds himself having to justify his pity for Prometheus. 'Why are you hesitating and pitying him in vain?' (36), Kratos asks him. What, in other words, is the purpose of pity other than some empty bourgeois or aesthetic gesture? But Hephaestus replies: 'Kinship and friendship are strangely powerful' (39). In the course of the play, Prometheus builds up powerful alliances between himself and the chorus of Oceanides, and between himself and Io, all based upon pity. These alliances weigh in the balance of power in the world and ensure that Prometheus and Io remain steadfast in guarding the future course of history.

To focus upon sympathy and emotion in political tragedy is to recover the importance of the material as well as the theoretical aspects of radical thought. It is to remind the revolutionary enthusiast about the cost of defiant upheaval and his responsibility to the casualties. Only then, when we remember the constraints and intractable difficulties of living under oppression, the shared tragedies, can we develop a realistic politics. 'I am convinced that we should solve many things if we all went out into the streets and uncovered our griefs, which perhaps would prove to be but one sole common grief', wrote Unamuno.[74] This shared 'communality of meaning', in Eagleton's words, would prove more effective than abstract theory or treatises on political thought.[75] 'A *Miserere* sung in common by a multitude tormented by destiny has as much value as a philosophy', Unamuno went on. Attending to the particular, giving expression to emotion and grief, sharing in a collective lament: these are the hallmarks of tragic performance. After all, Eagleton noted, 'suffering is a mightily powerful language to share in common' (p. xvi). For this reason, the productions of Greek or Shakespearean tragedy which have come out of Eastern Europe, with its legacy of communism and ready understanding of collective living and lamenting, have been some of the most effective and affecting in recent years.[76]

But the problem with Williams' or Eagleton's otherwise convincing accounts of a politicised tragedy is that they ignore the question of the aesthetic. These plays might depict the communality of suffering and the need for effective pity, but what about the fact that they merely 'represent' these things, rather than engage in serious political intervention? Is feeling sympathy for the suffering Galileo or Woyzeck enough? Tony Harrison's film *Prometheus*, made for Channel 4, addresses this question most explicitly. 'There has never been an artwork more aware of its own contextual mode and means of production', notes Edith Hall.[77] In the film, a gold statue of Prometheus is transported around Europe, reminding viewers of the tradition of labour and of political activism. Prometheus, after all, stole fire from the gods, thus, according to Harrison's film, allowing mortals work (mining) and pleasure (smoking). But at the beginning of the film, the statue is created, under the command of Hermes, from the melted-down tools of unemployed miners. By making a statue instead of offering the workers a regular job, Hermes seems to be part of the modern tendency to turn industry like coal mining into heritage. In other words, Hermes substitutes the aesthetic for full employment and economic labour. Tragedy as an art form has a vexed relationship with political reality. It can arguably displace attention from real suffering, just as viewers concentrate

6. Bureaucratic, compliant chorus. National Theatre of Romania's *Oresteia*, directed by Silviu Purcarete, 1998. © Geraint Lewis

upon the gold statue rather than the dilapidated factories which have closed down all over Europe. But it can allow injustice and hardship to be viewed from a different, startling perspective. The huge statue is floated on a barge down the Rhine or bussed through Greece, hardly fitting into the frame. We are jolted out of our everyday acceptance of economic decline and political inertia by this vision. Thus the awkwardness of this visual image testifies to the startling 'interruption' offered by tragedy in a climate of resigned capitalism.

Case studies 3: Gender

Feminists have traditionally been wary of tragedy. They have associated tragedy with masculinity and comedy with femininity. Linda Bamber, for example, wrote of the 'powerful misogyny in the tragedies' of Shakespeare, and Dympna Callaghan has confirmed that 'comedy is the preferred genre of feminist criticism'.[78] Comedy offers an optimistic view of possibility and women's empowerment; we might think of Rosalind in *As You Like It* or even Aristophanes' Lysistrata. Tragedy, on the other hand, has often seemed to feminists to crush any chance of social progress and to confirm the status of women as victims or *femmes fatales*. 'In the comedies Shakespeare seems if not a feminist then at least a man who takes the woman's part', Bamber continues. 'In the tragedies, however, Shakespeare creates such nightmare female figures as Goneril, Regan, Lady Macbeth and Volumnia.'[79] For a political movement such as feminism, this is hardly encouraging and thus even recent studies of the genre have strenuously sought out the positive, morale-boosting aspects of the plays, somewhat against the grain.

Tragic theory has also appeared unconsciously masculine or phallocentric in its concerns. Ever since Aristotle, it has concentrated upon what it posits as 'universal', moving away from the specific plays to a debate about the unchanging principles of tragedy and archetypal, teleological plot structures. It locates the tragic sense in some transcendent realm, whether it be in eternal justice (Hegel) or in the aesthetic (Nietzsche) or in consciousness (existentialism). And it focuses upon the individual (male) hero and his tortured or spiritual mind. 'The "universal" subject of liberal humanist tragic aesthetics is always male', commented Dympna Callaghan.[80] Moreover if women have been the subject of critical attention, it has been because they are productive metaphors for wider anxieties within tragedy. They represent the 'other' and are therefore good to think with. Critics tend to treat gender in a way that turns it into something else, or makes it cease to matter. Treating gender as merely symbolic serves to downplay its gravity or importance, and it continues the masculine emphasis upon the principle rather than the concrete, upon the 'general' rather than the particular. 'In criticism, alas, love, marriage, and family and all socio-cultural systems of organization . . . are too often read as mere tropes used by the author to discuss the really meaningful, philosophical dimensions of tragedy, "man and his universe" ', notes Callaghan.[81]

Yet despite these scruples, feminists have played an important role in revealing the gendered hierarchy behind tragic structures, whether or not this is symbolic or substantial. They have also pointed out the ubiquity of what are considered particular female concerns in tragedy, which male critics have arguably neglected: issues such as love, the sacrifice of virgins, marriage, the nineteenth century 'New Woman' question. In highlighting these issues, critics draw attention to the fundamental questions behind feminist approaches to tragedy. Does the fact that women play quite a central role in tragedy, in contrast to the marginal position they have invariably held within society, suggest that tragedy is subversive? Or does tragedy merely offer a licensed space which allows fictional women relative freedom and prominence, without implicating external society? Do the negative, 'nightmare' roles given to many women within this licensed space serve to confirm male misogyny?

These questions are focused around the problem of female transgression in tragedy. Women, it has been noted, are either portrayed as victims or *femmes fatales* in tragedy; in other words, they are either the repositories of the drama's moral sense or they rupture it, causing the downfall of the hero through their subversive or even evil strategies.[82] So for example, Iphigenia's or Cordelia's or Desdemona's innocence, figured by natural imagery, acts as a touchstone by which to measure the iniquity of the male world which kills them. So, also, Medea or Lady Macbeth call upon the aid of magical or demonic powers to ensure that their terrible plans are more successfully diabolical. In all these cases, it can be argued that the socially constructed boundaries of morality and expected female behaviour are confirmed by these plays. The good women die but are admired for their sacrifice; the bad women are eventually suitably punished. Transgression tests the boundaries only to reaffirm them in the end.

But in fact the plays are more complicated and ambivalent than this simple dichotomy suggests. Medea, played originally by a male actor in front of a male audience, invites our sympathy for the female lot: 'Of everything that is alive and has a mind, we women are the most wretched of creatures . . . Men say of us that we live a life free from danger at home while they fight wars. How wrong they are! I would rather stand three times in the battle-line than bear one child' (230; 249–51) Lady Macbeth's 'unsex me here' speech is contrasted later in the play with her sleep-walking scene: 'All the perfumes of Arabia will not sweeten this little hand' (V.i.42–3). So the audience both identifies with these women and yet is also distanced from them, in an oscillating and troubling relationship which tests the audience's assumptions and self-identity. Similarly, Cordelia's and Desdemona's deaths are arguably partly the result of their initial transgressions: Cordelia refuses to obey her father and speak; Desdemona goes against her father's wishes and marries Othello. It is these acts of transgression which provoke the events of the play and cause the women's eventual punishment. Yet, since by the time of their deaths they are idealised as morally pure, the notions of transgression and female duty are interrogated along with the revelation of cosmic injustice. It all means that women 'serve not just to define limits but also to uncover the limiting structures in society', according to Callaghan (p. 63).

Recently there has been increasing interest among feminist critics in reviewing female practices which previously appeared passive and supplementary but which have now been shown to be powerfully subversive. In particular, critics such as Nicole Loraux, Helene Foley and Gail Holst-Warhaft have revealed the radical implications of female mourning in ancient Greek tragedy. Traditionally women weeping in public have been considered to be weakly resorting to stereotype. But in fact in fifth-century Athens, they were breaking the law. At the end of the sixth century, Solon legislated against the practice of female lamentation. According to the ancient historian Plutarch, he 'regulated women's appearances in public, as well as their festivals, and put an end to wild and disorderly behaviour . . . he abolished the practice of lacerating the flesh at funerals, of reciting set dirges, and of lamenting a person at the funeral ceremonies of another'.[83] Solon was motivated by a desire to keep public and private spheres separate and not to allow the 'unmanly and effeminate passions' of women to become visible. The regulation would be strictly policed; lawbreakers would 'be punished by the *gunaikonomos* [lawkeeper for women]', according to Plutarch (*Solon*, 21.5).

Public female lamentation was thus moved from the public agora to the theatre, where it features prominently in many tragedies. What does this mean? Several tragedies suggest that the dangerous implication of women mourning is being registered. Eteocles berates the chorus of women in *Seven Against Thebes* for publicly crying about the fate of the city: 'You, I ask, insufferable creatures that you are! is this the best course to save the town, does this hearten our beleaguered soldiers – to fling yourselves before the images of the gods that guard the city and shout and shriek and make decent folk detest you? . . . The fortunes of the foe without are thus aided best, while we are ruined from within by our own selves' (181–6; 193–4). He articulates the widely held fifth-century Athenian male view that 'shrieking' women lack control and that they therefore undermine the polis from within. But later, after his death, the chorus of women takes control of the stage, organising the public mourning for Eteocles and Polyneices and even guiding the sisters, Antigone and Ismene, in their lament: 'Through the city too passeth the sound of lamentation; the battlements lament; the land that loveth its sons laments. But for those who come after them their wealth abideth, for the ill-starred wretches the cause, aye, the cause whereby their strife came to its end in death'. Here the lament alters the balance of power in the city. The chorus weeps collectively for the dead brothers whose personal dispute caused the threat to the public polis and yet it also celebrates the safe passage of the city through the war. So it assumes the higher moral ground, subtly chastising the brothers for putting their private dispute before the public good of the city, and taking responsibility for the city's survival. Distinctions between public and private, male and female, authority and transgression, thus become subversively blurred.[84]

The staging of mourning goes to the heart of the problem of theatre's relation to politics. Is drama mere representation or does it, in Greg Nagy's words, constitute an archetypal re-enactment?[85] Loraux suggests that mourning can take place publicly in the theatre because it is conducted within a regulated civic setting. 'Tragedy takes some liberties with respect to norms, but, for the most part, orthodoxy is not damaged', she explains. 'The stage is taken over peacefully by a system of representations much more reassuring for the good functioning of the political sphere'.[86] But Foley, while mindful of the fact that the theatre is not a direct reflection of fifth-century Athenian life, maintains that Greek tragic lamentation was subversive, and that grieving women in tragedy disturbed the gender hierarchy upon which Athenian democracy was premised. 'A mourning woman is not simply a producer of pity, but dangerous. Yet the message her lament carries is never fully suppressed', she writes.[87]

A further reconsideration of traditional female roles continues to be focused upon the figure of Antigone, the woman who did not just mourn but actively buried the dead. Ever since Hegel, Antigone has been held up as a symbol of female transgression before the masculine law of the city, but critical and theoretical opinion is divided on the nature of this transgression. Is Antigone acting according to an alternative, feminine principle, the law of the gods and the family? Or is she merely a product of the Law of the Father, symbolically necessary as a counter to the masculine polis? According to Hegel, Antigone represented independent female concerns – blood, family, private life – which came into dialectical conflict with the male concerns in the city. Indeed, Hegel believed that Antigone acted according to the laws of matriarchy which prefigured and were replaced by the laws of patriarchy, and that therefore the play dramatises this historical moment of transition from matriarchy to patriarchy.[88] Incidentally, this belief about an ancient matriarchal society which was driven out by patriarchy has now been disproved by classical scholars. But, in any case, Hegel argued that the conflict between Antigone and Creon allowed the tensions in the polis to be resolved and enabled the community of Thebes to progress. Lacan, in contrast, argued that Antigone represented a projection of male anxiety and desire. She represented his desire for death and yet also warded it off at the same time: she 'pushes to the limit the realisation of something that might be called the pure and simple desire of death as such. She incarnates that desire.'[89] In contrast to both these male philosophers, Luce Irigaray claimed that Antigone's motivations cannot be understood from a masculine perspective of the city and the symbolic at all. Rather, Antigone is driven by her special bonds of blood with her brother, blood which is not to be considered as dialectically opposed to law or spirit (as it was for Hegel), but physical and therefore ungraspable by abstract, symbolic principles. She is also drawn along a path of identification with her mother: 'she will cut off her breath – her voice, her air, blood, life – with the veil of her belt, returning into the shadow (of a) tomb, the night (of) death, so that her brother, *her mother's desire*, may have eternal life'.[90] More recently Judith Butler has argued that Antigone's action and words are intimately, insidiously bound up within the state. In order to make her defiance public, Antigone must speak publicly before Creon, 'like a man' (484), and invoke the laws. She can defy Creon 'only through embodying the norms of power she opposes', Butler comments.[91] Moreover, the kinship invoked by Antigone to justify her deed is far from unproblematic. Polyneices is, after all, both her brother and her uncle, the product of Jocasta's and Oedipus' incestuous union. Antigone's love for her 'brother' is therefore not the natural tie of 'blood' invoked by Irigaray, but deeply ambiguous, policed by the state's laws about natural or unnatural kinship. There is no pre-political realm of the feminine, therefore, nor is there an alternative female act of defiance. Rather, Antigone is shaped by the ethics of the state, killing herself in the tomb. 'Hers becomes a politics not of oppositional purity but of the scandalously impure', comments Butler.[92]

Butler's account of Antigone is part of a new movement of approaching tragedy from the perspective of gender, rather than strictly of feminism. Gender is not peculiarly the province of women but socially constructed, an image which figures the forces of desire and constraint which permeate tragedy. A new form of criticism – a 'queer' reading of tragedy – attends to the way in which gendered metaphors are co-opted to describe confusions of identity and disrupted expectations. Characteristically, queer theory has lent itself more to comedy, since it celebrates playfulness, mobility and fluid identities. The cross-dressing in Shakespeare's comedies, for instance, is rich with possibilities for the queer theorist. But Pippa Berry has produced a fine example of how the 'angled or oblique point of view' offered by the playful attention to sexual metaphor in Shakespeare can reveal 'tragedy's double or multilayered significance'.[93] By exploring how the deaths of Shakespeare's heroes are described in bawdy, feminised terms, she mounts a case for a very different notion of Shakespearean tragedy, one which is 'scandalously impure', not concerned with Aristotelian teleology and catharsis but open-ended and genre-bending. 'While this multilayered, "earthy" and primitive sediment of meaning unsettles some of the seeming *gravitas* of tragedy, it has an obscure, philosophical and political weight of its own, as it challenges dominant cultural notions of what is "fundamental" and "final" both to tragedy and to human identity', Berry writes (p. 3).

In cinema, the queer gaze which disrupts fixed gender identities is ambivalent. It is playful, and comic if kept within carefully fixed boundaries; it is tragic, if it goes beyond those boundaries. So cross-dressing can be for comic effect in films like *Some Like It Hot* or *Tootsie,* when the straight orientation of the main characters is clearly apparent beneath the clothes. But it leads to disturbing crises in *The Crying Game* or even tragedy in *Boys Don't Cry.*[94]

In *The Crying Game*, the confusion over Dil's and Fergus/Jimmy's sexual orientation mirrors the confusions about their political loyalty, lending both a tragic gravity. And in both films, the moments of 'unmasking', of stripping the character to reveal the sex beneath, are not so much playful as shocking. Indeed, in *Boys Don't Cry*, conventional gender identity is violently reimposed upon Tina/Brandon with fatal consequences. But probably most disturbing for America was the 2005 Hollywood film, *Brokeback Mountain*. Finally homosexuality was depicted not in the marginal settings of comic cross-dressing or troubling a uniquely mixed-up individual woman, but within the traditional genre of the cowboy western, practised by two 'normal', straight-looking men. The director, Ang Lee, explores the tragic disjunction between the cowboys' private desires and the public social expectations of sexual conformity which they have internalised. The film thus addresses issues of repression and stifled expression with Chekhovian understatement, rather than the shocking sensationalism of the abnormal.[95]

Chapter 4

Non-dramatic tragedy

4.1 Visual culture

The emphasis in tragic drama has repeatedly been upon seeing things. Again and again, the playwright demands that we bear witness to the tragic climactic moment, whether it be the vision of Oedipus emerging from the palace blinded or Lear returning to the stage with Cordelia in his arms. These are iconic moments in theatre. And yet icons within visual culture are rarely considered for their tragic significance by academic critics. Back in 1766, Gotthold Ephraim Lessing suggested a few reasons why this might be the case in his book, *Laocoon: An Essay on the Limits of Painting and Poetry*. Literature, he wrote, is able to evoke the internal emotion of a person; visual art can only depict the external expression. Since 'we are generally unable to respond with the same degree of sympathy to physical pain as to other suffering', this external physical representation of anguish could not be deemed tragic.[1] Furthermore, art could only capture one moment and not the whole narrative or context. To reduce tragic experience to one moment might be to trivialise it: 'When a man of firmness and endurance cries out he does not do so unceasingly, and it is only the seeming perpetuity of such cries when represented in art that turns them into effeminate helplessness or childish petulance' (p. 20). Finally, art is governed by aesthetic criteria which run counter to the preoccupation of tragedy: 'The demands of beauty could not be reconciled with the pain in all its disfiguring violence, so it had to be reduced' (p. 17).

Lessing's scruples about tragic art owe much to specifically eighteenth-century assumptions about art. After all, we no longer believe that visual art has necessarily to be beautiful. But nevertheless, Lessing's points are useful in highlighting what he considers to be the crucial limits of visual culture – the lack of interior introspection, the reduction to the static moment, the aesthetic transformation of painful material – thus allowing us to think about their tragic potential. Some works of art are made consciously to overcome the limits which Lessing pinpoints. Indeed they derive their power precisely from their capacity to challenge the limits. But in other cases, it might be said that

158

tragic art unashamedly demonstrates the qualities which Lessing describes. In other words, works of art which might be termed tragic do indeed capture painful experience as a single moment or are undeniably beautiful. However, these cases raise the question of whether indeed written or dramatic tragedy is so very different. For, in its emphasis upon the aesthetic form of the work of art or upon the limits of our understanding of others' feelings, visual culture only highlights, in a more extreme way, the problems of tragic representation in general.

Physical externality

Some images are simply unambiguously tragic to look upon. Without knowing anything about the context or the story, we can respond to the clearly visible signs of dying and grieving. Narrative is not necessary, since the image in itself arrests us by its tragic poignancy. The ancient statue of the Laocoon, struggling against the ever-tightening coils of the sea monster to which his two sons have already succumbed beside him, is one example (despite Lessing's scruples about it). The ancient Greek vase painting of Achilles falling in love with the Amazonian queen Penthesilea at the moment of killing her in battle would be another. The contrast between violence and tenderness in both these images lends them a clear emotional charge. One feels the grief of Laocoon and Achilles, sharpened by the violent death of their loved ones. Within the Christian tradition, one could point to Mary holding the dead Jesus in her arms (the Pietà), as a quintessentially tragic image. Even without understanding anything about Christ's life or death, we can respond to the actual image as that of a mother grieving over her son and still appreciate its power.[2]

But in the case of many works of art, the tragic significance lies less in the physical depiction itself than in the knowledge of the context, either of its original composition or of its subsequent interpretation. For example, what one thinks of Christian religious art depends partly on one's interpretation of the gospel narrative. Is the crucifixion inherently tragic or not? (see pp. 184–88). The fifteenth-century German painters, like Matthias Grunewald, who portrayed Jesus on the cross wounded and contorted in pain, might well be said to be offering us a tragic picture of sacrifice and human suffering.[3] But what of the many paintings of the crucifixion which portray Christ's face as calm, his eyes cast heavenward to God or down to his people, while his body is tortured on the cross?[4] The contrast between Jesus' torture and his serene demeanour implies Christ's internal life. But is this internal life contented or is it deceived? Do we look at the physical suffering clearly experienced on the cross? Or do we try to imagine what cannot be seen, Christ's private reflections? The

7. Achilles killing Penthesilea, queen of the Amazons. Interior of an Attic cup, about 460 BC, in the Antikensammlungen, Munich. © AKG library

picture is either divinely transcendent or urgently questioning of God's purpose, depending upon one's interpretation,

Besides the representations of the crucifixion, there are, in the Christian tradition, depictions of events which in themselves appear harrowing but which were deemed necessary in the overall divine narrative: the beheading of John the Baptist or the deposition from the cross. Rubens' *Massacre of the Innocents* in part derives its power from the visual impact of what can clearly be seen. It depicts one of the most problematic events in the gospel, the slaughter of all newborn children in Bethlehem on the order of Herod in the hope of killing Christ, who in fact had been smuggled away to Egypt. The painting shows a circling spiral of violence as women attempt in vain to fight off the executioners and save their babies. Bodies lurch and fall towards the viewer, drawing him

8. A tragic picture of sacrifice and human suffering. The Crucifixion, by Matthias Grunewald. Painted around 1510. In Kuntsmuseum Basel, Switzerland. © AKG library

dramatically into the scene through the striking use of perspective. Is it tragic? As Jonathan Jones commented, while this painting 'rages against cruelty', it is 'also a cruel painting' because it is concerned with the skill of its depiction: 'there is a fascination with the technical, physical problem of depicting heightened action in a tight group'.[5] It provokes admiration but also a deep unease in the viewer, throwing his feelings into turbulence. It also raises the question of the context in which a painting is viewed. Originally it was probably hung in a private patron's picture gallery, designed to 'engender a sense of learned pleasure on the part of the connoisseur' who might recognise motifs from well-known classical statuary in the composition of the figures.[6] This aesthetic, intellectual provenance suggests that the painting is not tragic. But since its first creation, the painting has been viewed by artists like Picasso as an emotive protest against political violence. Was it therefore coincidence that it was loaned to London's National Gallery, amid great publicity, just a month before the war on Iraq in 2003? It seemed to many that the painting's tragic overtones, of state-sponsored violence inflicted upon the most innocent, could not be ignored.[7]

These are examples of works of art where the meaning of the painting lies beyond what is immediately apparent before us. We have the external image of crucifixion or massacre or beheading which is horrific in its violence. But the question of whether or not it is to be considered tragic depends upon the context in which the image is viewed. But, despite Lessing's doubts, there are also works of art which suggest an internal life, behind the external, visible image. These paintings explore mental as well as physical suffering. Massaccio's fresco of the 'Expulsion from the Garden of Eden', in the Brancacci's chapel in Florence, is unusual in that it successfully captures the mental despair of this event. Adam's and Eve's nakedness is the visible sign of their shame, but their torment is clearly more internal, as Massaccio depicts Adam covering his eyes to contemplate inner sorrows and guilt to come, while Eve casts her eyes imploringly to heaven. Nearly five centuries later, August Rodin's huge sculptural work, the *Gates of Hell*, achieves a comparable anguished interiority, since the tumble of tortured figures falling into the abyss is presided over by Rodin's well-known figure of the Thinker, contemplating his destiny.

In the last hundred years or so, artists have experimented with interrupting the viewer's gaze upon their work. Instead of a single perspective upon the work of art, the artist suggests the possibility of multiple perspectives. By allowing for different, subjective interpretations of his work, the artist implies a unique, inner life both within the viewer and also within what is viewed. Cubist art is concerned precisely with this issue of multiple perspectives, and nowhere is it used to greater effect than in Picasso's painting, *Guernica*. Initially a reaction to the bombing of the town of Guernica during the Spanish Civil War, the painting references Rubens' *Horrors of War*, the crucifixion and many other tragic icons in the artistic canon. But it also dismantles artistic techniques in its attempt to suggest annihilation and brutality. 'To mark Guernica the event, Picasso began to draw as if he were at the beginning of art, like a child; he tried to unteach himself'.[8]

Recently artists have been returning to classical preoccupations with the human body and its mortality but deliberately breaking up its stable surface to suggest inner fragility. Marc Quinn's 'Self' is a sculptured head, made out of the frozen blood of the artist. As the sculpture is exhibited, it is under constant threat of melting, the surface cracking to expose more frozen blood below. Only the refrigeration unit hidden in the sculpture's plinth prolongs its life. As Peter de Bolla, who has written about this artwork most movingly, notes, 'this work is "about" mortality, making art in the age of AIDS, the futility of art's wager against time'.[9]

Static moment

Marc Quinn's head points to another issue in tragic art. Not only does it successfully represent the internal, fragile life of the subject but it is also in a constant state of change, from liquefaction to solidification and vice versa. We witness the making and unmaking of art, which seems to replicate the human, mortal condition. Some artists recently have explored the possibility of art which depicts the natural processes of weariness and decay. That these were traditional concerns of artists is evident from the fact that their work references well-known religious and still-life pieces from the fifteenth and sixteenth centuries, but they portray these processes through installation or video loop. So Sam Taylor Wood's video of a bowl of rotting fruit picks up Renaissance preoccupations with mortality evident in still-life painting, or her 'Pietà', a video of her holding the actor Robert Downey Jr in the same pose as Michelangelo's famous statue, shows her visibly struggling to bear his weight in a way which revises our view of Michelangelo's marble perfection. It might be said that works like Sam Taylor-Wood's, which reduce theological art to its literal, physical dimensions, parody tragic profundity. But it could also be argued that they draw upon iconic images from religious art in order to give their work the gravity which they are seeking.

In referencing well-known works of art, documentary photographs attempt to make chaotic history iconic. While their subject matter is the real world, their images sometimes recall – either by design or chance – familiar, static images from the traditional canon of art. The photographs, indeed, gain additional power from that iconic resonance. Eugene Smith's famous photograph of 'Tomoko in her bath' illustrates the devastating effects of industrial mercury poisoning in Japan.[10] A mother bathes her seriously disabled child, whose limbs are withered and contorted by fetal mercury poison. The story, which tells of the youth of a whole town maimed and killed by business corruption and cover-up, is horrific. But the photograph brings out a certain humanity and compassion for the subject, by recalling, in the mother and child's pose, Michelangelo's *Pietà*. The exhibition at the 2005 'VISA pour l'image' photography festival at Perpignan by award-winning photographer Kristen Ashburn picked up the iconic image again. Her subject matter was the unspeakably grim situation in Zimbabwe, where 35 per cent of the population is infected with AIDS. But her photographs, portraits of sufferers in the last hours before death, possessed a stark, static beauty. One photograph, of a grandmother holding her grandson, was fortuitously posed as a modern *Pietà*, the stillness of the image poignantly at odds with the turbulence (the deaths, the poverty and despair) described in the caption.[11]

Photographs capture movement in a static image. Arguably, they perform the very monumentalisation of fleeting experience into 'seeming perpetuity' which Lessing warned against in tragic art. It is photography's capacity to depict the 'decisive moment', in Henri Cartier-Bresson's phrase, which lends it tragic significance. The moment caught on film gives ephemeral experience permanence, so that we can return to it and reflect on its meaning emotionally and intellectually. We might think of Robert Capa's well-known picture of the volunteer soldier in the Spanish Civil War, falling backwards after being shot dead. Or Eddie Adams' Pulitzer prize-winning photograph, of General Loan, South Vietnam's police chief, executing a Vietcong rebel in the street. There is actually also film footage of this event, since both cameramen and photographers were all present.[12] In the film, one can see the man walking along the street with the soldiers beforehand, apparently little suspecting what was about to happen, and, a few seconds later, after the shooting, the man lying dead in the street, surrounded by witnesses. In the moving-image version, this seems just a depiction of casual murder, because we see the banal context of the street and the walk, and indeed this film footage has now been forgotten. But the photograph continues to have power, because it gives the scene a stillness and gravity, and it became one of the iconic images of the Vietnam war.

Other photographs rely upon the caption to place the static image in context and ensure its tragic significance. The spectator is aware of future events, unknown either to the subject or the photographer at the time, which lend the photograph tragic poignancy. The photograph, in other words, preserves a moment of innocence, to which the viewer can never return. In this regard, the family photographs of Jews in Germany before the Holocaust have a particular power. Roman Vishniac's photographs of the Jewish quarters 1935–8, collected as 'Children of a Vanished World', were taken as a testimony to a community before it was violently destroyed. We need to know the context, of the impending doom facing these children, to feel the full poignancy of the image. But beyond that haunting knowledge, details are not needed to appreciate the power of these pictures and indeed, for Vishniac's exhibition later in New York, extensive captions including places, names and dates, were omitted.[13]

Aesthetics

The discussion of documentary photographs composed to suggest well-known works of art raises the further issue of the beauty of visual culture. Should tragedy appeal to the eye? Should it be attractive to look at or should the nature of its subject matter negate the question of aesthetics? 'You might think that the image of something is beautiful when what you are seeing is something ugly', said war photographer, Don McCullin. After taking a picture of troops carrying their wounded colleague in Vietnam, he realised the image recalled the crucifixion: 'You have to be careful how you frame your shot'.[14] In many ways, the problem McCullin identifies here picks up the age-old question about tragedy in general: why does tragedy give pleasure? It can, after all, be argued that audiences are drawn to tragic plays because they appreciate the way that they are structured, the way that they tell the story. Narratives and plays draw upon aesthetic frameworks to organise their material and that very organisation becomes part of the meaning of the tragedy. The representation of suffering on stage offers some kind of explanation for that suffering. So too visual culture organises its subject in order to try to make sense of things and thus to find significance in it. One might think, for example, of David's paintings produced in revolutionary France such as the *Oath of the Horatii*, in which three patriotic brothers prepare to wage war on a rebel army led by the husbands of their sisters. The eye moves from the stoic men swearing their oath of allegiance to the Roman republic in the centre of the picture out to the corner where the women sit in paroxysms of grief over the slaughter to come. Although one needs to know the story to get the full meaning of the painting, it is possible to read the image, with its basic contrast between the men and the women, like a narrative.

There are works of art whose tragic import has been seriously undermined by the exquisite manner – some might say kitsch – in which they are depicted. While the numerous medieval paintings of the martyrdom of saints were commissioned to inspire admiration and piety, it appears that many artists seized the opportunity which the stories of bindings and flayings afforded them to portray naked, male flesh with aesthetic relish. St Sebastian, who was used as target practice for Roman archers, was a particular favourite. His naked, youthful body, pierced by arrows, in paintings by Mantegna, Pollaiuolo and Guido Reni among others, has become an 'icon of sex appeal', according to art historian Nigel Spivey.[15] On non-religious subjects, there are the mawkish paintings of some of the Pre-Raphaelites: Henry Wallis' picture of the death of the young poet Chatterton, stretched out in marble whiteness in his garret, or Millais' drowned Ophelia floating downstream, every strand of hair and petal of flower minutely rendered in brushstrokes. Even Lessing noted that 'the more we see, the more we must be able to imagine' (p. 19), but these artists revel in showing everything in painstaking detail. As a result, these pictures have replaced tragic concern over the subject matter with a self-regarding obsession

9. Starving child watched by waiting vulture in Sudan. Photograph by Kevin Carter, 1993. © Corbis

with the medium, and the result is a treacherous transformation of feeling into melodrama.

Photographers also run the danger of another charge. In their quest for the arresting photograph, they seek out the most critical, heart-breaking experiences but do not intervene. They merely bear witness, rather than alleviate the situation in a practical way. One could think of Kevin Carter's Pulitzer prize-winning photograph of a starving child watched over by a waiting vulture. Or the extremely controversial photographs by Horst Faas of the police bayoneting dissidents in Dacca, Bangladesh, in 1972.[16] In these cases, photojournalism raises more acutely and more vividly the question which Brecht posed: what is the use of tragic representation (in theatre, in art, in photography) if it changes nothing? Photographers could be accused of shielding their emotional response behind a lens, viewing atrocity, starvation and grief as a human-interest story to be composed beautifully and dramatically. But we, the consumers of tragedy, are perhaps even more guilty of dissociating aesthetic response from ethical action.

Jaded by images of tragedy from around the world in today's media, are we still capable of responding appropriately to visual culture which depicts suffering? Is tragic art still possible? The days of magazines publishing the work of independent, professional photographers are fading, and arguably the most iconic photograph of the present War on Terror was shot on an amateur's camera: the hooded, electric 'crucifixion' at Abu Ghraib prison.[17] The reasons

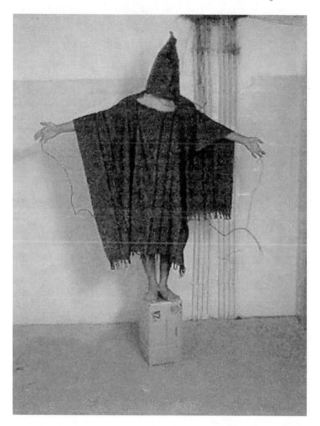

10. Hooded prisoner endures 'electric crucifixion' torture. Abu Ghraib prison, Baghdad. This photograph was originally published in the *New Yorker* (10 May 2004)

why this photograph was taken and how it came to be published are complex. But suffice it to say that there is still a natural human hunger to see images of atrocity as a way to make sense of it, to respond to it appropriately. We can see this evident in the New York exhibition of photographs of 9/11, to which anyone could contribute a picture, and in the numerous pictures of funerals in the West Bank and Gaza taken by the Palestinian brothers, Ahmed Jadallah, Suhaib Salem and Mohammed Salem.[18] In both these cases – one amateur and the other professional – the images were repeated endlessly and could have provoked fatigue in the viewer. But instead, they were compelling for their act of witness. They confirm that somebody marked the event and took a photograph;

this significant act of witnessing will be perpetuated when the photograph is viewed subsequently. Only by looking at these kinds of photographs will we be encouraged, in Susan Sontag's words, 'to pay attention, to reflect, to learn, to examine the rationalisations for mass suffering offered by established powers'.[19] As Jean-Francois Leroy, director of the 'VISA pour l'image' photo festival at Perpignan, put it: 'We have the duty to know. We have the duty to understand the world in which we live.'[20]

4.2 Novels

Traditional definitions of tragedy seem antithetical to the novel. According to Aristotle, tragedy should have a simple, unitary plot and it should deal with general truths, rather than with specific facts, places or people. But neither of these desired criteria (unitary plot and general truths) are usually to be found in novels since multiple narratives and referentiality are two of the most characteristic aspects of the novel. Indeed, the novel is typically constructed from what Bakhtin has called the 'dialogical imagination', which incorporates many voices and different perspectives. And ever since *Robinson Crusoe* and most spectacularly in *Ulysses*, the novel has also been concerned with objects, real locations and 'particular facts'.

So, given these serious generic obstacles, can one talk about the tragic novel at all? Thomas Hardy's novels might reasonably be termed tragic, in that he attempted to impose a classical tragic structure upon the non-classical landscape of Wessex. References to the gods in *Tess*, or Fate in the *Mayor of Casterbridge*, or even the ancient past which recurs to haunt the protagonists in *Return of the Native*, constitute attempts, on Hardy's part, to fit the events of the novel into an orthodox model based upon Greek tragedy. The effort appears forced at times, and it might be argued that the frequently noticed oppressive nature of Hardy's landscape symbolises vividly the weight of tragic structure bearing down upon the otherwise multitudinous business of the novel. So, for example, most strikingly we see Tess hacking up turnips with her friend in the harsh winter fields as the gods might look down upon Oedipus, or indeed the tragedian might organise the chaotic mess of life: 'the two girls crawling over the surface of the [field] like flies'.[21]

More interesting, I believe, are those great nineteenth-century novels, by George Eliot, Stendhal and Tolstoy, which explored how the new medium of the novel might produce a very different kind of tragedy. These novelists self-consciously posit the traditional models of tragedy only to modify them during the course of the novel, finding a new tragic sense located precisely in those aspects of representation excluded by Aristotle, in the multiple voices and referentiality. They depict heroes and heroines with classical aspirations. Julien Sorel in *Le Rouge et le Noir* dreams of being Napoleon; Dorothea Brooke imagines herself a St Theresa or an Antigone. Even Anna Karenina's passion is portrayed by Tolstoy to be just as intense and single-minded as Phaedra's.[22] But these aspirations are thwarted by the very medium in which these protagonists find themselves. The intensity of Anna's passion is not reciprocated because the minute, myriad ties of society pull upon Vronsky's consciousness. Her refusal to yield to the many concerns of society, unlike Vronsky, is further modified by the comparison with Levin, who is driven by similar feelings of yearning and dissatisfaction. A few years earlier, after watching his brother die, Levin 'realising that for every man, and himself too, there was nothing ahead but suffering, death, eternal oblivion, . . . had decided that to live under such conditions was impossible – he must either find an explanation to the problem of existence which would make life seem something other than the cruel irony of a malevolent spirit, or he must shoot himself'.[23] But instead, he carries on living, finding that by mingling with the local peasants on his estate he can become caught up in their daily fluctuations between sorrow and joy and mitigate his single-minded, obsessive quest with their little concerns.

In short, Anna's tragedy, driven to commit suicide because she cannot accept Vronsky's compromises and concessions, is offset by Levin's spiritual awakening. The single, linear tragic plot is qualified by the pressure of all the other lives and stories which surround it. This is a process which George Eliot notes in *Middlemarch* too, that society is a web which complicates the Hegelian view of history as linear. History for Eliot is made up from 'the stealthy convergence of human lots', during which 'some [slip] a little downward, some [get] higher footing' and where the 'less marked vicissitudes . . . are constantly shifting the boundaries of social intercourse'.[24] So by a Bakhtinian dialogic vision of society and plot structure, Lydgate's disappointment is arguably set against Fred Vincy's redemption and quiet happiness with Mary Garth.

But this web of interdependence and 'vicissitude' also becomes the very medium within which individual aspiration is imprisoned and crushed. Both Dorothea and Lydgate are 'embroiled' in the same thick medium, the same 'hampering threadlike pressure of small social conditions, and their frustrating complexity' (p. 210), which dampens and wastes their idealistic ambition to make a mark upon the world. When they meet, they recognise the parallels in their fate. 'For years after Lydgate remembered the impression produced in him by this involuntary appeal – this cry from soul to soul, without other consciousness than their moving with kindred natures in the same embroiled medium, the same troublous fitfully-illuminated life' (p. 324). Lydgate's insight into the 'embroiled medium' comes to have greater and greater significance for him as the novel progresses, when we witness his initial determination to find a cure for cholera become dissipated in the daily medical drudgery necessary to keep his wife Rosamund in the material luxury she demands. We are left with the image of Rosamund as a basil plant feeding on her husband's brains, in a reference to the story of Isabella and the pot of basil.[25] And Dorothea's idealistic energy is similarly exhausted by the events of the novel, the pun on her name – 'Brooke' – allowing Eliot to end the novel with quiet disappointment at her decline: 'Her finely-touched spirit had still its fine issues, though they were not widely visible. Her full nature, like that river of which Cyrus broke the strength, spent itself in channels which had no great name on the earth' (p. 896).

Of course, in their tenacious concern with consciousness, both Tolstoy and Eliot address the question of the location of the tragic sense, which dogs any discussion of the tragic novel. Are these protagonists aware of their tragic predicament, in the way dramatic heroes necessarily must be? Or is the tragic consciousness to be found rather in the narrative voice, in the author's perspective? Eliot offers us images of the narrative voice illuminating the tangled web of the novel's business, which could suggest that the sharp, agonised consciousness is hers alone:

> Your pier-glass or extensive surface of polished steel made to be rubbed by a housemaid, will be minutely and multitudinously scratched in all directions; but place now against it a lighted candle as a centre of illumination, and lo! the scratches will seem to arrange themselves in a fine series of concentric circles round that little sun. It is demonstrable that the scratches are going everywhere impartially, and it is only your candle which produces the flattering illusion of a concentric arrangement, its light falling with an exclusive optical selection.   (p. 297)

The sense of Dorothea's failure to be a tragic heroine is voiced by the author, rather than by the character herself, and could be the product of Eliot's heightened awareness of the novel's 'medium':

> A new Theresa will hardly have the opportunity of reforming a conventual life, any more than a new Antigone will spend her heroic piety in daring all for the sake of a brother's burial: the medium in which their ardent deeds took shape is for ever gone.   (p. 896)

But both novels describe a process of the deliberate numbing of the consciousness on the part of the protagonists. In other words, Dorothea and Levin succeed in their active quest not to think in order to shield themselves precisely from

Eliot's tragic sense of futility and disappointment. So Levin *realises* that he was able to survive without shooting himself, because he had lived like his placid, unexceptional wife Kitty, without intellectualising things: 'He had gone on living, thinking and feeling, had even at that very time married, had experienced many joys and been happy whenever he was not pondering on the meaning of life' (pp. 831–2). And Dorothea's lonely grief in her marriage is set in the context of the need to 'wad' ourselves with 'stupidity':

> That element of tragedy which lies in the very fact of frequency, has not yet wrought itself into the coarse emotion of mankind; and perhaps our frames could hardly bear much of it. If we had a keen vision and feeling of all ordinary human life, it would be like hearing the grass grow and the squirrel's heart beat, and we should die of that roar which lies on the other side of silence. As it is, the quickest of us walk about well wadded with stupidity. (p. 226)

This 'stupidity' in Tolstoy and Eliot, as defence against the tragic, is qualititatively different from the 'stupidity' in Flaubert. In *Madame Bovary*, the general stupefaction, felt particularly after Emma's death, is not born out of an agonised decision on the part of the characters not to feel or think but rather from the novelist himself, who empties the world of the novel of all significance. His description of Emma's milieu, of her frustrated aspirations and her ghastly death from arsenic poisoning, repeatedly returns to the figure of nothingness, the empty circle, the black hole. This is a novel of disgust, rather than tragedy.[26]

But in Tolstoy and Eliot, the characters' consciousness is set in a context in which illumination comes and goes 'fitfully', and can shine at times into their lives. Anna enjoys a moment of revelation, just a second before her suicide: 'suddenly the darkness that had enveloped everything for her lifted, and for an instant life glowed before her with all its past joys. But she did not take her eyes off the wheels of the approaching second truck' (p. 801). Levin, in a paradoxically enlightened and self-aware moment, recognises that his survival through living rather than thinking has eschewed 'enlightenment', while it has brought a quiet fulfilment. And Dorothea, whose survival might be said to be dependent upon her calculated 'wadding' of her 'keen vision', concludes in the flickering, *half* light of hidden but worthwhile insignificance:

> But the effect of her being on those around her was incalculably diffusive: for the growing good of the world is partly dependent on unhistoric acts; and that things are not so ill with you and me as they might have been, is half owing to the number who lived faithfully a hidden life, and rest in unvisited tombs. (p. 896)

The density of the world, which these lives briefly illuminate, bears down upon character and reader alike, cushioning the acuteness of classical tragedy but preventing also its intense, cathartic release.

4.3 Film

Film is not traditionally considered a tragic art form. Books on tragedy and film actually focus upon dramatic tragedy which is adapted for film: 'Shakespeare in film' or 'Greek tragedy in film'. This implies that tragic film as such does not exist, since the original tragic writing is assumed to take place in the theatre, upon which film is predicated. But if we believe that every culture invents art forms to respond to its particular experience of pain and suffering, then we would assume that film, as the most popular art form of the late twentieth and early twenty-first centuries, must fulfil a role in shaping our response to these experiences today.

So what are the difficulties in defining film as tragic? The problem seems to lie partly in the cultural, social context of cinema. It is generally believed that cinema is the venue for mass popular culture, in contrast to the theatre, and that mass culture craves entertainment and escapism, rather than the disturbance of tragedy. 'Nobody seriously questions the principle that it is the function of mass culture to maintain public morale, and certainly nobody in the mass audience objects to having his morale maintained', wrote film critic Robert Warshow.[27] The problem also can be found in film's characteristic emphasis upon the gaze. Viewing film in the cinema is associated with pleasure, since, in the words of Laura Mulvey, 'cinematic codes create a gaze, a world and an object, thereby producing an illusion cut to the measure of desire'.[28] Cinematic tragic pleasure is, of course, at odds with Aristotle's strictures on spectacle in tragedy: 'Spectacle is emotionally potent but falls quite outside the art and is not integral to poetry: tragedy's capacity is independent of performance and actors, and besides, the costumier's art has more scope than the poet's for rendering effects of spectacle' (*Poetics*, 1450b16–20).[29]

But certain genres of films address precisely these issues and find, in their experiments with visual images and the spectator's gaze, a new language of tragic cinema. As with tragic drama, the emotional power of these films is partly derived from their resistance to commercial 'morale-boosting' and partly from their self-conscious development of, and simultaneous departure from, fixed generic expectations. The Hollywood genre of *film noir*, for example, which emerged in the post-war America of the 1940s, acquired a set of conventions which were immediately recognisable and almost as immediately inverted to lend particular moments in certain films extra poignancy and interest.[30] The films were distinctive for what one critic has described as 'their dark, visual style and their black vision of despair, loneliness and dread', evoked by their nocturnal, urban settings, the isolation of the main protagonist, and the anxiety inherent in their typical plot-lines. The shadowy lighting in the films resists the spectator's gaze to prevent the films from becoming 'spectacle'. Characteristically the films are structured through the use of flashbacks, which add to the tragic sense of fatalism, since the hero's doom is already known as he tells his story. *Double Indemnity* (1944) opens with the hero Walter Neff crawling, wounded, to an office so that he can dictate his story into his colleague's stenograph; *Out of the Past* (1947) operates through a series of flashbacks, as Jeff Bailey tells his new fiancée of his inextricable entanglement in a murky past, caught by the *femme fatale* Kathie. In each case, the hero expresses the horror of his entrapped situation, which is re-enforced by the film's structure. *Double Indemnity*, for example, famously draws on the metaphor of the trolley-car ride to ponder tragic fate: 'They've committed murder and that's not like taking a trolley ride together where each can get off at a different stop. They're stuck with each other. They've got to ride all the way to the end of the line. And it's a one-way trip, and the last stop is the cemetery.'

There are numerous adaptations of *film noir*, but I will focus upon just a couple to show how they experiment with these conventions and disturb them to powerful effect. The hero, Dix Steele, in Nicholas Ray's film, *In a Lonely Place* (1950), like all Ray's existential heroes, is an alienated and violent individual for whom nothing appears to have any value. But, unlike most *film noir* protagonists, he is a writer, rather than a detective or a criminal, with the result that the film becomes self-consciously reflexive. At times, he appears to write his own script. He fancifully generates the suspicion that he could be a murderer, or at least he does nothing to quell it. As a result, the suspicion becomes strong enough to threaten his relationship with his fiancée Laurel and thus the one chance he has for success and happiness. By the time the police telephone with the news that they have caught the murderer, the relationship is beyond repair. 'Yesterday this would have mattered so much to us. Today it doesn't matter at all', Laurel tells them. The implication is that we invent romantic love just as we invent the paranoiac suspicions inherent in *film noir*. Once both fictions are destroyed, nothing matters 'at all'. Laurel closes by wistfully quoting a line from Dix's script to describe their vanished love, blurring once again the distinction between fiction and fact: 'I was born when she kissed me. I died when she left me. I lived a few weeks while she loved me.'

Martin Scorsese's *Taxi Driver* (1976) also makes the spectator's gaze grimly ironic, by viewing the nocturnal, *film noir*-ish world through the eyes not of a jaded screen-writer but of a New York cabbie. A Vietnam-vet, Travis wishes, as he puts it, to 'clean up the streets', but he lacks, like Ibsen's Hedda Gabler, any alternative values to counter what he sees as the inadequacies of the world around him. His response is simply more violence. But at the film's close, Scorsese develops Nicholas Ray's sense of the meaninglessness of society's ideals to even more devastating effect. For Travis' unprovoked and purposeless massacre of men in a brothel is converted by the media into an act of heroism. Scorsese uses the overhead camera shot of the massacre – derived from Hitchcock – to suggest the irony of this supposed objective perspective: 'As flies to wanton boys are we to the gods'. If Travis is a hero, then heroism and the distinction between good and evil mean nothing any longer in post-Vietnam America.

Film noir uses the visual language of cinema (and mainstream Hollywood cinema to boot) to interrogate alienated subjectivity with tragic effect. In contrast, around the same time Italian cinema was exploring the shocking reality of post-war conditions apparently objectively. Directors like Rossellini filmed real people, rather than actors, and preferred the documentary genre rather than the narrative plot. But it was when that strain of neo-realist cinema was combined with an interest in individuals, played by professional actors, that the films could be described as tragic. (Fellini's *La Strada* (1954), for example). Bunuel's *Los Olvidados* (1950) brought together the influence of Italian neo-realism, in its depiction of the harsh life in Mexico City's shanty town, with surrealist dream sequences which lent a poignant humanity to the most forgotten and illiterate of subjects. This combination of realism and surrealism offers a disturbing and unsentimental vision of redemption, in that Pedro, who has tried in vain throughout the film to extricate himself from the criminal clutches of Jaibo ('I want to be good but I don't know how', he tells his unfeeling mother), is tipped onto a garbage heap after he has been killed, like throwaway trash, while Jaibo, who has terrorised the neighbourhood and destroyed Pedro's life, hears, as he lies dying, the surreal, ghostly, loving voice of the mother he never knew.

The 'morale-boosting' capacity of cinema is based partly on the human need for heroes. One thinks of Hollywood's dependence upon the celebrity movie-star system. But the film genres discussed so far throw that hero-worship into question: *film noir* by deconstructing the means by which heroes are created in movies, neo-realism by dispensing with movie-stars altogether. The epic film, as typified by the work of director David Lean, appears at first to comply with Hollywood's demand for a hero, in that films like *Lawrence of Arabia, Bridge Over the River Kwai* and *Dr Zhivago* revolve around the martyrdom and idealisation of their central characters. But Lean achieves this effect by self-consciously disavowing cinema's pleasure in the body and its appetites, in an effort to impose a tragic structure (as Thomas Hardy does in the novel) derived from supposedly higher art forms. Lawrence refuses to drink as he crosses the desert; Colonel Nicholson is prepared to spend days in 'the oven' without water rather than sacrifice a principle. Thus Lean creates figures who, arguably like Antigone, are willing to give up their bodily desires (the object of cinema's spectacle) for an abstract idea or principle. And thus, Lean implies, his films are not mere cinema as entertainment but tragedies with the profundity of classical drama.

But, of course, Lean's anti-cinema films are belied by the sheer cinematic beauty of the camera-work. Lawrence's martyrdom is offset in interesting ways by the arresting spectacle of the Moroccan desert and the physical beauty of the actor Peter O'Toole. In this case, the recent developments in the Western epic, which combine the stunning visual effect of the desert with a tragic cynicism about whether there are any principles worth sacrificing oneself for, might seem more knowingly cinematic. Sergio Leone's great trilogy, for example (*A Fistful of Dollars, For a Dollar More* and *The Good, The Bad and The Ugly*), traces a growing scepticism, through each film, about the traditional values upon which pioneering American society depends, until, by the end of the last film, all endeavour seems tragically futile. The film closes with a series of images of pointlessness: the army suffering massive casualties in a fight for a bridge which gets blown up; Tuco digging up the wrong grave in the search for dirty money; a three-way duel, waged in the empty desert with one gun unloaded.

Recent European films have experimented with resisting the spectator's gaze altogether. Krzysztof Kiéslowski attempts, in his *Three Colours* trilogy, to separate the audience's eye from the ear, by splicing visual material with aural dialogue and music. Watching is consequently made difficult, not a matter of indulgence nor the exercise of spectatorial power. In *Blue* (1993), for example, the viewer is disorientated by seeing first Julie's (Juliette Binoche) eye in close-up, then a blank screen with a blast of music, then a shadowy man's profile from Julie's head-on-pillow perspective, then another blast of music. The sensory fragmentation replicates Julie's state of post-traumatic stress, as she recovers from the shock of losing her husband and daughter in a car crash. Her normal human response to emotion is turned upside-down. 'Why are you crying?', she asks her housekeeper. 'Because you are not', is the reply. But gradually she learns to mourn, and the viewing for us becomes easier, as she is able to 'restitute her fantasy frame' (Slavoj Žižek's words) and reassumes the ordinary, inauthentic practices of everyday life.[31]

The Danish director Lars Von Trier's 'Dogma' school of film-making has specialised in making watching film difficult. Movies like *Breaking the Waves*

(1996), *Festen* (*The Celebration*) (1998) and *Dancer in the Dark* (2000), all arguably tragedies, are shot using 16 mm film and hand-held camera to give the impression of the home video and thus of an amateurish authenticity. The form of the film offsets the high-concept, theological dimension of the narrative. In *Breaking the Waves*, for example, the naïve heroine, Bess, accepts her paralysed husband's demand that she have sex with other men so that he can live her experience vicariously. In doing this, she sacrifices her good reputation in her small, Calvinist community. Ultimately, under the mistaken belief that she needs to take more sexual risks to help her declining husband, she is violently gang-raped and left to die. The community, scandalised by her behaviour, buries her coffin in unhallowed ground and condemns her to hell. But her husband, who is miraculously cured when she dies in what amounts to a highly problematic spiritual transaction, arranges to con the village elders by filling the coffin with sand and burying his wife at sea. The film raises timeless tragic questions about virtue, about sacrifice and about love, while searing our emotions by the rawness of the camera work. It closes with the over-head shot as if from God's perspective (again derived from Hitchcock and Scorsese) of bells ringing in heaven over the scene of the sea burial. Is this ironic or has Bess received divine redemption? Has Bess's sacrifice been pointless or is it recognised and given grace by a God, by some objective, judicial sanction? The surrealism of the scene leaves the film open, available to both a nihilist and a religious interpretation, in the spirit of the best Shakespearean tragedy.

4.4 Psychoanalysis

Psychoanalysis might be said to work analogously with tragedy and to offer insight into the pleasure of the process of watching tragedy. For if, as Roy Morrell observes, 'Tragedy's function is to get under control life's most chaotic and difficult parts', then psychoanalytic therapy exemplifies this function in its effort to master the turbulence of psychic disturbance.[32]

Psychoanalysts believe that people originally learn to manage their emotions through play. According to Freud, growing up is basically a tragic experience. It involves losing the original closeness to one's mother enjoyed as a baby at the breast and it is exacerbated by the realisation that one is alone in a world which is larger than the mere creation of our wishes. Children effectively act out the experience of the loss of their mother in games they invent and control. Freud describes watching one child play with a toy, which he repeatedly 'loses' and regains:

The child had a wooden reel with a piece of string tied around it . . . What he did was to hold the reel by the string and very skillfully throw it over the edge of his curtained cot, so that it disappeared into it, at the same time uttering his expressive 'o-o-o-o'. He then pulled the reel out of the cot again by the string and hailed its reappearance with a joyful 'da'. This, then, was the complete game – disappearance and return.[33]

The child manages to conquer his feelings of bewilderment on being left alone by means of two crucial aspects of the game: repetition and control. By repeating the experience over and over again, he becomes inured to its impact. He may not understand it logically but he becomes used to the feeling of abandonment. Moreover, by pulling the string and thus deciding when to witness the return, he can actively control his emotions and not be passively overwhelmed by them.

Play is also one of the central metaphors for the process of psychoanalytic therapy. Now the subject is not just going through the difficult process of growing up, but has suffered some specific crisis which has affected him deeply and upset his emotional, psychic balance. In therapy, he is helped to view his experience objectively, with some distance, rather than passively allowing it to overwhelm him. Through repeatedly describing the event, the patient is able to detach himself gradually from the experience. 'The physician . . . must get [the patient] to re-experience some portion of his forgotten life, but must see to it, on the other hand, that the patient retains some degree of aloofness, which will enable him, in spite of everything, to recognise that what appears to be reality is in fact only a reflection of a forgotten past', writes Freud.[34] His account here of successful therapy, during which a patient 'works through' a terrible experience with an analyst, shares common ground with Aristotle's account of the witnessing of theatrical tragedy in a healthily functioning city. Aristotle maintained that the audience responded to what was represented on stage with a mixture of pity and fear. In other words it felt a helpful mixture of identification and distance from what was performed, allowing it to analyse its implications both emotionally and rationally. In encouraging the patient to 'detach' himself from his experience, Freud also focuses upon the role of 'aloofness' and distance when witnessing again the traumatic events in one's past life.

Like the staging of Greek tragedy, Freud saw the consulting room as a demarcated space in which it was possible for the patient to confront the most terrible experiences which were too unbearable for him to attend to elsewhere. During the therapy sessions, the patient transfers his real, troubling feelings about people in his life to his therapist, so that he comes to identify aspects of his mother, father, or other close characters, in his therapist. The therapy can thus take the form of a licensed play, since the patient comes to realise the various 'artificial' substitutions his mind makes in order to shield itself from viewing the original trauma. 'The new condition has taken over all the features of the illness; but it represents an artificial illness which is at every point accessible to our intervention', Freud explains. 'It is a piece of real experience, but one which has been made possible by especially favourable conditions, and it is of a provisional nature.'[35] These substitutions are put under the spotlight, so to speak, in the consulting room, so that they can be played out once again and gradually understood. In this 'playing out' or what Freud also calls 'working through', we can arguably see correspondences with Aristotle's description of catharsis. Through watching tragedy, the audience member is cleaned of his emotions; through analytic transference, the patient overcomes his psychological resistances and works through his painful memories.

Thus psychoanalytically, tragedy effects a physiological catharsis, controlling and evacuating violent and disturbing feelings, according to one critic's interpretation of Freud.[36] But what about the experience of watching tragedy which is not cathartic, which is less certain and focused, and leaves us filled with bleak despair? Freud actually distinguished between 'mourning' and 'melancholia', precisely according to this question of 'focus'. 'Mourning', he argued, focuses upon a particular source of grief, and thereby is able to gradually detach itself from that object: 'Each single one of the memories and expectations in which the libido is bound to the object is brought up and hypercathected, and detachment of the libido is accomplished in respect of it'.[37] In contrast, melancholia lacks a specific source of grief: 'melancholia is in some way related to an object-loss which is withdrawn from consciousness' (p. 245). Could tragedies without catharsis be described as melancholic? One might think immediately in this context of *Hamlet*, where the source of Hamlet's difficulty could be said to be 'withdrawn from consciousness'. Indeed, Walter Benjamin, who developed Freud's distinctions in his study of tragedy, posited *Hamlet* as nearly a melancholic play, transformed into conventional tragedy by its Christian ending:

> For the *Trauerspiel* Hamlet alone is a spectator by the grace of God; but he cannot find satisfaction in what he sees enacted, only in his own fate. His life, the exemplary object of his mourning, points, before its extinction, to the Christian providence in whose bosom his mournful images are transformed into a blessed existence. Only in a princely life such as this is melancholy redeemed, by being confronted with itself.[38]

Melancholia causes disturbing confusion because of its lack of a clear-cut cause or source. But the blank bewilderment experienced in watching some tragic drama also shares correspondences with the confused understanding following traumatic events. In other words, work on trauma can elucidate some of the processes involved in staging and witnessing tragic drama. Freud's theories about trauma were influenced by his experience with shell-shocked soldiers after the First World War. He found that the soldiers were caught in a loop of repeated memory, 'obliged to repeat the repressed material as a contemporary experience instead of, as the physician would prefer to see, remembering it as something belonging to the past'. In a state of trauma, the patient is unable to gain the crucial distance needed for successful therapy, and finds himself *in medias res*, as if re-enacting the same scene over and over again. This repetition means that the patient never attains an understanding of his situation and thus cannot develop a protective, psychological defence against it.

Later work on trauma has further developed Freud's notion of the trauma patient's lack of understanding and his or her inability to describe the situation. It is now thought that the trauma is actually caused by the failure to understand or to represent the feelings of disturbance, rather than simply the direct experience of the original, horrific event. Freud's 'dream of the burning child' has become the test case to which theorists have repeatedly returned. In this story, a sick child has just died. The father, exhausted by tending to the dying child, goes away to his room to sleep, leaving somebody to watch over the dead body. In his sleep, the father dreams that the child appears beside his bed, saying 'father, don't you see I'm burning?' At this point, the father wakes up, rushes into the child's room and finds that one of the candles has fallen over and that the bed coverings and one of the child's arms have been burnt. Freud was interested in the reason for the father's dream, arguing that the father dreamt that the child was still alive, standing beside his bed, because he wanted to ward off the unspeakable trauma of his death. The pleasure of the dream, even though it was tinged with nightmare, was preferable to the unbearable tragedy of caring for the child as he died.[39]

But later commentators are more interested in what happens when the father wakes up from his dream. For them, it is not the experience of the original trauma which fascinates but the subsequent ways one tries to represent it or to shield oneself from it. Lacan focuses upon the fact that the father dreams that he is woken up by the child; in other words, he focuses upon the fantasy wakening, rather than the subsequent real awakening. He argues that the death of a child is an impossible experience to comprehend. In Lacan's words, it is the 'real' which cannot be encountered directly. The father has thus inevitably failed to respond to it appropriately. The dream therefore rehearses again the father's failure to treat his child properly, in this case to keep the child from burning, by representation rather than presentation. Being woken by the child in the dream is thus both a wish fulfilment (this time he will respond to the child's plea in time) and also a nightmarish reproach. 'Is not the dream essentially . . . an act of homage to the missed reality – the reality that can no longer produce itself except by repeating itself, endlessly, in some never attained awakening?', writes Lacan.[40] This interpretation focuses, in typical Lacanian fashion, upon the disturbing combination of loss and desire inherent in the process of coping with trauma.

More recently, Cathy Caruth has written most interestingly about the real moment of waking up. At this point, the father must leave all fantasies and dreams aside, rescue his son's body from the flames and, most importantly, realise that he has to go on living. 'Awakening', she writes, 'is itself the site of a trauma, the trauma of the necessity and impossibility of responding to another's death'.[41] The father feels guilty, both about letting the child's body burn and also about continuing to live while his child has died. One failure comes to substitute for the other, and both are represented by the dream, which itself is about guilt, neglect and the failure to see harm until too late. This failure and guilt itself becomes the source of further trauma, Caruth argues, because they cannot be properly understood or confronted. She explains: 'To awaken is thus to bear the imperative to survive: to survive no longer simply as the father of a child, but as the one who must tell *what it means not to see*, which is also what it means to hear the unthinkable words of the dying child'.[42] Trauma lies in the limits of understanding. The implications of this for tragedy lie in the well-attested limitations upon the audience's ability to explain the play it has just witnessed and the nature of its response to it. Tragedy, we might say with Caruth, thus 'simultaneously defies and demands our witness'.[43]

The connections between trauma and tragedy are explored by Toni Morrison in her great tragic novel, *Beloved*. The book addresses the horror of slavery in America in the nineteenth century and the difficulty for African Americans of confronting one of the worst periods in their history. It emerges, through the course of the narrative, that the main character, Sethe, was brutally raped and abused by the family who owned her in Kentucky. She escaped, pregnant, to Ohio in the north, where slavery had been abolished and where she had already sent her three children on to her mother-in-law, Baby Suggs. But, after nearly dying along the road, giving birth to her baby on the banks of the Ohio river and eventually finding sanctuary with Baby Suggs, she learned that her owners had arrived in pursuit, to drag her back south. Terrified at the prospect, she killed her elder daughter, to protect her from the slavers' clutches, and was only just prevented from murdering the other children by Stamp Paid. She was imprisoned for three months, and her younger daughter, Denver, was cared for by Baby Suggs.

All this happened long before the novel opens. Indeed, *Beloved* is concerned with the way this story comes to light and with the impact that it has had upon Sethe and her family. The narrative is provoked by the arrival of a mysterious stranger at Sethe's home, years after the traumatic events of the murder and imprisonment. The stranger, Beloved, could be the ghost of Sethe's murdered child, or perhaps, as Denver says, 'she was – more'.[44] At any rate, she unsettles the comfortable amnesia which has settled over the household, causing Sethe to revisit the past and Denver to learn what really happened. For Sethe, the past experience in Kentucky is a traumatic memory, which has not been 'worked through' but reified, haunting her tangibly like the physical scars on her back which will not disappear or like the enigmatic ghostly Beloved. 'Even though it's all over – over and done with – it's going to always be there waiting for you', Sethe explains to Denver, and she responds: 'If it's still there, waiting, that must mean that nothing ever dies'.[45]

The narrative structure of the novel is extremely complex, replicating the tangled loops of Sethe's traumatised memory. Since 'nothing ever dies', the past presses upon the mind simultaneously with the present; different time periods are interspersed without apparent, rational order. The effect is claustrophobic, phantasmagorical; episodes are repeated and fragmented, as the narrative unfolds. The characters, bewildered and terrified by the process, cannot understand what is going on when Beloved teases, seduces and harries them. But ultimately, painful as the narrative is, the story proves to be cathartic. Sethe finds relief in telling her tales to Beloved: 'perhaps it was Beloved's distance from the events, or her thirst for hearing it' (p. 58). Denver is liberated enough to get work outside home, and Paul D, Sethe's lover and another ex-slave haunted by his past, can start thinking about the future: 'we got more yesterday than anybody. We need some kind of tomorrow' (p. 273). Beloved, and the painful memory she represents, disappears and is forgotten once again. 'It was not a story to pass on', writes Morrison (p. 275).

The novel, then, works as tragedy and as trauma, exploring the relationship between the two. It reveals the way that characters eventually move on, converting the suffering into narrative. They are held fast in history and thus paradoxically liberated to let go of 'yesterday'. But the novel also is itself traumatic, 'passing on' the story which supposedly should not be passed on, and thus reopening the wound once again.[46] The tragic close, when Beloved disappears, could then just be the start of another traumatic opening, when her ghost might reappear. And in that case, no proper telling of the story, which fully represents the trauma, can achieve tragic clarity.

4.5 Theology

'Tragedy is only possible to a mind which is for the moment agnostic or Manichean', wrote the literary critic I. A. Richards in 1924. 'The least touch of any theology which has a compensating Heaven to offer the tragic hero is fatal.'[47] This assumption has largely persisted. Religious belief is thought to be inimical to tragedy. Religion gives its adherents hope; tragedy presents its audience with despair. Religion assumes that a God or gods watch over the world and protect it; tragedy depicts man isolated and alone. Religion suggests that death is not the end and that there will be some reward or 'compensation' (Richards' word) in heaven; tragedies usually end with death. No wonder then that Karl Jaspers can declare that 'Christian salvation opposes tragic knowledge. The chance of being saved destroys the tragic sense of being trapped without chance of escape. Therefore no genuinely Christian tragedy can exist.'[48]

But it can be countered that some of the most fundamental concerns of tragedy are deeply theological in nature. Whether it be the problem of evil or the nature of suffering, the search for understanding or the quest for a sense of closure or catharsis, these are issues which theologians and religious believers have been agonising over for centuries. Richards' premise is that religious faith is based upon certainty, solutions and salvation, while tragedy offers uncertainty and, perhaps, damnation. But in fact both tragedy and theological enquiry enjoin a careful balance of uncertainty and certainty, or in other words, question and answer, in their proponents. 'Some find the essence of tragedy in the power with which the question cries out; others in the difficult final resolution', writes Helen Gardner in her T. S. Eliot Memorial Lectures on 'Religion and Tragedy'. 'Ultimately, I think, we must accept that the way men read the image of life that a tragedy presents will depend on the bias of their temperaments.'[49] So too with religious belief. While some evangelicals will read the Bible simply to provide the answers, others will find their faith through wrestling with doubt and intractable difficulty at the heart of the text. For them, the process of questioning constitutes the complexity of religious belief itself.

Central to the theological concern with tragedy are the questions of causality and narrative: what is the relationship between the means and the end? What is the relationship between suffering and redemption? What, from a Christian perspective, is the relationship between the crucifixion and the resurrection? These questions could be described as the tragic concern with 'Saturday', to coin George Steiner's term. In the narrative of Easter, Friday is the day of crucifixion while Sunday witnesses the resurrection. Friday symbolises despair while Sunday brings joy, hope and redemption. But Saturday is the day in between, in which we wonder about the connection between despair and hope, whether one is the inevitable consequence of the other or whether indeed Sunday compensates for Friday. Saturday is the middle day in the narrative, when perhaps the longed-for end will never come.

> Ours is the long day's journey of the Saturday. Between suffering, aloneness, unutterable waste on the one hand and the dream of liberation, of rebirth on the other. In the face of the torture of a child, of the death of love which is Friday, even the greatest art and poetry are almost helpless. In the Utopia of the Sunday, the aesthetic will, presumably, no longer have logic or necessity. The apprehensions and figurations in the play of metaphysical imagining, in the poem and the music, which tell of pain and of hope, of the flesh which is said to taste of ash and of the spirit which is said to have the savour of fire, are always Sabbatarian.[50]

Saturday is the day of contingency and doubt, when it is still uncertain whether Sunday will arrive and resolve things. It is also a day which can linger in the memory, overshadowing any joy which may come with the end of the symbolic weekend. What if, indeed, Sunday never comes and life is just one long Saturday, without narrative closure? Saturday, says Steiner after all, 'has become the longest of days'.[51]

One can detect this 'Saturday' concern – the concern with the middle part of the narrative – in the three biblical stories which are considered to carry the greatest tragic implications: Abraham's thwarted sacrifice of Isaac; the testing of Job; and Christ's crucifixion.[52] Abraham's attempt to sacrifice his son in obedience to God's command formed the starting point for Kierkegaard's reflections on doubt and belief, which shaped his tragic vision (see pp. 129–31). It is well known that, at the moment when Abraham held a knife to Isaac's throat, an angel pointed out a ram to him in substitution so that Isaac was spared. But according to Kierkegaard this fact should have no bearing upon the gravity of the story. Abraham was prepared to kill what was most precious to him, against all logical and ethical precept, in order to please a mysterious God. And no final substitution can diminish the apparent malevolence of God and the mad obsession of Abraham which the middle part of the story exposes. This story, which as Carol Delaney has observed, 'became the model of faith at the foundation of the three monotheistic (Abrahamic) religions: Judaism, Christianity and Islam', reveals an inherently tragic world in which ethics and reason count for nothing and unthinking obedience to an unfathomable God is all that matters.[53] It is a world that does not make sense and whose very meaninglessness apparently allows hideous atrocities, like the killing of an innocent child, to happen.

The book of Job dramatises another trial. Job's faith is tested by having the worst deprivation and suffering inflicted upon him. Again the story is about a world which does not make sense according to human understanding. Job's friends try to comfort him by telling him that God is just and that he punishes the wicked while rewarding the good and therefore Job's suffering must be caused by his sinfulness. But Job assures them, correctly, that he has done everything right and that there is no wickedness in him. He demands to know the reason for his suffering: 'let me know why you contend against me' (Job 10.2). And he wants to know what kind of God it is to whom he must continue to cling.[54] Since God has apparently overthrown all the rules of justice, trust and mercy, it is impossible any longer to know what to believe or how to behave. 'How can a mortal be just before God?', he asks. 'How can I answer him, choosing my words with him?' Like Isabella in *Measure for Measure*, Job must 'appeal for mercy to my accuser' (Job 9.15). But God responds to Job with a whirlwind of mighty fear and strength – 'Where were you when I laid the foundation of the earth?' (Job 38.4) – teaching him a lesson in humility. His argument is that Job cannot hope to understand the mind of God. God deals with superhuman forces – the ocean, the sun, the stars, the giant monsters like leviathan and behemoth – and is not concerned with the minutiae of human justice and logic, the *quid pro quo* economy. 'Shall a fault-finder contend with the Almighty' (Job 40.2), God scoffs. In the end, Job is reduced to a gibbering wreck of contrition, and promises, like a typical Greek chorus, in the future not to think too much: 'Therefore I have uttered what I did not understand, things too wonderful for me, which I did not know' (Job 42.3). And, heartened by this, God miraculously restores everything that Job lost: his children, his animals, his prosperity. As in the *Winter's Tale*, family members are magically brought back to life so that tragedy may be averted. But the tragic irrationality at the heart of the world has been exposed by the story. And moreover the unreliability of God has been revealed. After all, God effectively lies. He claims to be uninterested in transactions, in reducing himself to contending logically with any other being. And yet Job's suffering is initially caused by God's *wager* with Satan that Job's faith will withstand any test. This is a capricious God, reminiscent of the Greek gods, whose arbitrariness constitutes the shaky foundation for chaotic, violent injustice.

Christians believe that Abraham's sacrifice of Isaac prefigures the ultimate sacrifice, that of Jesus on the cross. This is supposedly part of God's divine purpose in order to bring about salvation, but, unlike the earlier two stories, there is no Euripidean-type substitution of the victim for a ram at the close or Shakespearean magical restitution. Jesus bears his ordeal right through to the end, when the curtain of the temple is torn in two, the earth shakes and rocks split. The extreme suffering of Jesus on the cross begs the question of the cost of salvation and the nature of the relationship between good and evil. How can the crucifixion be justified? How can God allow it to happen? According to some theologians, we can understand the presence of God's compensating goodness even at the worst moments of the crucifixion, by various signs of its symbolic significance. In other words, Jesus' physical suffering – the blood, the thirstiness, the mental torment of being abandoned – carries underlying purpose and can be considered teleological, leading to the resurrection and redemption. Even his words on the cross, which appear to be simply expressions of pain, are also quotations from psalms. 'I thirst', for example, is both an indication of Jesus' physical condition and also, as John's gospel says, to fulfil scripture. Jesus' death is thus set in a wider context of biblical promise, which arguably justifies the crucifixion and mitigates its horror.

Of course it should be added that this interpretation of Jesus' suffering as providential depends on which gospel version is studied. St Mark's gospel originally finished at chapter 16, verse 8, which ends with the empty tomb, without proof of the resurrection: 'And they went out quickly, and fled from the sepulchre; for they trembled and were amazed: neither said they any thing to any man; for they were afraid'. Mark's is arguably the most tragic account of the crucifixion, because it refuses to draw out any significance in the event and closes with fear and uncertainty, with the death of the hero and an empty tomb. St John's gospel, on the other hand, is imbued with symbolism and the sense of God's purpose behind events, from Judas' betrayal of Christ – 'Verily, verily, I say unto you, that one of you shall betray me; . . . He it is, to whom I shall give a sop, when I have dipped it. And when he had dipped the sop, he gave it to Judas Iscariot' (John 21.26) – to Jesus' last words before his death: 'When Jesus therefore had received the vinegar, he said, It is finished (*teleitai*): and he bowed his head, and gave up the ghost' (John 19.30). As in the *Oresteia*, the Greek word *teleitai* (*telos*) is used in both its senses here: 'finished' and 'fulfilled'. So while one theologian, Donald Mackinnon, writes of the 'tragic irony' in St John's gospel in its presentation of God's purpose, a 'triumph purchased at the price of appalling catastrophe', nevertheless it is arguably the case that John offers the most teleological version of Christ's death and therefore the account which most explains and justifies suffering.[55]

According to the interpretation of the crucifixion outlined above, God's suffering – losing himself when he feels himself abandoned in the cross, 'emptying' himself out in the physical figure of Jesus – is part of a grander plan of drawing the world back to him, of letting humanity fill that emptiness in. Sacrifice and loss take their place in a wider context of love – God's love. 'God so loved the world that he gave his only begotten son', and so on. Consequently suffering for those who accept God can become mitigated by the thought of that wider context, that joy and meaningfulness. Meanwhile for those who do not accept God, suffering simply is meaningless and brings about annihilation. Evil, according to this theory, arises from the deprivation of God. Graham Ward explains:

> There is a suffering which is rendered meaningless because it has no part in redemption. This is a suffering which rejects and fights against redemption. It has no truth, no existence in Augustine's ontology of goodness, because it is privative – it deprives and strips creation of its orders of being . . . But there is a suffering which is intrinsically meaningful because it is a continuation, a fleshing out, and a completing of the suffering of Christ.[56]

This is a tragic view of the world, in that it views suffering as necessary for knowing God, for attaining that love and redemption. 'With the darkest nights of the soul, in which is evident the inseparability of consciousness, subconsciousness and the sensitivities of the flesh, come the profoundest awareness of participation in the divine', writes Ward.[57] But it is only tragic in the sense that the teleological, Hegelian interpretation of the *Oresteia* might be said to be tragic. 'We must suffer into truth' (Chorus, *Agamemnon* 177).

In contrast, other Christian theologians maintain that it is important that the darkness of Easter Saturday is not glossed over in the feverish anticipation of the resurrection the next day. Jesus' resurrection, in other words, does not mitigate the suffering of his crucifixion and his death. At the heart of Christian belief is the Incarnation, or the notion that Jesus was human as well as God, that he took on our humanity. So in his death on the cross, he experienced the most extreme pain and despair that it is possible for man to suffer. The night before he was crucified, in the garden of Gethsemane, he was in such mental agony that he sweated blood, asking God not to make him go through the ordeal and feeling utterly abandoned: 'sleepest thou? couldest not thou watch one hour?' (Mark 14.37), he reproaches the disciples. And on the cross, between the two thieves, he voices the utmost desolation: 'My God, my God, why hast thou forsaken me' (Mark 15.34). If evil means the deprivation of God, then this cry of Jesus from the cross, forsaken by God, articulates the greatest experience of evil imaginable.[58]

The emphasis upon Jesus' physical suffering, in this interpretation of the crucifixion, points to the fact that God shares our humanity, that God became man and suffered the most extreme pain that can ever be inflicted upon us. Under this theory, the evil of the cross is offset by the thought of divine purpose or redemption, but it is endured by Jesus in a very human, realistic way. Consequently evil is not conquered nor used as a test of faith, but God suffers under it too. And this shared experience of suffering becomes the one source of goodness or of strength. From now on, when tragedies happen or when suffering occurs, we can say that God has trodden that path before us and shares in the experience with us. This is the only religious consolation, that there is divine compassion even at the darkest hour. 'When God becomes man in Jesus of Nazareth, he not only enters into the finitude of man, but in his death on the cross also enters into the situation of man's godforsakenness', writes Jurgen Moltmann in *The Crucified God*. 'He takes upon himself the eternal death of the godless and the godforsaken, so that all the godless and the godforsaken can experience communion with him.'[59] This fellow compassion has a transformative force. Indeed, to pick up George Steiner's 'Saturday' metaphor again, the Christian capacity to feel compassion arguably transfigures every Friday into a Saturday:

> The best use, usually, of Friday prayers is against injustice done to others, is an aspect of our solidarity with poverty and suffering. But then, the strange thing is that, in such solidarity, we learn from others the gleam of joyfulness in pain, of patient courage, which we lacked. Thus we discover that it is not Friday, after all, but Saturday.[60]

But for one theologian, Donald Mackinnon, even these accounts which focus upon Christ's humanity and suffering, fall short of doing justice to the darkness of the cross. He acknowledges that 'Christianity takes the history of Jesus and urges the believer to find, in the endurance of the ultimate contradictions of human existence that belongs to its very substance, the assurance that in the worst that can befall his creatures, the creative Word keeps company with those whom he has called his own'.[61] But any attempt to allow that 'keeping company' to *explain* suffering or to transmute pain into a 'gleam of joyfulness' must be resisted because it does not attend to the specific horror adequately. Having lived through the Second World War, the revelation of the Holocaust and the dropping of the atom bomb on Hiroshima, like Jurgen Moltmann, Mackinnon was haunted by the darkness of the human heart and of what it was capable of perpetrating. His conclusion, as a theologian, was that evil cannot be explained away theologically, and that the depth of suffering in the world can neither be understood nor fully plumbed. The only possibility is to describe and redescribe concrete particulars, without analysis or explication. The crucifixion, after all, was a particular event, a 'deed done in history', and must not be abstracted by metaphysics or philosophical rationalisation. 'A doctrine of the atonement is the projection of a raw piece of human history in a way calculated to admit the man who attends to it to some perception of its inwardness and universal significance', he explains. 'But such a doctrine inevitably fails if it encourages the believer to avert his attention from the element of sheer waste, the reality of Christ's failure'.[62]

In his claim that evil or the crucifixion cannot be understood but just repeatedly described and attended to, Mackinnon controversially advocates a concept of God as unknowable and of tragedy ultimately as mystery. Indeed, under this belief, tragedy and religion become analogous, both marking the moments when rational understanding fails. 'It is a lesson to be learnt from tragedy that there is no solution of the problem of evil; it is a lesson which Christian faith abundantly confirms, even while it transforms the teaching by the indication of its central mystery.' Confronted by mystery, the appropriate human response is often silence. And on God's side the response might be a further question rather than a glib consolation. 'Part of the finality of the Christian story is an actualisation of the "whole tragic potentiality" of human history on the cross', writes one theologian, Ben Quash. 'Part of the finality . . . is the realisation in history of God's eternal attitude of *response*, which in its very ultimacy preserves the value of the questioning – questioning which frequently has a tragic quality.'[63]

Some theologians imagine that the mystery, silence and questioning can ultimately lead to good, to God's glory. The whole point of claiming God and tragedy as mysterious is that we do not ultimately know the answers about their nature and function. As Gardner said, making assumptions about the final scheme of things, whether they are optimistic or pessimistic, probably depends upon one's temperament. Recognising the tragic heart of the Christian story might finally lead one to a deeper understanding of suffering and its place in the world and therefore carry some purpose. But as far as Mackinnon was concerned, any attempt to 'move beyond tragedy', by explaining the mystery or seeing in it a 'traceable providential order', was deeply suspect. Only by returning again and again to the contemplation of the cross, as one might go to repeated performances of a play or become trapped in the circular loop of traumatic experience, only then, looking at the desolate and wasted figure of Christ, can one attend to tragic suffering theologically.

Chapter 5

Coda: tragic sites

Particular places take on tragic resonance. Indeed, sites where terrible things have happened become the focus for the public mourning of past history. One could think, for example, of the Battlefield of the Somme, of Auschwitz, of Ground Zero in New York. These sites are now places of pilgrimage, to which survivors, relatives of the dead and the concerned public come to remember and reflect. Tours are offered to Auschwitz-Birkenau to view the surviving prison blocks, gas chamber and crematorium where one-and-a-half million people were killed between 1940 and 1945.[1] Empty now, the huts of Auschwitz or the sixteen acres once filled by the twin towers of the World Trade Center testify to the lives that were lost here, to the terrible five years of the holocaust or the 105 minutes from first plane crash to second tower collapse on 9/11. Time, in these cases, has been remembered as place. Events become reified in the public imagination as geographical sites, arguably converted into objects like Freud's traumatic memories.

Except that the significance of these tragic sites, and their power to move the modern visitor, lies in what is missing rather than in what is present. Freud's traumatic memory cannot be absorbed or properly remembered because it resists the mind's 'working through'; it sticks out, hard, opaque, ill-understood. But the tragic power of Ground Zero or Auschwitz stems from the imaginative gulf between the place and what it commemorates, between the land which we can see and the dead which have disappeared. In the aftermath of 9/11, this gulf became acutely apparent. For eight months, the firemen raked through the debris of the twin towers looking for the remains of the 2,752 people reported missing. But it became clear that many bodies were never going to be found and that they had simply been vaporised by the intense heat of the fire. One fireman commented on his desperate search to identify the many dead, as the months wore on and the piles of debris disappeared. 'It's not over, but it's definitely winding down', he told the *New York Times*. 'You've got a great number of people that you want to find, and you've got a certain amount of dirt that's left. And there's a gap. That gap is going to be a sorrowful one. But we can't make more dirt.'[2] It is often to this gap, it seems to me, that tragedy

189

attends. The gap between the indifferent natural world and the lives that once beat within it; the gap between what is visibly present before us and what we acknowledge is missing; the gap between questions and answers: this is what continues to intrigue and trouble the public as it deals with the aftermath of any tragedy.

In recent years, the 'gaps' in the form of literal missing bodies have, in some places, been marvellously filled. The techniques and legal practices of forensic archaeology have so advanced that it has become possible to excavate the mass graves of victims of genocide and to bring some of the perpetrators to account. In Argentina, the mothers of the disappeared, the 'madres de la Plaza de Mayo', invited forensic archaeologists from the United States to investigate the fate of the victims of the 1976–83 junta. Estimates of the number of disappeared vary between 9,000 and 30,000. Since the forensic evidence has not yet been used in a trial, because of the amnesty law passed in 1987, the statistics are not yet definitively known, but in June 2005 this amnesty was overturned so trials can now go ahead. It may be, therefore, that the past, in the form of human remains, could soon come to haunt the members of that junta. In Rwanda, where over one million Tutsis were killed in just a hundred days in 1994, the United Nations-appointed International Criminal Tribunal has been using evidence gleaned from forensic archaeology in the prosecution of key leaders who incited the violence.

The excavation of these graves reveals the existence of a grim form of justice. They prove that the history of atrocity is not always erased but can be held fast in the ground and dug up at a later date, to confirm private or unofficial memories of loss. The perpetrated wrong is not left unpunished or unanswered but, in Macbeth's words, 'returns to plague the inventor'. And it can be confronted in the form of a body in a particular place, dug up from the ground. This is the same possibility of justice which prompted the Chilean writer Ariel Dorfman's novel, *Widows*, the story of women claiming dead bodies washed up on a river bank. As each body is washed up, one of the women demands it back from the authorities, claiming that it is that of her dead relative and that she wants to give it a proper funeral. The effect is to force the authorities to acknowledge that these men have been killed.[3] The physical body forces that confrontation with atrocity more urgently than a story ever could do. But, in fact, in *Widows*, it is not possible for the women or the authorities to identify each dead body specifically; the extent of physical decomposition reminds us of how much of the individual person has been lost.[4]

In contrast, after September 11th 2001, when so many bodies could not be found, the city of New York could only focus its attention on the names of the victims, rather than their physical remains. In the months following the catastrophe, the *New York Times* published short biographies, entitled 'Portraits of Grief', of each of the victims, accompanied by a photograph. And on the wall erected around the Ground Zero site were listed the 2,757 people who lost their lives that day. The ceremony held on the anniversary of 9/11 each year takes the form of a name call of the dead, which lasts several hours. In its emphasis upon the names of the dead, listed one after another, New York City follows a modern tradition of memorialisation which attempts to confront the problem of the sheer number and anonymity of the dead in war and natural disaster. Whether it be the First World War dead or the numbers of the casualties in Vietnam, memorials combine attention to statistics (the devastating length of the list) with a focus upon the individual (the careful naming of each victim). As Tom Laqueur notes in his essay on First World War commemoration, 'the sources of modern memory . . . derive their meaning from their intrinsic lack of it and bear testimony to their own artifice . . . They are like the army of the living, both democratic and individual in their singularity, mere numbers in their aggregate.'[5] So the memorial for the dead at Ground Zero named each person individually but also mourned them as a group, devastating in their huge number. The Vietnam War memorial, designed by Maya Lin, allows families to touch the name of their particular dead relative and to mourn his individual death. But the memorial as whole also commemorates a tragic episode in US history, symbolising, by cutting a trench into the ground, the open wound in America's national memory.[6]

Memorials, therefore, like the Vietnam War Memorial in Washington or the 'Portraits of Grief' in the *New York Times*, arguably share correspondences with the tragic drama which I have been examining in this book. Through listing names, memorials attempt, as did Euripides in *The Trojan Women*, to prevent the preciousness of each individual from being lost in the general, wide-scale disaster. And they make what might have been ephemeral into something lasting and therefore meaningful, just as Hecuba hopes her suffering will be turned into song. They transform the terrible atrocities into stone; they shape the chaos of experience into aesthetic pattern which can be confronted, reflected upon and lamented. Of course, as with the analogy with excavation mentioned above, this suggests that tragedy is to be considered essentially retrospective, an act of response. Is it therefore 'tragic' to witness or report or mourn the genocide in Rwanda but not to participate in it? Is the ceremony to remember the dead at Vietnam a 'tragedy' but not the war itself? Can one talk about the 'tragic' graves of the First World War or the 'tragic' poems of Wilfred Owen, but not Owen's actual death on Armistice Day, 1918?

In these tortured enquiries about event and representation, about the act of participation or the act of witnessing, about time present and time past, lie the intractable difficulties of tragedy. Here, we can say, is the gap between question and answer which cannot be filled but which continues to challenge us. Here is the paradox of tragedy, both on and off the stage. This book can only hope to begin to pose these questions, not to solve them.

Notes

1 Approaching the subject

1. Yeats, Preface to *The Oxford Book of Modern Verse* (Oxford: Oxford University Press), p. xxxiv. Yeats was commenting specifically on his decision to omit First World War poetry from his anthology, but set this decision in the broader context of the nature of tragedy: 'I have rejected these poems for the same reason that made Arnold withdraw his *Empedocles on Etna* from circulation; passive suffering is not a theme for poetry. In all the great tragedies, tragedy is a joy to the man who dies; in Greece the tragic chorus danced. When man has withdrawn into the quicksilver at the back of the mirror no great event becomes luminous in his mind; it is no longer possible to write *The Persians, Agincourt, Chevy Chase*: some blunderer has driven his car on to the wrong side of the road – that is all.'

2. Steiner, *The Death of Tragedy*, p. 3. The belief that Greek conventions define tragedy has led Steiner to argue that no real tragedy has been written since the seventeenth century.

3. Reiss, *Tragedy and Truth*, p. 2. Reiss goes on to explain the difference between tragedy and the tragic: 'This absence of significance, this impossibility of attaining to meaning in discourse, is rendered . . . as what we call the tragic. Tragedy is the discourse that at once produces and absorbs that absence called the tragic' (p. 3).

4. Williams, *Modern Tragedy*, p. 49.

5. Eagleton, *Sweet Violence: The Idea of the Tragic*, p. 15. Eagleton is of course being bitingly sarcastic here. Ato Quayson has offered a useful reading of a 'real-life event' (the execution of Ken Saro-Wiwa) in the light of theories of 'literary tragedy'. See chapter 4 of his book *Calibrations: Reading for the Social* (Minneapolis: University of Minnesota Press, 2003). 'It is the question of discursive and structural relations that allows the deployment of the tragic trope in the first place, because like literary tragedy, the significance of a real-life event may be grasped as inhering in the very constitution and later fragmentation of the cultural, symbolic, personal and political, the "enunciative modalities" that, in Foucauldian terms, give it coherence and solidity' (p. 60).

6. The scene was recorded by photographer Robert Wallis. For details of the *ekkyklema*, see Taplin, *Greek Tragedy in Action*, pp. 11–12; and Wiles, *Tragedy in Athens*, pp. 162–5.

7. Unamuno, *The Tragic Sense of Life*, p. 34. Unamuno's interpretation of tragedy as fundamentally irrational owes much to Nietzsche, and can be seen to share correspondences with other mystical, modernist approaches to the topic at the time.

8. Lamb, 'On the Tragedies of Shakespeare, Considered with Reference to their Fitness for Stage Representation' (1811), in *Romantic Critical Essays*, p. 66; Bradley, *Shakespearean Tragedy*, pp. 205, 202.

9. Unamuno, *The Tragic Sense of Life*, p. 43.

10. Eagleton, *Sweet Violence*, p. xv.

11. Strindberg, Preface to *Miss Julie*, in Strindberg, *Plays*, trans. Michael Robinson, pp. 57–8.

12. Guy Debord, *The Society of Spectacle*, trans. Donald Nicholson-Smith (New York: Zone Books, 1994).

13. Sontag, *Regarding the Pain of Others*, p. 102.

14. *Ibid.*, p. 114.

15. Seaford, *Reciprocity and Ritual*, p. 369.

16. Vernant, 'Tensions and Ambiguities in Greek Tragedy', in Vernant and Vidal-Naquet, *Myth and Tragedy*, p. 33. Richard Seaford counters: 'the privileging . . . of ambiguity, transgression, and instability – the exclusively intellectualist view that the essence of tragedy is to question rather than to affirm – is to abstract the tragic text from Athenian cultic and political practice'; *Reciprocity and Ritual*, p. 365.

17. Hall, Macintosh and Wrigley, *Dionysus Since 69*, p. 44. For details of these productions, see Fiona Macintosh, 'Tragedy in Performance: Nineteenth- and Twentieth-century Productions', in *The Cambridge Companion to Greek Tragedy*, ed. Easterling, pp. 282–323; Hall, 'Sophocles' *Electra* in Britain', in *Sophocles Revisited*, ed. Griffin, pp. 261–306. For details of many other productions of Greek tragedy, see Hall, Macintosh and Wrigley, *Dionysus since 69*.

18. Bushnell (ed.), *Blackwell Companion to Tragedy*, p. 3.

19. Vernant and Vidal-Naquet, *Myth and Tragedy*, p. 27.

20. Rosslyn, *Tragic Plots*, p. 6.

21. Peter Szondi sees tragic theory as intimately bound up with the subject it attempts to gain a perspective upon; in other words, theories of tragedy are themselves, inadvertently, exercises in tragic failure, resembling 'the flight of Icarus'. See *An Essay on the Tragic*, p. 49.

22. *Ibid.*, p. 56.

23. See, for example, Bushnell, 'Introduction', and Boedeker and Raaflaub, 'Tragedy and City', in Bushnell (ed.), *Blackwell Companion to Tragedy*, pp. 1, 109–10.

2 Tragic drama

1. Before and after the Peloponnesian war, the performances lasted four days because more comedies were staged; during the Peloponnesian war, the performances lasted only three days. See Pickard-Cambridge, *Dramatic Festivals of Athens*, p. 66.

2. Goldhill, 'The Great Dionysia' in Winkler and Zeitlin (eds.), *Nothing to Do With Dionysus?* p. 102.

3. Plato, *Symposium*, 194b2–4. Agathon goes on to point out that he is more concerned about being judged by 'a few men of wit' in the private drinking party (or symposium) than by a 'host of fools' in the 'playhouse'.

4. Edith Hall explores the range of types of ancient performance from rhetoric and athletics to theatre in her chapter on 'Performance' in Cartledge (ed.), *Illustrated History of Ancient Greece*, pp. 219–49.

5. Pindar, *Pythian Ode* 8, ll. 95–6, trans. Nisetich.

6. Schlegel, *Lectures on Dramatic Art and Literature*, trans. Black, vol. 1, pp. 128–30: 'to exhibit the determination and the deed of Antigone in their full glory, it was necessary that she should have no support and no dependence'.

7. This ambiguous open-ended nature of the play's close has been highlighted in various recent productions (Zoe Wanamaker, 1997; Cambridge Greek Play, 2001), with Electra resuming the same abject position of mourning she adopted at the beginning. The Zoe Wanamaker *Electra*, directed by David Leveaux, began and ended with Electra in her father's old coat, covering her face with a tragic mask. In the Cambridge Greek Play, directed by Jane Montgomery, Electra began and finished contemplating a corpse which hung over the stage. This corpse could have signified the dead Agamemnon (focus of Electra's obsession), the murdered Clytemnestra (source of her murderous hatred) or even herself (wallowing in her sense of victimisation). See fig. 2.

8. See Goldhill, *Reading Greek Tragedy*, pp. 200–3, 222–43. For more on the Sophists, see Kerferd, *The Sophistic Movement.*

9. There is a debate over whether Aeschylus was the author of *Prometheus Bound*, partly because of the negative depiction of Zeus in the play: see Griffiths, *The Authenticity of Prometheus Bound.* But since the play has been read as if Aeschylus were the author for centuries and the real author is not known, it is reasonable to consider *Prometheus Bound* alongside the other Aeschylean plays.

10. Dodds, *The Greeks and the Irrational*, pp. 17–18.

11. Vernant, 'Ambiguity and Reversal: On the Enigmatic Structure of *Oedipus Rex* ', in Vernant and Vidal-Naquet, *Myth and Tragedy in Ancient Greece*, p. 134.

12. Vernant, 'Intimations of the Will in Greek Tragedy', in Vernant and Vidal-Naquet, *Myth and Tragedy*, p. 80.

13. The Loeb edition, edited by David Kovacs (1994), even notes, apparently without irony, his doubts about the text at this point: 'among the reasons for considering these lines spurious is that they are internally inconsistent' (p. 393).

14. See Michael Billington's review in *The Guardian* (1 February 2001): 'Where Euripides offers his murdering heroine mythical flight, Warner allows Medea no such consolation'; and Ben Brantley's review in the *New York Times* (4 October 2002): '[Jason and Medea's] most rancorous arguments are punctuated by perverse sexual sparks.... Ms. Shaw and Ms. Warner have created one of the most human Medeas ever'. See also Macintosh, 'Introduction: The Performer in Performance', in Hall, Macintosh and Taplin (eds.), *Medea in Performance*, pp. 28–9. The text, of course,

does not give stage directions, so the traditional assumption that Medea should appear at the end in a chariot pulled by serpents is based on evidence from vase paintings, rather than on Euripides' words. See Taplin, 'The Pictorial Record', in Easterling (ed.), *The Cambridge Companion to Greek Tragedy*, pp. 78–81; and Wiles, *Tragedy in Athens*, p. 122.

15. Vernant, 'The Historical Moment of Tragedy in Greece', in Vernant and Vidal-Naquet, *Myth and Tragedy*, p. 24.

16. Goldhill, 'Collectivity and Otherness: The Authority of the Tragic Chorus', in Silk (ed.), *Tragedy and the Tragic*, p. 248.

17. In her production for the National Theatre, London, in 1999, the director Katie Mitchell conveyed the importance of this confrontation between the chorus and Aegisthus by having Aegisthus actually shoot at the chorus to assert his authority. The production used Ted Hughes' translation.

18. Foley, *Ritual Irony*, p. 67. Details about the authorship of the ending can be found in Edith Hall's introduction to the Oxford World's Classics edition, p. xxv.

19. Foley, *Ritual Irony*, p. 78. Foley's whole chapter on *Iphigenia* (pp. 65–105) offers an excellent discussion of the problem of irony in Euripides.

20. Zeitlin, 'Thebes: Theater of Self and Society in Athenian Drama', in Winkler and Zeitlin (eds.), *Nothing To Do With Dionysus?* p. 131.

21. Oliver Taplin was not impressed by the African setting of the film and its ambivalent politics: 'The best minutes of the film are at the beginning and the end, set in contemporary Italy. Everything in between is Africanized. Is Pasolini making profound points about cultural relativity and 'la pensée sauvage', or is it rather that he was fascinated with photographing the Moroccan landscape and its inhabitants?' (Oliver Taplin, *TLS*, no. 4085 (17 July 1981).

22. Padel, 'Making Space Speak', in Winkler and Zeitlin (eds.), *Nothing To Do With Dionysus?* p. 358.

23. Wiles, *Tragedy in Athens*, p. 178.

24. Pucci, *The Violence of Pity in Euripides' Medea*, p. 28.

25. Racine, 'First Preface to *Andromache* ', in *Andromache and Other Plays*, trans. Cairncross, p. 40.

26. Tobin, *Racine and Seneca*, pp. 158–62.

27. Levitan, 'Seneca in Racine', p. 209.

28. *Ibid.*, p. 206.

29. Seneca, *Epistle* 110.

30. Lyons, *Kingdom of Disorder*, p. 406.

31. Barthes, *On Racine*, trans. Howard, p. 26.

32. Pascal, fragment 72, quoted in Goldmann, *The Hidden God*, trans. Thody, p. 36.

33. Peter Brook, Introduction, *Seneca's Oedipus*, adapted by Ted Hughes (New York, 1972), p. 5. Indeed, Brook's production was staged with the actors seated throughout the performance, remaining outwardly static in order to liberate their inner turbulence and irrationality.

34. For more information on Stoic philosophy and the *proficiens* in Seneca, see Tarrant's concise account in *Seneca's Thyestes*, pp. 22–5.

35. Caryl Churchill's translation was published by Nick Hern Books in 1995. It was first performed at the Royal Court Theatre Upstairs, London, on 7 June 1994, with Sebastian Harcome playing The Fury and Young Tantalus and Ewan Stewart playing the ghost of Tantalus and Thyestes.

36. 'A gently rising valley-side, which encloses the intervening space, slopes up in the form of a theatre', says the messenger; 'most of the shallow mob detested the crime – and gazed' (Fitch's translation in the Loeb edition).

37. Levitan, 'Seneca in Racine', pp. 198, 199.

38. Barthes, *On Racine*, p. 20.

39. See discussion on pp. 146–47.

40. Parrish, *Racine: The Limits of Tragedy*, p. 263.

41. Lough, *Seventeenth-Century French Drama*, p. 20.

42. Steven Connor, 'Watching the Birdie', located on his Birkbeck Blog: http://www.bbk. ac.uk/eh/skc/birdie. Connor goes on to explain: 'The Wooster group specialize not in passion brought to a pitch, or a focus, but what Antonin Artaud called "le souffrance de dubbing" – the suffering of dubbing, the passion of the synch. A suffering that is just to the side of itself is keyed in to the suffering of being just to the side of yourself. But there, what we name as *ecstasy* [literally standing outside oneself] has traditionally been thought of as being not all there.'

43. Pascal, *Pensées*, fragment 233, in Goldmann, *The Hidden God*, p. 292. This quotation comes from part of Goldmann's excellent chapter on 'The Wager' in tragic thought.

44. Pascal, *Pensées*, fragment 70, in Goldmann, *The Hidden God*, p. 205.

45. Goldmann, *The Hidden God*, p. 318.

46. Barthes, *On Racine*, p. 45.

47. Reiss, *Tragedy and Truth*, pp. 240–81.

48. Jean Racine, *Phèdre*, in a new version by Ted Hughes (Faber and Faber, 1998), pp. 74–5. This translation was used for the Almeida production of the play, directed by Jonathan Kent and performed at the Albery theatre in London in 1998.

49. Rossiter, 'Shakespearean Tragedy', in *Angel With Horns*, p. 265.

50. McAlindon, 'What is a Shakespearean Tragedy?' in McEachern (ed.), *The Cambridge Companion to Tragedy*, p. 1. See also Muir, *Shakespeare's Tragic Sequence*, p. 12.

51. Philip Sidney, *A Defence of Poetry*, ed. van Dorsten, p. 67: 'all their plays be neither right tragedies, nor right comedies, mingling kings and clowns . . . so as neither the admiration and commiseration, nor the right sportfulness, is by their mongrel tragic-comedy obtained'. Samuel Johnson, *Preface to Shakespeare*, in Green (ed.), *Samuel Johnson*, p. 423.

52. Headlam Wells, *Shakespeare, Politics and the State*, p. 6. This theory, of the divine chain of being, was most fully explored by Tillyard in *The Elizabethan World Picture*.

53. Puttenham, *The Arte of English Poesie* (1589), ed. Willcock and Walker, p. 26.

54. Dollimore, *Radical Tragedy*, p. 7; Lever, *The Tragedy of State*, p. 5.

55. Machiavelli, *The Prince* (1514), trans. Dacres (1640); 'another Elizabethan' was T. B., *Observations Political and Civil*, previously thought to have been written by

Sir Walter Raleigh, cited in Hattaway, 'Tragedy and Political Authority', in McEachern (ed.), *The Cambridge Companion to Shakespearean Tragedy*, p. 107.

56. Sidney, *A Defence of Poetry*, p. 45.

57. Bradley, *Shakespearean Tragedy*, pp. 13–16; Rossiter, *Angel With Horns*, p. 261.

58. See Sanders, *The Dramatist and the Received Idea*, p. 35; Massington, *Christopher Marlowe's Tragic Vision*, pp. 14–55; Bartels, *Spectacles of Strangeness*, pp. 60–1.

59. On this belief about the king's public and private body, see Kantorowicz, *The King's Two Bodies*.

60. Greenblatt, Introduction to *Macbeth, The Norton Shakespeare*, p. 2560.

61. Shuger, *Habits of Thought*, p. 70.

62. Greenblatt, *Hamlet and Purgatory*, pp. 235–57.

63. Thomas Dekker, *The Wonderfull Yeare* (1603), in *The Plague Pamphlets of Thomas Dekker*, ed. Wilson, p. 29. For more on the plague pits and early seventeenth-century religious belief, and despair, see Michael Neill, *Issues of Death*, pp. 1–48, and Wallace, *Digging the Dirt*, pp. 129–39.

64. Diehl, 'Religion and Shakespearean Tragedy', in McEachern (ed.), *Cambridge Companion to Shakespearean Tragedy*, p. 97.

65. See Greenblatt's chapter on 'Shakespeare and the Exorcists' in his *Shakespearean Negotiations*, p. 118.

66. Bradley, *Shakespearean Tragedy*, p. 235.

67. Barber, 'The Family in Shakespeare's Development: Tragedy and Sacredness', in Schwartz and Kahn (eds.), *Representing Shakespeare*, p. 200. See also Muir's Arden edition (1952), p. lix.

68. The current critical reception was inspired by Peter Brook's 1962 production for the RSC. His production was greatly influenced by Jan Kott's essay, '*King Lear*, or Endgame', which Brook read in French in 1962 and which was published in English in his book *Shakespeare Our Contemporary* in 1964. An example of the critical scepticism can be seen in Elton, *King Lear and the Gods*. For details of more recent productions of *King Lear*, see Alexander Leggatt, *King Lear*, Shakespeare in Performance (Manchester, 1991) and Peter Holland, *English Shakespeares*. One particularly bleak response to the play is Edward Bond's version of *Lear* (1970).

69. For good surveys of the pre-Shakespearean English tragedy, see Bushnell, 'The Classical and Medieval Roots of English Renaissance Tragedy', in Bushnell (ed.) *The Blackwell Companion to Tragedy*, pp. 289–306, and Dillon, *The Cambridge Introduction to Early English Theatre*, pp. 141–70.

70. The 2004 film, directed by Michael Radford, closed with Jessica wistfully fingering the ring she took from her father for her marriage to Lorenzo.

71. *Henry V*, Prologue, 17–18.

72. For Kemp's jigging ability, see Wiles, *Shakespeare's Clown*, pp. 43–60. Will Kemp left the company in 1599 and was replaced by Robert Armin, a much more serious, intellectual clown, who probably influenced the darker nature of the later comedies and tragedies. But the early tragedies – *Richard III, Richard II, Romeo and Juliet, Merchant of Venice* – were first staged in the heyday of Will Kemp.

73. See Neill, *Issues of Death*, pp. 265–304.
74. 'Inward liberty and external necessity are the two poles of the tragic world', wrote Schlegel, *Lectures on Dramatic Art and Literature*, vol. 1, p. 73.
75. Coleridge, 12th lecture, on *Hamlet*, in his series of *Lectures on Shakespeare*, delivered at the Royal Society in London (2 January 1812): in *Coleridge: Oxford Authors*, ed. Jackson, p. 655.
76. Schlegel, *Lectures on Dramatic Art and Literature*, vol. 1, p. 112–13.
77. Byron's letter to John Murray, 12 October 1817.
78. Schlegel, *Lectures on Dramatic Art and Literature*, vol. 1, pp. 128–30.
79. In the 2003 RSC production of the play directed by Adrian Noble and starring Ralph Fiennes, the avalanche was created by blinding white light, revealed by the collapse of the grey, protective wall at stage rear. The searing effect of the light caused Brand to buckle whilst at the same time it rewarded him, as one reviewer noted, with 'transcendent illumination'.
80. Forster, 'Ibsen the Romantic'.
81. Durbach, '*Ibsen the Romantic*'.
82. Northam, *Ibsen's Dramatic Method*, p. 13.
83. One 1906 production of *Ghosts*, by Max Reinhardt, for example, employed the symbolic suggestiveness of the set: 'the combination of colours and the shape of the furniture breathed a spirit of oppressiveness, of grief and of the sense of destiny which broods over this tragedy'.
84. Stina-Ewbank, 'The Last Plays', in Macfarlane (ed.), *The Cambridge Companion to Ibsen*, p. 127.
85. Ellis-Fermor on the late plays in her introduction to the Penguin edition of *The Master Builder*, p. 7. *Hedda Gabler* is conventionally designated a 'middle-period play' but I believe it makes more sense if it is viewed as characteristic of the late plays.
86. Simon Williams, 'Ibsen and the Theatre 1877–1900', in Macfarlane (ed.), *The Cambridge Companion to Ibsen*, p. 167.
87. Ivo von Howe's 2004 New York production of *Hedda Gabler* experimentally staged Ibsen against this grain, showing everything and leaving nothing unsaid or only imagined. See David Finkle's review: www.hotreview.org/articles/gettingahedda.htm.
88. Kate Paul, leaflet text for the Strindberg exhibition, Tate Modern, London, April–May 2005.
89. Strindberg did not adopt the conventional structuring of plays into acts and scenes, much after his early career (*Miss Julie* being the last play to use that structure). So I give only the page references here to Michael Robinson's Oxford World's Classics edition of the plays.
90. In its day, the play was so controversial that it was banned from public performance until 1939.
91. Chekhov's radical ambition of theatrical deconstruction is parodied in Trepliov's own theatrical experiment in *The Seagull*, but it has influenced productions since,

most recently the 2003 production in Edinburgh, directed by Peter Stein, in which the set was stripped back to reveal the theatre wings.

92. Chothia, *Forging a Language*.

93. Miller, 'Tragedy and the Common Man', in Martin (ed.), *The Theatre Essays of Arthur Miller*, p. 3.

94. *The Haunted*, Act IV, p. 161. The mad isolation envisaged by Vinnie here was accentuated in the 2004 National Theatre production by an additional scene set inside the house in which Vinnie collapsed onto the floor to begin her long solitary vigil, while the shutters were being nailed closed.

95. In the 1966 film, starring Richard Burton and Elizabeth Taylor, the husband and wife sit at the end, silent and exhausted by the night's cathartic action, but still touching, still showing signs of affection.

96. Shannon, *The Dramatic Vision of August Wilson*, p. vii.

97. This quotation from a member of the cast, Mary Alice, can be found in Shannon, *Dramatic Vision of August Wilson*, p. 112. Wilson also felt that Gabriel offered a spiritual connection with African American culture. His comic dance, misunderstood by Shorenstein and other white, American critics, owed its origins to African Americans' cultural past in African ritual.

98. Harper says to Prior, who is weeping, about the diorama: 'You shouldn't do that in here, this isn't a place for real feelings, this is just storytime'; *Perestroika*, Act III, scene 3, p. 40.

99. The HBO production in 2003, directed by Mike Nichols, which cast Emma Thompson as the main angel, was unabashed in its depiction of the wires involved in getting Thompson to fly and crash through the ceiling at the end of Part I.

100. Steiner, *The Death of Tragedy*, p. 3: the 'representation of personal suffering and heroism which we call tragic drama is distinctive of the western tradition'.

101. Gilbert and Tompkins, *Post-Colonial Drama*, p. 16.

102. For more on Sam Mendes' RSC production of *The Tempest* in 1993, see Christine Dymkowski (ed.), *The Tempest*, Shakespeare in Production (Cambridge, 2000), pp. 47–8, 327. For one influential post-colonial reading of the *Tempest*, see Paul Brown, ' "This Thing of Darkness I Acknowledge Mine": *The Tempest* and the Discourse of Colonialism', in Dollimore and Sinfield (eds.), *Political Shakespeare*, pp. 48–71.

103. Katrak, *Wole Soyinka and Modern Tragedy*, p. 55.

104. However the 2005 production at the Arcola Theatre, London, directed by Femi Elufowoju, was obviously influenced by Western ideas of democracy, by performing in the round and therefore including the audience as part of the community. 'I am just an ordinary man, like you and you', said Mo Sesay's Odewale, pointing at a couple of audience members sitting next to him.

105. Soyinka, 'The Fourth Stage', in *Art, Dialogue and Outrage*, p. 29. Soyinka also explains: 'Yoruba traditional art is not ideational however, but "essential". It is not the idea (in religious arts) that is transmitted into wood or interpreted in music or movement, but a quintessence of inner being' (p. 28).

106. Soyinka, 'The Fourth Stage', p. 31.
107. Soyinka, 'Author's Note', in Gikandi (ed.), *Death and the King's Horseman*, p. 3.
108. Biodun Jeyifo, *The Truthful Lie: Essays in a Sociology of African Drama* (1985), reprinted in Gikandi (ed.), *Death and the King's Horseman*, p. 171.
109. Femi Osofisan, *No More the Wasted Breed*, in *Morountodon and Other Plays; Another Raft*. Osofisan draws upon Brechtian aesthetic techniques. 'So that's how we shall proceed tonight, with all our tricks laid bare', says Yemosa Two, at the beginning of *Another Raft*, p. 3.
110. Williams, 'Ritual as Social Symbolism: Cultural Death and the King's Horseman', in Ogunba (ed.), *Soyinka: A Collection of Critical Essays*; reprinted in Jeyifo (ed.), *Modern African Drama*, p. 562.
111. Gilbert and Tomkins, *Post-Colonial Drama*, p. 23.
112. Wertheim, *The Dramatic Art of Athol Fugard*, p. 90.
113. Fugard, *Sizwe Bansi is Dead*, in Biofran Jeyifo (ed.), *Modern African Drama*, pp. 100, 103.
114. *The Sought-for Grave (Motomezuka)*, in Keene (ed.), *20 Plays of the No Theatre*, p. 47.
115. Yeats, 'Certain Noble Plays of Japan', in *Essays and Introductions*, p. 232.
116. Chorus, *The Sought-for Grave*, p. 48.
117. Bergson, *Laughter: An Essay on the Meaning of the Comic*, p. 21. For more on Bergson and comedy, see *Comedy: Developments in Criticism*, ed. D. J. Palmer, and the forthcoming *Cambridge Introduction to Comedy*.
118. Cavell, *Must We Mean What We Say?* p. 119.
119. *Ibid.*, p. 153; Vladimir exits, apparently to the backstage lavatory, 'end of the corridor, on the left', Act I, p. 35.
120. Georg Lukacs, *The Meaning of Contemporary Realism*, ed. J. and N. Mander (London, Merlin Press, 1962), pp. 25, 20, 21.
121. Williams, 'Theatre as a Political Forum', in Tony Pinkney (ed.), *The Politics of Modernism: Against the New Conformists* (London, Verso, 1989), p. 94. For more on the debate about Beckett's politics, see Birkett and Ince (eds.), *Samuel Beckett*, pp. 10–16.
122. Kott, *Shakespeare Our Contemporary*, p. 141.
123. Adorno, 'Trying to Understand *Endgame*', in *Notes to Literature*, p. 251. For more on the political implications of Beckett's disintegrating selves, see Stephen Watt, 'Beckett by Way of Baudrillard: Toward a Political Reading of Beckett's Drama', in Burkman (ed.), *Myth and Ritual in the Plays of Samuel Beckett*, pp. 103–23.
124. Beckett's 'note' on the Auditor's movement demands that it 'consists in simple sideways raising of arms from sides and their falling back, in a gesture of helpless compassion' (p. 375).
125. Kott, *Shakespeare Our Contemporary*, pp. 132, 133.
126. Adorno, 'Trying to Understand *Endgame*', p. 249.
127. Charles R. Lyons, '*Happy Days* and Dramatic Convention', in Brater (ed.), *Beckett at 80 / Beckett in Context*, p. 94.

128. *Waiting for Godot* was premièred in French in Paris in 1953; the English version was first performed in London in 1955. *Endgame* was premièred in London in French in 1957. *Happy Days* was premièred in New York in English in 1961. *Act Without Words* was originally written and published in French but first performed at the Royal Court Theatre, London, in 1957.

129. For more on the politics and place in Beckett's work, see, for example, the exhibition catalogue produced by Eoin O'Brien, *The Beckett Country*. Beckett's most political play is *Catastrophe* which he dedicated to Václav Havel.

130. See, for example, details of the Beckettian production of Eugene O'Neill's *The Iceman Cometh* in 1956, described in Normand Berlin, 'The Tragic Pleasure of *Waiting for Godot*', in Brater (ed.), *Beckett at 80*, p. 61.

131. Artaud, 'Theatre and Cruelty' (1933), in *Theatre and its Double*, trans. Corti, pp. 64–5.

132. Posthumus describes the tablet that he finds on his body later as 'senseless speaking' (V.v.240). Samuel Johnson complained of 'much incongruity' in the play; Warren, *Cymbeline*, notes that the whole play depends upon 'the placing of potentially tragic situations within a context of elaborate theatricality' (p. 12) and that therefore an analysis of different theatrical performances of the scene is essential (pp. 15–18).

133. McLuskie and Uglow (eds.), *The Duchess of Malfi*, p. 151. For another good analysis of the performance issues of the play see White, *Renaissance Drama in Action*, pp. 88–100.

134. The fact that the same actor would probably have played both Pentheus and Agave adds an extra dramatic irony to this moment. The 'Pentheus' actor effectively holds the 'Pentheus' mask in his hands. In Peter Hall's 2002 production at the National Theatre, London, William Houston played Agave and Pentheus. See fig. 5.

135. Since Agave's question is not answered, it is clear that some text is missing here. But it is not known how many lines are missing. There is an ancient third-century AD source, which described Agave's 'lament', so some scholars believe that this lament occurred at this point in the text. See Edith Hall's note in Euripides' *Bacchae and Other Plays*, trans. Morwood, pp. 191–2, and also Seaford's commentary on lines 1300–1 in Seaford (ed.), *Euripides' Bacchae*.

136. Jonathan Bate's introduction to his Arden edition of *Titus Andronicus*, p. 63

137. Peter Brook's production was staged in 1955; Deborah Warner's was staged in 1987. For the performance history, see Bate, *Titus Andronicus*, pp. 48–69. And for an even more detailed account, see Dessen, *Titus Andronicus*.

138. Edwardes, *Time Out*, January 1995; cited in Sierz, *In-Yer-Face Theatre*, p. 95; Sierz, *In-Yer-Face Theatre*, p. 99.

139. John Peter, *The Sunday Times* (29 January 1995).

140. Sarah Kane explained: 'The form is a direct parallel to the truth of the war it portrays – a traditional form is suddenly and violently disrupted by the entrance of an unexpected element that drags the characters and the play into a chaotic pit without logical explanation'. Quoted in Saunders, *'Love Me or Kill Me': Sarah Kane and the Theatre of Extremes*, p. 45.

141. The original Royal Court production was necessarily stylised rather than explicit, with 'deliberately' unrealistic mutilation, so that it could explore the ambivalent redemption brought about by torture and love; Sierz, *In-Yer-Face Theatre*, p. 114. Sarah Kane commented: 'I think the less naturalistically you show these things the more likely people are to be thinking what is the meaning of this act rather than "fucking hell, how do they do that"!'; quoted in Saunders, *'Love Me or Kill Me'*, p. 89. The Oxford Stage Company production, directed by Sean Holmes at the Arcola Theatre, placed Grace and Rod at opposite sides of the stage, so that their shared 'final moment of epiphany' (Michael Billington, *The Guardian* (9 November 2005)) was suggested by visual symmetry, rather than by physical contact.

142. See Rebellato, 'Sarah Kane: An Appreciation', p. 280: 'the play strips romantic love of all its unknowable promises, its claims of eternity, and asks what is left ... This irreducible core is the extraordinary and hard-won affirmation of the play'.

143. Barker, *Arguments for a Theatre*: 'Fortynine Asides for a Tragic Theatre', p. 19; 'The Consolations of Catastrophe', pp. 51–4; 'Beauty and Terror in the Theatre of Catastrophe', pp. 55–60.

144. Scarry, *The Body in Pain*, p. 4.

145. *Ibid.*, p. 6.

146. The most impressive moment of the 2004 Cambridge Greek Play (*Oedipus the King*) was Matilda Dratwa's messenger speech, delivered with striking stillness and lack of drama. The effect was to let the words do the work, while she remained seemingly in a state of awed shock by what she had seen.

147. Goldhill, *Reading Greek Tragedy*, p. 10.

148. *Ibid.*, p. 2.

149. Reiss, *Tragedy and Truth*, p. 2.

150. Vannier, 'Theatre of Language', *Tulane Drama Review* (Spring, 1963), p. 182, cited in Kennedy, *Six Dramatists in Search of a Language*, p. 169.

151. Pinter, 'Writing for the Theatre' (1962), in *Harold Pinter*, p. xii.

152. Knowles, '*The Caretaker* and the "Point" of Laughter', in Scott (ed.), *Harold Pinter*, p. 160.

153. Drew Milne, 'Pinter's Sexual Politics', in Raby (ed.), *The Cambridge Companion to Pinter*, p. 195.

154. Deleuze, 'L'épuisé', in *Quad et autres pièces pour la television* (Paris: Minuit, 1992), p. 104, cited in Critchley, *Very Little ... Almost Nothing*, p. 180.

155. Critchley, *Very Little ... Almost Nothing*, p. 180.

156. Paul Taylor, *The Independent* (30 June 2000). On the staging of the Royal Court production, and the effect of the mirror, see Saunders, '*Love Me or Kill Me*', 115–17.

157. Tangram Theatre's production thus focused upon the theatricality of the play's last moments, staging its suicide under the dim theatre lights like Sylvia Plath's poem, 'Lady Lazarus'. In contrast, the Royal Court interpreted the call to 'open the curtains' as an invitation to let in the outside world, ending the solipsism of performance and exposing the play to wider, social responsibilities.

3 Tragic theory

1. Aristotle, *Poetics*, 1448a28–29. The Greek word 'dran' means 'to do'.
2. Plato, *The Republic*, trans. Cornford, x.605 (p. 330).
3. Ato Quayson has usefully defined this paradox as 'form' and 'content': 'One of the key questions that remains unresolved in the Aristotelian formation is whether tragedy, and indeed literary art, is a form or a content'; *Calibrations: Reading for the Social*, p. xvii.
4. See Nuttall, *Why Does Tragedy Give Pleasure?* pp. 1–28.
5. On the meaning of *hamartia*, see Jones, *On Aristotle and Greek Tragedy*, pp. 12–20.
6. In the 1995 Loeb edition quoted here, Stephen Halliwell refuses to translate the Greek word 'katharsis' and leaves it simply as the word now familiar in English, 'catharsis'. W. H. Fyfe, in the previous Loeb edition, translated this phrase as: 'through pity and fear [tragedy] effects relief to these and similar emotions'.
7. On *katharsis* in Aristotle, see Stinton, '*Hamartia* in Aristotle and Greek Tragedy', and Nussbaum, *The Fragility of Goodness*, pp. 382–3.
8. *Rhetoric*, II.5.1; II.8.2.
9. Hegel, *Reason in History*, p. 11.
10. One interesting example of the didactic possibilities of tragedy for Hegel and his followers is the production of *Antigone* in 1841 at the Prussian court. This production was praised by some Hegelian writers because they believed it bolstered the rational foundations of the Prussian state. I am grateful to Dr Mark Berry for this reference.
11. Hegel is wrongly associated with a rigid theory of history based on thesis, antithesis, synthesis. This actually came from Fichte, not Hegel, but Hegel became associated with its mechanical formalism, as exemplified by Kierkegaard's criticism. See Kaufmann, *Hegel: Reinterpretation, Texts and Commentary*, p. 161. However, the notion of 'dialectics' or the 'dialectical process' *does* originate with Hegel. This means that historical progress is reached through the tension and conflict between opposing ideas or forces, leading ultimately to a resolution; it also means that truth can be reached through a dialectical method, i.e. through debating and confronting opposing points of view.
12. Hegel, *Reason in History*, quoted in Kaufmann, *Hegel: Reinterpretation, Texts and Commentary*, p. 256.
13. Hegel, *Aesthetics: Lectures on Fine Arts*, trans. Knox, vol. II, p. 1213.
14. Kaufmann, *Tragedy and Philosophy*, p. 202. See also Bradley: 'The essentially tragic fact is the self-division and intestinal warfare of the ethical substance, not so much the war of good with evil as the war of good with good'.
15. *Libation Bearers*, 461–2 (Loeb translation). Herbert Weir Smyth's translation for the 1926 Loeb edition captures the symmetry and word-play of the Greek here better than any other.
16. Recently, Hegel's polarisation of Antigone and Creon has come in for some radical critique, from Luce Irigaray, Judith Butler and others. See pp. 155–56.

17. Brecht privileged 'history' or 'epic' theatre over 'dramatic' or 'tragic' theatre in his manifesto for a new type of theatre, and preferred to see how the individual was affected by large historical forces: see Willett (ed.), *Brecht on Theatre*, p. 37. Shakespeare's history plays dramatise the tragic victims of the larger historical dialectical identified by Hegel.

18. Hegel, *Aesthetics: Lectures on Fine Arts*, vol. II, p. 1198.

19. *Ibid.*, vol. II, p. 1215.

20. On this paradox, see Paul Gordon, *Tragedy After Nietzsche*, pp. 74–5: 'Nietzsche maintains that chaotic Dionysian suffering and destructiveness beget soothing objective realities such as the *principium individuationis* that save humanity from the turbulent, oceanic flux surrounding it . . . It is wrong to argue, then, that either redemption or the lack thereof is incompatible with tragedy, for it is their interplay that produces both nihilism and its denial in the work of art.'

21. Schopenhauer, *The World as Will and Representation*, trans. Payne, vol. I, p. 164.

22. Nietzsche, *The Birth of Tragedy*, trans. Whiteside, p. 16.

23. Schopenhauer, *The World as Will*, vol. I, p. 254.

24. Nietzsche, *The Birth of Tragedy*, p. 47. Given the fact that Nietzsche is interested in the temporal structure of tragedy, rather than its static, iconic resonance, it is strange that he has very little to say about Euripides' play *The Bacchae*, in which Dionysus is literally present before us on stage, tearing down the Apolline pretensions of Pentheus. The explanation is that Nietzsche considered Euripides a 'rational' writer inspired by the 'daemon' of Socrates, rather than by the Apollonian and Dionysias drives. *Birth of Tragedy*, pp. 59–64.

25. *Birth of Tragedy*, p. 40. We enjoy artistic representations of other people's suffering: see Nietzsche, *Beyond Good and Evil*, pp. 229ff.; and *On the Genealogy of Morals*, vol. II, p. 7. On the aesthetic treatment of suffering in Nietzsche, and the complex relation between art and metaphysic in *The Birth Of Tragedy*, see Silk and Stern, *Nietzsche on Tragedy*, pp. 288–96.

26. This ritualistic approach to tragedy is shared by Wole Soyinka: see the chapter on post-colonial tragedy.

27. Alasdair Macintyre draws out the inconsistencies of Kierkegaard's *Either/Or*, based fundamentally on the 'mode of its presentation and its central thesis'; *After Virtue*, p. 38. He explains: 'the principles which depict the ethical way of life are to be adopted *for no reason*, but for a choice that lies beyond reasons, just because it is the choice of what is to count for us as a reason . . . The notion of authority and the notion of reason are . . . mutually exclusive' (p. 41).

28. Kierkegaard, 'The Ancient Tragical Motif As Reflected in the Modern', in *Either/Or*, p. 142.

29. *Ibid.*, p. 143.

30. Kierkegaard, 'Problema I: Is There a Teleological Suspension of the Ethical?' in *Fear and Trembling*, trans. Hannay, pp. 83–95.

31. *Ibid.*, p. 88.

32. Kant, *Religion Within the Limits of Reason Alone*, trans. Greene and Hudson, p. 175.

33. Kierkegaard, *The Concept of Anxiety* (1844), trans. Thomte, pp. 44–6. 'The prohibition induces in him anxiety, for the prohibition awakens in him freedom's possibility. What passed by innocence as the nothing of anxiety has now entered into Adam, and here again it is a nothing . . .' (p. 44).

34. According to Penelhum, belief in God for Kierkegaard is 'a matter of making a voluntary leap which the Skeptic declines to make'; *God and Skepticism*, p. 84.

35. Nietzsche, *The Gay Science*, trans. Nauckhoff, pp. 119–20.

36. Sartre, *Existentialisme est un Humanisme* (1946), trans. Mairet as *Existentialism and Humanism*, p. 56.

37. Sartre, *Existentialism and Humanism*, p. 34.

38. Sartre, *Huis Clos* (1944), trans. Gilbert, in *Huis Clos and Other Plays*, p. 223.

39. Camus, *The Myth of Sisyphus*, trans. O'Brien, p. 19.

40. Sartre, *Nausea*, trans. Baldick, p. 20.

41. Camus' *The Outsider*, trans. Laredo, pp. 116–17.

42. Jonathan Dollimore has been the most outspoken in his criticism of the existential view of tragedy: 'both ethical and existential humanism are in fact quasi-religious: both reject the providential and "dogmatic" elements of Christianity while retaining its fundamental relation between suffering, affirmation and regeneration. Moreover they, like Christianity, tend to fatalise social dislocation; its causes are displaced from the realm of the human; questions about them are raised but only rhetorically, thus confirming man's impotence to alleviate the human condition': *Radical Tragedy*, p. 193.

43. For example, James George Frazer, *The Golden Bough: A Study in Magic and Religion* (originally published London: Macmillan, 1922; new edn London: Penguin, 1996).

44. See, for example, Claude Levi-Strauss, *The Raw and the Cooked*, trans. John and Doreen Weightman (New York: Harper and Row, 1969; reprinted Harmondsworth: Penguin, 1986).

45. A semiotic system is one in which meaning is denoted by certain signs and symbols and can be decoded easily once the sign-system is known.

46. On the *pharmakos* and sacrifice, see Girard, *Violence and the Sacred*, pp. 93–6. Plato discusses the ambiguity of the *pharmakon* in the *Phaedrus*, in relation to the Sophists and the equivocal benefits of rhetorical language; Derrida famously discussed this in an essay, 'Plato's Pharmacy', published in *Dissemination*, trans. Johnson, pp. 63–171.

47. See Kierkegaard, *Either/Or*, p. 147: 'Even if the individual moved freely, he still rested in the substantial categories of state, family and destiny. This substantial category is exactly the fatalistic element in Greek tragedy, and its exact peculiarity. The hero's destruction is, therefore, not only a result of his own deeds, but is also a suffering, whereas in modern tragedy, the hero's destruction is really not suffering, but is action . . . Our age has lost all the substantial categories of family, state and race. It must leave the individual entirely to himself, so that in a stricter sense he becomes his own creator.'

48. A recent exception to the widespread neglect of this topic is Basterra's *Seductions of Fate.*

49. For an account of oracles and fiction, which combines the second and third fields listed here (that is, literature and anthropology), see Wood, *The Road to Delphi: The Life and After-Life of Oracles.*

50. Aristotle, *Nicomachean Ethics*, trans. Rowe, p. 125: 1111a1–a5, 1111a19.

51. Vidal-Naquet, 'The Shields of the Heroes', in Vernant and Vidal-Naquet, *Myth and Tragedy in Ancient Greece*, p. 295.

52. *The Seven Against Thebes*, trans. Dawson, ll. 653–55. See Zeitlin, *Under the Sign of the Shield.*

53. Yeats, 'The Tragic Theatre', in *Essays and Introductions*, pp. 241, 245.

54. Synge, *Riders to the Sea* (1905), in *The Playboy of the Western World and Riders to the Sea* (London: Unwin, 1979), p. 91.

55. See, for example, Freud's explanation of the formation of the psyche in *The Ego and the Id* (1923), *SE*, vol. XIX, pp. 13ff. Of course, the relation between the conscious and the unconscious is so complex in Freud that what one might think of as one's consciousness or conscience is, in fact, shaped and determined by one's unconscious. Thus Fate can be believed to be derived from one's moral conscience, a 'punitive agency of our childhood', when, in fact, it is embraced paradoxically by one's unconscious and repressed desires: see 'An Experience on the Acropolis', *SE*, vol. XXII, p. 243.

56. Lorca was a great admirer of Synge and was greatly influenced by *Riders to the Sea*: see Christopher Maurer's introduction to the Penguin edition, p. xv.

57. *Mayor of Casterbridge*, chapter XVII, World's Classics edition, p. 115.

58. George Eliot, *Mill on the Floss*, World's Classics edition, pp. 401–2. It is possible that Hardy was quoting from Eliot, rather than directly from Novalis, in his comment about 'Character is fate', in which case Eliot's qualification of this assertion might also have been latently in his mind.

59. *Mayor of Casterbridge*, chapter XVII: World's Classics edition, p. 115.

60. *Mayor of Casterbridge*, chapter XL, p. 286; chapter XLIII, p. 313.

61. Benjamin, 'Fate and Character', pp. 126, 127. Andrew Benjamin 'explains' Walter Benjamin's difficult essay: 'Shoah, Remembrance and the Abeyance of Fate, in Marcus and Nead (eds.), *The Actuality of Walter Benjamin*, pp. 135–55. In essence, Benjamin is concerned with 'the problem of the temporality of history once the dominant directional determining forces of chronology and teleology have been discarded' (p. 139); fate, then, when severed from time and linear history, becomes hard to distinguish from fiction and can only be redeemed if one holds onto the idea of the 'moment', of Oedipus at the crossroads.

62. Steiner, *The Death of Tragedy*, p. 8.

63. Dollimore, *Radical Tragedy*, p. 190.

64. For example, Brecht's essay 'Shouldn't We Abolish Aesthetics?': 'the usual superstition which holds that a play has to satisfy *eternal* human urges when the only eternal urge that it sets out to satisfy is the urge to see a play'; *Brecht on Theatre,*

trans. Willett, p. 20. See also Augusto Boal on the dangers of Aristotelian catharsis in 'Aristotle's Coercive System of Tragedy', in *Theater of the Oppressed*, pp. 1–52.

65. Strindberg, Preface to *Miss Julie*, in Strindberg, *Plays*, trans. Robinson, p. 57.

66. Robert Leach, 'Mother Courage and Her Children', in Thomson and Sacks (eds.), *The Cambridge Companion to Brecht*, pp. 128–38. Leach is most interesting on the theme of 'interruption' in Brecht.

67. Bentham, *The Panopticon Writings*, ed. Bozovic; Foucault, *Discipline and Punish*, pp. 200ff. See also Foucault's 'The Eye of Power' in *Power/Knowledge*, pp. 146–65.

68. For example, 'The Spectre of Ideology' in Wright and Wright (eds.), *The Žižek Reader*, pp. 53–86.

69. Büchner, *Woyzeck*, scene 6, p. 120, in *Complete Plays*, trans. John Reddick.

70. Two recent productions of the play – the 2002 production directed by Robert Wilson in the London Barbican and the Icelandic production directed by Gisli Orn Gardasson in 2005 – have confronted the fragmentary nature of the text by privileging theatrical images over language. Gardasson's production, performed in and around a large, swimming tank of water, assaulted the audience with a series of startling 'flashy theatrics' and challenges to conventional taste. See reviews in *The Times* (14 October 2005), *The Independent* (14 October 2005) and *The Guardian* (13 October 2005).

71. Williams, *Modern Tragedy*, p. 53.

72. Thomson, *Aeschylus and Athens*, p. 306: 'The view of human progress expressed by Aeschylus is not far removed from the position of modern dialectical materialism'.

73. Williams, *Modern Tragedy*, pp. 61–84.

74. Unamuno, *The Tragic Sense of Life*, p. 17.

75. Eagleton, *Sweet Violence*, p. xvi.

76. I am thinking particularly, for example, of Silviu Purcarete's production, for the National Theatre of Romania, of Aeschylus' *Oresteia* in 1997. See fig. 6.

77. Hall, 'Tony Harrison's *Prometheus*: A View from the Left', p. 132. The script of the film was published in 1998 by Faber.

78. Bamber, *Comic Women, Tragic Men*, p. 4; Dympna Callaghan, *Woman and Gender in Renaissance Tragedy*, p. 38.

79. Bamber, *Comic Women, Tragic Men*, p. 2.

80. Callaghan, *Woman and Gender*, p. 49. See also Belsey, *The Subject of Tragedy*, pp. ix–x.

81. Callaghan, *Woman and Gender*, p. 35.

82. Figes, *Tragedy and Social Evolution*, p. 118.

83. Plutarch, *Solon*, 21.4. For a good discussion of Greek legislation on funerals, see Alexiou, *The Ritual Lament in Greek Tradition*, chapter 1.

84. For a longer discussion of the choral lamentation in *Seven against Thebes*, see Foley, *Female Acts in Greek Tragedy*, pp. 45–54.

85. Nagy, Foreword to Loraux's *Mothers in Mourning*, p. x.

86. Loraux, *Mothers in Mourning*, pp. 54, 65. Holst-Warhaft also believes that tragedy 'appropriated the rhetorical passion of women's laments', thereby 'usurping a female

art form', but she argues that 'behind the new masculine poetics of tragedy' we can detect, though less and less as the fifth century progressed, 'a female art form, half-submerged and potentially explosive'; *Dangerous Voices*, pp. 126, 157, 130.

87. Foley, *Female Acts*, p. 55. Other recent discussions of the politics of the representation of women in Greek tragedy, as opposed to in fifth-century Athenian life, include Wohl, *Intimate Commerce*.

88. Hegel, *The Phenomenology of Spirit* (1807), pp. 279–89.

89. Lacan, *Seminar 7*, in *The Ethics of Psychoanalysis 1959–60*, trans. Potter, p. 282.

90. Irigaray, 'The Eternal Irony of the Community', in *Speculum of the Other Woman*, trans. Gill, p. 219.

91. Butler, *Antigone's Claim*, p. 10.

92. *Ibid.*, p. 5. For a useful account of all these critics on Antigone, see the chapter on Antigone in Battersby, *The Phenomenal Woman: Feminist Metaphysics and the Patterns of Identity*, pp. 103–24. Battersby offers a particularly favourable account of Irigaray's interpretation (pp. 112–18), which serves as a good counter to Butler's more negative analysis.

93. Berry, *Shakespeare's Feminine Endings*, p. 6.

94. Hayward, *Cinema Studies: The Key Concepts*, pp. 181–4.

95. There was a fierce debate when the film was first released over whether it was a 'gay' film. On the one hand, the film's subject was homophobia in the mountain states and the private unhappiness it caused. On the other hand, the film could be seen to follow Ang Lee's general interest in the public pressure upon people to conform and their inability to choose their own private happiness. In that case, the homophobia was only contextual, rather than essential, to the film's concerns. For a good essay on the debate and Lee's directing vision, see Stephen Hunter, *The Washington Post* (2 February 2006).

4 Non-dramatic tragedy

1. Lessing, *Laocoon: An Essay on the Limits of Painting and Poetry*, trans. McCormick, p. 24.

2. I am thinking particularly of Michelangelo's statue in St Peter's, Rome.

3. See fig. 8. This painting of the crucifixion by Grunewald contrasts the grotesque physical nature of Jesus' tortured body on the cross with the unquestioning devotion of his family, followers and even one soldier, converted by this experience, at the foot of the cross. The interesting juxtaposition of pain and piety makes the image tragic. In contrast, the 1515 crucifixion painting by Grunewald from the Isenheim Altarpiece is more satirical than tragic, in that it portrays the figures around the cross as either indifferent to Christ's suffering or even as mocking.

4. For example, the fifteenth-century crucifixion scene by Antonello de Messina, in London's National Gallery.

5. Jones, *The Guardian* (27 February 2003).

6. David Jaffe and Amanda Bradley, 'Rubens: Massacre of the Innocents', *Apollo Magazine*, 67.496 (2003), p. 9.

7. Jones: 'for the same reason that *Guernica* is an undying protest against war, Rubens' *Massacre of the Innocents* is a universal image of atrocity'.

8. Spivey, *Enduring Creation*, p. 248. The tragic implications of the painting are indicated by the public outcry which followed the decision to cover over the reproduction, hanging in the United Nations in New York, during Colin Powell's presentation of the case for war on Iraq there in 2003.

9. Bolla, *Art Matters*, p. 144.

10. Eugene Smith, 'Tomoko in her bath', was first published as part of a photo essay on Minamata in *Life* magazine in 1972. See Jim Hughes' essay on the photograph in *The Digital Journalist: A Multimedia Magazine for Photojournalism in the Digital Age*, 7 (2000).

11. A few images from Contact photographer Kristen Ashburn's photographic essay, 'AIDS and faith in Zimbabwe', which won second prize in the Best of Photojournalism 2006 awards, may be viewed via Google Image.

12. Film footage of the execution of Vietcong rebel Bay Lop was filmed by South Vietnamese cameraman Vo Suu and acquired by NBC.

13. See also Tom Laqueur's essay on Serge Klarsfield's photographs: 'The Sound of Voices Intoning Names', *London Review of Books* (5 June 1997); and Golding, 'Photography, Memory and Survival'.

14. *Beyond Words: Photographers of War*, directed by Greg Kelly and Eric Foss, for CBC Newsworld, November 2005. See http://www.cbc.ca/beyondwords. The particular photograph which McCullin was referring to here is published in his biography, *Unreasonable Behaviour*, p. 108.

15. Spivey, *Enduring Creation*, p. 99.

16. South African freelance photographer Kevin Carter won the Pulitzer Prize in 1994 for his photograph of a famine-stricken child in the Sudan, first published in *The New York Times* (26 March 1993). Associated Press photographer Horst Faas won the Pulitzer Prize in 1972 for his picture series, 'Death in Dacca'. Both these examples are very controversial. For a further discussion of these issues, see John Long's letter, *Fineline: The Newsletter on Journalism Ethics*, 2.8 (November/December 1990), p. 6. See also Marinovich, *The Bang Bang Club*.

17. The photograph was first published in *The New Yorker* in May 2004.

18. The 9/11 photographs, including around 5,000 photographs sent in by the general public, were originally mounted as an exhibition and later published as a book: Alice Rose George, Charles Traub, Gilles Peress and Michael Shulan, *Here is New York: A Democracy of Photographs* (Zurich: Scalo, 2002). The photographs of Reuters photographers, Ahmed Jadallah, Suhaib Salem and Mohammed Salem, who happen to be brothers, were collected in an exhibition at Perpignan 2005, but may be viewed individually via Google Image.

19. Sontag, *Regarding the Pain of Others*, p. x.

20. Quoted from *Beyond Words: Photographers of War*.

21. Hardy, *Tess of the D'Urbervilles*, p. 360.
22. Anna herself is clear-sighted in her analysis of her single-minded passion: "'My love grows more and more passionate and selfish, while his is dying, and that is why we are drifting apart", she went on musing. "And there's no help for it. He is all in all to me, and I demand that he should give himself more and more entirely up to me. And he wants to get farther and farther away from me . . . If I could be anything but his mistress, passionately caring for nothing but his caresses – but I can't, and I don't want to be anything else. . . . And where love ends, hate begins'" (p. 796).
23. Tolstoy, *Anna Karenin*, p. 831.
24. Eliot, *Middlemarch*, ed. Harvey, p. 12.
25. In Keats' poem, 'Isabella; or, the Pot of Basil', Isabella's husband is murdered by her brothers. She secretly continues to mourn and cherish him, by hiding his severed head in a pot and growing a basil plant in the earth above it. His decomposing brain fertilises the basil and she waters it each day with her tears. In Rosamund's case, she has reduced her husband's brain to a decomposing mush, useful only in its capacity to support financially her extravagant, parasitic lifestyle: 'He once called her his basil plant; and when she asked for an explanation, said that basil was a plant which had flourished wonderfully on a murdered man's brains' (p. 893).
26. On the images of emptiness in the novel, see Tanner, *Adultery in the Novel*: 'One horror that the book explores is what happens when the wedding ring comes to mean as little as the napkin ring, part of the more general sense of disappearing distinctions that pervades the book. The related horror is the notion that the deformed energies of the artist and the bourgeois (jealousy and possessiveness) may combine in this manic *production* of nonmeaning, cluttering up not only the house but society and the world itself with these palpable things that are nonthings' (pp. 255–6).
27. Warshow, 'The Gangster as Tragic Hero', pp. 240–4.
28. Mulvey, 'Visual Pleasure and Narrative Cinema', in Rosen (ed.), *Narrative, Apparatus, Ideology*, p. 208.
29. The amount we see, and how we see it, seems to be crucial for determining generic distinctions in cinema. Charlie Chaplin once famously observed that 'life is a tragedy when seen in close-up, but a comedy in long-shot'. Does this suggest that large-scale spectacle is therefore necessarily comic, or, at least, not tragic?
30. Susan Hayward describes *film noir* as melodrama, and indeed there is no entry for tragedy among her 'key concepts' in cinema. This is just symptomatic of the reluctance of cinema theorists to engage with the tragic aspect of film; Hayward, *Cinema Studies*, pp. 236–48.
31. Žižek, *The Fright of Real Tears*, p. 169.
32. Morrell, 'The Psychology of Tragic Pleasure', p. 24. See also Freud's comment on the paradoxical pleasure of watching tragic drama in *Beyond the Pleasure Principle*: 'A reminder may be added that the artistic play and artistic imitation carried out by adults, which, unlike children's, are aimed at an audience, do not spare the spectators (for instance, in tragedy) the most painful experiences and yet can be

felt by them as highly enjoyable. This is convincing proof that, even under the dominance of the pleasure principle, there are ways and means enough of making what is itself unpleasurable into a subject to be recollected and worked over in the mind' (*SE*, vol. xviii, p. 17).

33. Freud, *Beyond the Pleasure Principle, SE*, vol. XVIII, p. 15.
34. *Ibid.*, p. 19.
35. Freud, 'Remembering, Repeating and Working Through', *SE*, vol. XII, p. 154.
36. Nuttall, *Why Does Tragedy Give Pleasure?* pp. 29–56.
37. *Mourning and Melancholia, SE*, vol. XIV, p. 245.
38. Benjamin, *The Origin of German Tragic Drama*, p. 158. In contrast the 'German *Trauerspiel* was never able to inspire itself to new life; it was never able to awaken within itself the clear light of self-awareness'.
39. Freud, *The Interpretation of Dreams, SE*, vol. V, pp. 509–10.
40. Lacan, 'Tuche and Automaton', in *The Four Fundamental Concepts of Psychoanalysis*, trans. Sheridan, p. 58.
41. Caruth, *Unclaimed Experience*, p. 100.
42. *Ibid.*, p. 105.
43. *Ibid.*, p. 5.
44. Morrison, *Beloved*, p. 266.
45. *Ibid.*, p. 36.
46. Ramadanovic, *Forgetting Futures*, pp. 98–105, discusses the 'haunting', trauma and repetition in the novel.
47. Richards, *Principles of Literary Criticism*, p. 246.
48. Jaspers, *Tragedy is Not Enough*, p. 38.
49. Gardner, 'Religion and Tragedy', in *Religion and Literature*, p. 34.
50. Steiner, *Real Presences*, p. 232.
51. *Ibid.*, p. 231.
52. Donald Mackinnon has even asserted that 'Christianity demands to be presented as the tragedy of Jesus': 'Theology and Tragedy', p. 168.
53. Delaney, *Abraham on Trial*, p. 5.
54. Ticciati, 'Does Job Fear God for Nought?'.
55. Mackinnon, 'Order and Evil in the Gospel', in *Borderlands*, p. 91.
56. Ward, 'Suffering and Incarnation', in Ward (ed.), *The Blackwell Companion to Postmodern Theology*, p. 201.
57. *Ibid.*, p. 198. Ward is careful to point out that his theory is not a 'theodicy', a 'theological rationale for human tragedy' (p. 202), which is traditionally the criticism cast against his line of argument.
58. Of course, Jesus' despairing cry picks up the line from Psalm 22: 'My God, my God, why hast thou forsaken me? Why art thou so far from helping me, and from the words of my roaring.' So while Jesus' words express an personal sense of abandonment, they are paradoxically given divine strength by the support of biblical precedent and prophecy.
59. Moltmann, *The Crucified God*, p. 286.

60. Lash, 'Friday, Saturday, Sunday', p. 117.
61. Mackinnon, 'Order and Evil in the Gospel', p. 93.
62. Mackinnon, 'Atonement and Tragedy', in *Borderlands*, pp. 102–3.
63. Quash, *Theology and the Drama of History*, p. 94. Quash's quotation – the 'whole tragic potentiality' – is from Mackinnon, *Explorations in Theology*, p. 83.

5 Coda: tragic sites

1. Clearly a whole book could be written – and many have been written – just on Auschwitz and tragedy, and I can only touch on the issue here. Writers have reacted variously to the assault upon the consciousness mounted by the holocaust, from Primo Levi's celebration of the human spirit's capacity to survive the concentration camp's horrors, in *If This Is A Man*, to Maurice Blanchot's sense that writing after Auschwitz can only be fragmentary (*The Writing of Disaster*). One recent contribution to this debate, about the relation between writing and the holocaust, is Cohen, *Interrupting Auschwitz: Art, Religion, Philosophy*. More problematically, a sense of the response of many ordinary people today to Auschwitz can be gleaned from the public feedback posted on the websites of the tour companies offering tours to Auschwitz: see, for example, www.escape2poland.co.uk/testimonials.html.
2. *New York Times* (17 March 2002). For more on the excavation of Ground Zero and the 'tragic gap', see my article ' "We Can't Make More Dirt": Tragedy and the Excavated Body'.
3. Ariel Dorfman, *Widows*, trans. Kessler. Michael Ondaatje confronts a similar concern with political atrocity, justice, forensic archaeology and tragic repercussions in his novel, *Anil's Ghost*. For a discussion of this novel and the tragic catharsis offered by forensic archaeology, see my *Digging the Dirt*, pp. 198–9.
4. Indeed, forensic archaeologist Margaret Cox has explained that the excavation of mass graves can be conducted for two different purposes: either to identify the individual dead so that their relatives can mourn them, or to gather forensic information about some exemplary cases of atrocity which can stand as evidence in court. One allows for specific mourning; the other can be used to bring perpetrators to justice. But they can often involve two completely different methods of excavation. See my article on Margaret Cox and forensic archaeology in *The Times Higher Education Supplement* (24 September 2004). So the unearthing of bodies can lead to very different acts of interpretation and mourning, which are analogous to the varying priorities in tragic drama: i.e. political justice and individual lamentation.
5. Tom Laqueur, 'Memory and Naming in the Great War', in Gillis (ed.), *Commemorations: The Politics of National Identity*, p. 164. There are more than 58,000 names on the Vietnam memorial. A ceremony in which the names are read out has taken place three times, in 1982, 1992 and 2002. In 2002, the reading of the names took a total of sixty-five hours, over four days.

6. Maya Lin, 'I thought about what death was, what a loss is. A sharp pain that lessens with time, but can never quite heal over. A scar. The idea occurred to me there on the site. Take a knife and cut open the earth, and with time the grass would heal it': quoted in Robert Campbell, 'An Emotive Place Apart', *AIA Journal*, 72 (May 1983), p. 151. See also Sturken, *Tangled Memories*, and Holst-Warhaft, *The Cue for Passion*, pp. 185–92.

Bibliography

1 Approaching the subject

Bushnell, Rebecca (ed.), *The Blackwell Companion to Tragedy* (Oxford: Blackwell, 2005)

Drakakis, John, and Naomi Conn Liebler (eds.), *Tragedy* (London: Longman, 1998)

Eagleton, Terry, *Sweet Violence: The Idea of the Tragic* (Oxford: Blackwell, 2003)

Nuttall, A. D., *Why Does Tragedy Give Pleasure?* (Oxford: Clarendon Press, 1996)

Poole, Adrian, *Tragedy: A Very Short Introduction* (Oxford: Oxford University Press, 2005)

Quayson, Ato, *Calibrations: Reading for the Social* (Minnesota: University of Minnesota Press, 2003)

Reiss, Timothy, *Tragedy and Truth: Studies in the Development of a Renaissance and Neoclassical Discourse* (New Haven: Yale University Press, 1980)

Rosslyn, Felicity, *Tragic Plots: A New Reading from Aeschylus to Lorca* (Aldershot: Ashgate 2000)

Sontag, Susan, *Regarding the Pain of Others* (New York: Picador, 2003)

Steiner, George, *The Death of Tragedy* (London: Faber and Faber, 1961)

Szondi, Peter, *An Essay on the Tragic*, trans. Paul Fleming (Stanford, CA: Stanford University Press, 2002)

Unamuno, Miguel de, *The Tragic Sense of Life*, trans. J. E. Crawford Fitch (1921; republished New York: Dover Publications, 1954)

Williams, Raymond, *Modern Tragedy* (1966; republished, London: Hogarth Press, 1992)

2.1 The Greeks

Plays and translations

Aeschylus, *Suppliant Maidens, Persians, Prometheus, Seven Against Thebes*, trans. H. Weir Smyth (Cambridge, MA: Loeb Classical Library, 1922)

Agamemnon, Libation Bearers, Eumenides, trans. H. Weir Smyth (Cambridge, MA: Loeb Classical Library, 1926)

Prometheus Bound, ed. Mark Griffith, Cambridge Greek and Latin Classics (Cambridge: Cambridge University Press, 1983)

The Oresteia, a new version by Ted Hughes (London: Faber and Faber, 1999)

The Oresteia, trans. Tony Harrison (1981), in Harrison, *Theatre Works 1973–1985* (Harmondsworth: Penguin, 1986)

The Oresteia, trans. Robert Fagles (Harmondsworth: Penguin, 1977)

Euripides, *Cyclops, Alcestis, Medea*, trans. David Kovacs (Cambridge, MA: Loeb Classical Library, 1994)

Children of Heracles, Hippolytus, Andromache, Hecuba, trans. D. Kovacs (Cambridge, MA: Loeb Classical Library, 1995)

Iphigenia at Aulis, Rhesus, Hecuba, Daughters of Troy, Helen, trans. A. S. Way (Cambridge, MA: Loeb Classical Library, 1912)

Electra, Orestes, Iphigenia in Taurica, Andromache, Cyclops, trans. A. S. Way (Cambridge, MA: Loeb Classical Library, 1912)

Bacchanals, Madness of Hercules, Children of Hercules, Phoenician Maidens, Suppliants, trans. A. S. Way (Cambridge, MA: Loeb Classical Library, 1912)

Medea, and Other Plays, trans. James Morwood, World's Classics (Oxford: Oxford University Press, 1998)

Bacchae, and Other Plays, trans. James Morwood, World's Classics (Oxford: Oxford University Press, 1999)

The Trojan Women, and Other Plays, trans. James Morwood, World's Classics (Oxford: Oxford University Press, 2001)

Euripides' Bacchae, ed. with commentary by Richard Seaford (Warminster: Aris and Phillips, 1996)

Homer, *The Iliad*, trans. Robert Fagles (Harmondsworth: Penguin, 1990)

The Iliad, trans. Martin Hammond (Harmondsworth: Penguin, 1987)

Pindar, *Pindar's Victory Songs*, trans. Frank J. Nisetich (Baltimore: Johns Hopkins University Press, 1980)

Plato, *The Symposium*, trans. W. F. M. Lamb (Cambridge, MA: Loeb Classical Library, 1925; reprinted 1967)

The Republic, trans. F. M. Cornford (Oxford: Clarendon Press, 1941)

Sophocles, *Oedipus the King, Oedipus at Colonus, Antigone*, trans. F. Storr (Cambridge, MA: Loeb Classical Library, 1912)

Ajax, Electra, Trachiniae, Philoctetes, trans. F. Storr (Cambridge, MA: Loeb Classical Library, 1913)

Sophocles I and II, ed. D. Greene and R. Lattimore (Chicago: University of Chicago Press, 1957; republished 1991)

Electra and Other Plays, trans. E. F. Watling (Harmondsworth: Penguin, 1953)

Antigone, Oedipus the King, Electra, trans. H. D. F. Kitto, World's Classics (Oxford: Oxford University Press, 1994)

The Three Theban Plays, trans. Robert Fagles (Harmondsworth: Penguin, 1984)

The Cure at Troy, a Version of Sophocles' Philoctetes by Seamus Heaney (London: Faber and Faber, 1990)

Secondary sources

Cartledge, Paul, *The Greeks: A Portrait of Self and Others* (Oxford: Oxford University Press, 1993)

Cartledge, Paul (ed.), *Illustrated History of Ancient Greece* (Cambridge: Cambridge University Press, 1997)

Dodds, E. R., *The Greeks and the Irrational* (Berkeley: University of California Press, 1951)

Easterling, P. E. (ed), *The Cambridge Companion to Greek Tragedy* (Cambridge: Cambridge University Press, 1997)

Easterling, P. E., and Edith Hall (eds.), *Greek and Roman Actors: Aspects of an Ancient Profession* (Cambridge: Cambridge University Press, 2002)

Foley, Helene, *Ritual Irony: Poetry and Sacrifice in Euripides* (Ithaca: Cornell University Press, 1985)

Goldhill, Simon, *Language, Sexuality, Narrative: The Oresteia* (Cambridge: Cambridge University Press, 1984)

Reading Greek Tragedy (Cambridge: Cambridge University Press, 1986)

Griffin, Jasper (ed.), *Sophocles Revisited: Essays Presented to Sir Hugh Lloyd-Jones* (Oxford: Oxford University Press, 1999)

Griffiths, M., *The Authenticity of Prometheus Bound* (Cambridge: Cambridge University Press, 1977)

Hall, Edith, *Inventing the Barbarian: Greek Self-Definition Through Tragedy* (Oxford: Clarendon Press, 1989)

Hall, Edith, Fiona Macintosh and Oliver Taplin (eds), *Medea in Performance 1500–2000* (Oxford: Legenda, 2000)

Hall, Edith, Fiona Macintosh and Amanda Wrigley (eds.), *Dionysus Since 69: Greek Tragedy at the Dawn of the Third Millennium* (Oxford: Oxford University Press, 2004)

Kerferd, G., *The Sophistic Movement* (Cambridge: Cambridge University Press, 1981)

Knox, Bernard, *The Heroic Temper: Studies in Sophoclean Tragedy* (Berkeley: University of California Press, 1964)

Padel, Ruth, *In and Out of the Mind: Greek Images of the Tragic Self* (Princeton: Princeton University Press, 1992)

Pickard-Cambridge, Arthur, *The Dramatic Festivals of Athens* (1953; 2nd rev. edn, London: Oxford University Press, 1968)

Poole, Adrian, 'Total Disaster: Euripides' *Trojan Women*', *Arion*, ns 3 (1976), pp. 257–87

Tragedy: Shakespeare and the Greek Example (Oxford: Blackwell, 1987)

Pucci, Pietro, *The Violence of Pity in Euripides' Medea* (Ithaca: Cornell University Press, 1980)

Rehm, Rush, *Greek Tragic Theatre* (London: Routledge, 1992)

The Play of Space: Spatial Transformation in Greek Tragedy (Princeton: Princeton University Press, 2002)

Schlegel, A. W., *Lectures on Dramatic Art and Literature*, trans. John Black
    (London, 1815)
Seaford, Richard, *Reciprocity and Ritual: Homer and Tragedy in the Developing
    City-State* (Oxford: Clarendon Press, 1994)
Segal, Charles, *Interpreting Greek Tragedy: Myth, Poetry, Text* (Ithaca and London:
    Cornell University Press, 1986)
Silk, M. S. (ed.), *Tragedy and the Tragic: Greek Theatre and Beyond* (Oxford:
    Clarendon Press, 1996)
Taplin, Oliver, *Greek Tragedy in Action* (London: Methuen, 1978)
Vernant, J.-P., and P. Vidal-Naquet, *Myth and Tragedy in Ancient Greece*, trans.
    Janet Lloyd (New York: Zone Books, 1988)
Wiles, David, *Tragedy in Athens: Performance Space and Theatrical Meaning*
    (Cambridge: Cambridge University Press, 1997)
Winkler, J., and F. Zeitlin (eds.), *Nothing to Do With Dionysus?: Athenian Drama
    in its Social Context* (Princeton: Princeton University Press, 1989)

2.2 Seneca and Racine

Plays and translations

Corneille, *The Cid, Cinna, The Theatrical Illusion*, trans. John Cairncross
    (Harmondsworth: Penguin, 1975)
Pascal, *Pensées*, trans. A. J. Krailsheimer (Harmondsworth: Penguin, 1966)
Racine, Jean, *Andromache and Other Plays*, trans. John Cairncross
    (Harmondsworth: Penguin, 1967)
    Andromache, trans. Douglas Dunn (London: Faber and Faber, 1990)
    Phèdre, in a new version by Ted Hughes (London: Faber and Faber, 1998)
Seneca, *Tragedies*, 2 vols., ed. and trans. John Fitch (Cambridge, MA: Loeb
    Classical Library, 2002–4)
    Four Tragedies and Octavia, trans. E. F. Watling (Harmondsworth: Penguin,
    1966)
    Seneca's Oedipus, adapted by Ted Hughes (New York: Doubleday, 1972)
    Thyestes, trans. and intro. Caryl Churchill (London: Faber and Faber, 1995)

Secondary sources

Barthes, Roland, *On Racine*, trans. Richard Howard (New York: Hill and Wang,
    1964)
Boyle, A. J., *Tragic Seneca: An Essay in the Theatrical Tradition* (London:
    Routledge, 1997)
Braden, Gordon, *Renaissance Tragedy and the Senecan Tradition: Anger's Privilege*
    (New Haven: Yale University Press, 1985)
Brassilach, Robert, *Corneille* (Paris: Fayard, 1961)

Critchley, Simon, ' "I Want To Die, I Hate My Life": Phaedra's Malaise', *New Literary History*, 35.1 (Winter 2004), pp. 17–40

Goldmann, Lucien, *The Hidden God*, trans. Philip Thody (London: Routledge and K. Paul, 1964)

Levitan, William, 'Seneca in Racine', *Yale French Studies*, 76 (1989), pp. 185–210

Lough, John, *Seventeenth-Century French Drama* (Oxford: Clarendon Press, 1979)

Lyons, John D., *Kingdom of Disorder: The Theory of Tragedy in Classical France* (West Lafayette: Purdue University Press, 1999)

Maskell, David, *Racine: A Theatrical Reading* (Oxford: Clarendon Press, 1991)

Parrish, Richard, *Racine: The Limits of Tragedy* (Seattle: Papers on French Seventeenth Century Literature, 1993)

Segal, Charles, *Language and Desire in Seneca's Phaedra* (Princeton: Princeton University Press, 1986)

Tarrant, R. J., 'Senecan Drama and its Antecedents', *Harvard Studies in Classical Philosophy*, 82 (1978), pp. 213–63

Seneca's Thyestes, ed. with intro. and comm. R. J. Tarrant (Atlanta, GA: Scholar's Press, 1985)

Tobin, Ronald, *Racine and Seneca* (Chapel Hill: University of North Carolina Press, 1971)

2.3 Shakespeare

Plays and contemporary texts

Shakespeare, William, *The Norton Shakespeare*, ed. Stephen Greenblatt (New York and London: Norton, 1997)

Bond, Edward, *Lear*, with comm. and notes by Patricia Hern (London: Methuen, 1983)

Dekker, Thomas, *The Plague Pamphlets of Thomas Dekker*, ed. F. P. Wilson (Oxford: Clarendon Press, 1925)

Machiavelli, *The Prince* (1514), trans. and ed. Robert M. Adams (New York and London: Norton, 1977; rev. edn, 1992)

Puttenham, George, *The Arte of English Poesie* (1589), ed. G. D. Willcock and A. Walker (Cambridge: Cambridge University Press, 1936)

Sidney, Philip, *A Defence of Poetry*, ed. Jan van Dorsten (Oxford: Oxford University Press, 1966)

Secondary sources

Bartels, Emily, *Spectacles of Strangeness: Imperialism, Alienation and Marlowe* (Philadelphia: University of Pennsylvannia Press, 1993)

Bayley, John, *Shakespeare and Tragedy* (London: Routledge, 1981)

Bradley, A. C., *Shakespearean Tragedy* (1904; new edn, Basingstoke: Macmillan, 1974; reprinted 1985)

Bratchell, D. F. (ed.), *Shakespearean Tragedy* (London: Routledge, 1989)

Cavell, Stanley, *Disowning Knowledge: In Six Plays of Shakespeare* (Cambridge: Cambridge University Press, 1987)

Dillon, Janette, *The Cambridge Introduction to Early English Theatre* (Cambridge: Cambridge University Press, 2006)

Dollimore, Jonathan, *Radical Tragedy: Religion, Ideology and Power in the Drama of Shakespeare and his Contemporaries* (Brighton: Harvester, 1984; 3rd edn, 2004)

Dollimore, Jonathan, and A. Sinfield (eds.), *Political Shakespeare* (1985; 2nd edn, Manchester, 1994)

Elton, William, *King Lear and the Gods* (San Marino, CA: Huntington Library, 1966)

Everett, Barbara, *Young Hamlet: Essays on Shakespeare's Tragedies* (Oxford: Clarendon Press, 1989)

Greenblatt, Stephen, *Shakespearean Negotiations: The Circulation of Social Energy in Renaissance England* (Oxford: Clarendon Press, 1988)

  Hamlet in Purgatory (Princeton: Princeton University Press, 2001)

  Will in the World: How Shakespeare Became Shakespeare (New York: Norton, 2004)

Headlam Wells, Robin, *Shakespeare, Politics and the State* (London: Macmillan, 1986)

Holland, Peter, *English Shakespeares: Shakespeare in the English Stage in the 1990s* (Cambridge: Cambridge University Press, 1997)

Johnson, Samuel, *Preface to Shakespeare*, in *Samuel Johnson*, ed. Donald Greene (Oxford: Oxford University Press, 1984)

Kantorowicz, E. H., *The King's Two Bodies: A Study in Medieval Political Theology* (Princeton: Princeton University Press, 1957)

Kerrigan, John, *Revenge Tragedy: Aeschylus to Armageddon* (Oxford: Clarendon Press, 1996)

Kirsch, Arthur, *The Passions of Shakespeare's Tragic Heroes* (Charlottesville: University Press of Virginia, 1990)

Kott, Jan, *Shakespeare Our Contemporary* (New York: Doubleday, 1964; reissued, Norton, 1974)

Lamb, Charles, 'On the Tragedies of Shakespeare, Considered with Reference to their Fitness for Stage Representation' (1811), in *Romantic Critical Essays*, ed. D. Bromwich (Cambridge: Cambridge University Press, 1987)

Lever, J. W., *The Tragedy of State* (London: Methuen, 1971; new edn, 1987)

Liebler, Naomi Conn, *Shakespeare's Festive Tragedy: The Ritual Foundations of Genre* (London: Routledge, 1995)

McAlindon, T., *Shakespeare's Tragic Cosmos* (Cambridge: Cambridge University Press, 1991)

McEachern, Claire (ed), *The Cambridge Companion to Shakespearean Tragedy* (Cambridge: Cambridge University Press, 2002)

Masington, Charles G., *Christopher Marlowe's Tragic Vision: A Study in Damnation* (Athens, OH: Ohio University Press, 1972)

Miola, Robert S., *Shakespeare and Classical Tragedy: The Influence of Seneca* (Oxford: Clarendon Press, 1992)

Muir, Kenneth, *Shakespeare's Tragic Sequence* (London: Hutchinson, 1972)

Neill, Michael, *Issues of Death: Mortality and Identity in English Renaissance Tragedy* (Oxford: Clarendon Press, 1997)

Rossiter, A. P., *Angel With Horns: Fifteen Lectures on Shakespeare*, ed. Graham Storey (London: Longman, 1961; new edn, 1989)

Sanders, Wilbur, *The Dramatist and the Received Idea: Studies in the Plays of Marlowe and Shakespeare* (Cambridge: Cambridge University Press, 1968)

Schwartz, Murray M., and Coppelia Kahn (eds.), *Representing Shakespeare: New Psychoanalytic Essays* (Baltimore and London: Johns Hopkins University Press, 1980)

Shuger, Debora, *Habits of Thought in the English Renaissance: Religion, Politics and the Dominant Culture* (Berkeley: University of California Press, 1990)

Tillyard, E. M. W., *The Elizabethan World Picture* (London: Chatto and Windus, 1943)

Wiles, David, *Shakespeare's Clown: Actor and Text in the Elizabethan Playhouse* (Cambridge: Cambridge University Press, 1987)

Zimmerman, Susan (ed.), *Shakespeare's Tragedies* (Basingstoke: Palgrave Macmillan, 1998)

2.4 Romantic tragedy: Ibsen, Strindberg, Chekhov

Plays and translations

Byron, George, *Manfred*, in *Poetical Works of Byron*, ed. F. Page (Oxford: Oxford University Press, 1945; 3rd edn, corrected by John Jump, 1973)

Chekhov, Anton, *Plays*, trans. Elisaveta Fen (Harmondsworth, Penguin, 1959)

Goethe, Johann Wolfgang, *Faust*, trans. Phillip Wayne (Harmondsworth: Penguin, 1949)

Ibsen, Henrik, *Brand*, trans. Michael Meyer (London: Methuen, 1986)

Ghosts; A Public Enemy; When We Dead Wake, trans. Peter Watts (Harmondsworth: Penguin, 1964)

The Master Builder, and Other Plays, trans. Una Ellis-Fermor (Harmondsworth: Penguin, 1958)

Hedda Gabler and The Dolls House, trans. Christopher Hampton (London: Faber and Faber, 1989)

Strindberg, August, *Plays*, trans. Michael Robinson, World's Classics (Oxford: Oxford University Press, 1998)

Secondary sources

Coleridge, 'Lectures on Shakespeare', in *Samuel Taylor Coleridge*, ed. H. J. Jackson (Oxford: Oxford University Press, 1985)

Carlson, Harry G., *Strindberg and the Poetry of Myth* (Berkeley: University of California Press, 1982)

  Out of Inferno: Strindberg's Reawakening as an Artist (Seattle: University of Washington Press, 1996)

Cox, Jeffrey N., *In the Shadows of Romance: Romantic Tragic Drama in Germany, England and France* (Athens, OH: Ohio University Press, 1987)

Durbach, Errol, *'Ibsen the Romantic': Analogues of Paradise in the Later Plays* (London: Macmillan, 1982)

Forster, E. M., 'Ibsen the Romantic' (1928), in Charles Lyons (ed.), *Critical Essays on Henrik Ibsen* (Boston: G. K. Hall, 1987)

Gottlieb, Vera, and Paul Allain (eds.), *The Cambridge Companion to Chekhov* (Cambridge: Cambridge University Press, 2000)

Macfarlane, James (ed.), *The Cambridge Companion to Ibsen* (Cambridge: Cambridge University Press, 1994)

Northam, John, *Ibsen's Dramatic Method: A Study of the Prose Dramas* (London: Faber and Faber, 1953)

  Ibsen: A Critical Study (Cambridge: Cambridge University Press, 1973)

Robinson, Michael, *Studies in Strindberg* (Norwich: Norvik Press, 1998)

Shideler, Ross, *Questioning the Father: From Darwin to Zola, Ibsen, Strindberg and Hardy* (Stanford: Stanford University Press, 1999)

Tornqvist, Egil, *Strindbergian Drama: Themes and Structures* (Stockholm: Almqvist and Wiksell International, 1982)

2.5 American tragedy

Plays and editions

Albee, Edward, *Who's Afraid of Virginia Woolf?* (London and New York: Penguin, 1965)

Hansberry, Lorraine, *A Raisin in the Sun* (1959; London: Methuen, 2001)

Kushner, Tony, *Angels in America: Part One: Millennium Approaches* (London: National Theatre and Nick Hern Books, 1992)

  Angels in America: Part Two: Perestroika (London: National Theatre and Nick Hern Books, 1994)

Miller, Arthur, *The Portable Arthur Miller*, ed. Christopher Bigsby [including *Death of a Salesman* and *The Crucible*] (London and New York: Penguin, 1997; new edn, 2003)

  A View from a Bridge and *All My Sons* (Harmondsworth: Penguin, 1961; reprinted, 2000)

O'Neill, Eugene, *Mourning Becomes Electra* (London: National Theatre and Nick Hern Books, 1992)

Long Days Journey Into the Night (London: National Theatre and Nick Hern Books, 1991)

The Iceman Cometh (New York: Vintage International, 1999)

Williams, Tennessee, *Cat on a Hot Tin Roof* (New York and London: Signet, 1958)

A Streetcar Named Desire, and Other Plays, ed. Martin Browne (Harmondsworth: Penguin, 1962)

Wilson, August, *Ma Rainey's Black Bottom* (New York and London: Plume Books, 1985)

Fences (New York and London: Plume Books, 1986)

The Piano Lesson (New York and London: Plume Books, 1990)

Secondary sources

Bigsby, Christopher, *Critical Introduction to Twentieth-Century American Drama: II. Williams, Miller, Albee* (Cambridge: Cambridge University Press, 1984)

Chothia, Jean, *Forging a Language: A Study of the Plays of Eugene O'Neill* (Cambridge: Cambridge University Press, 1979)

Falk, Doris V., *Eugene O'Neill and the Tragic Tension: An Interpretative Study of the Plays* (New Brunswick: Rutgers University Press, 1958)

Fisher, James, *The Theater of Tony Kushner: Living Past Hope* (New York and London: Routledge, 2001)

Geis, Deborah, and Steven F. Kruger (eds.), *Approaching the Millennium: Essays on Angels in America* (Ann Arbor: University of Michigan Press, 1997)

Gross, Robert F. (ed.), *Tennessee Williams: A Casebook* (London and New York: Routledge, 2002)

Miller, Arthur, *The Theatre Essays of Arthur Miller*, ed. Robert A. Martin (London: Methuen, 1978; 2nd edn, 1994)

Robinson, James A., *Eugene O'Neill and Oriental Thought: A Divided Vision* (Carbondale: Southern Illinois University Press, 1982)

Shannon, Sandra G., *The Dramatic Vision of August Wilson* (Washington, DC: Howard University Press, 1995)

Williams, Dana, and Sandra G. Shannon, *August Wilson and Black Aesthetics* (Basingstoke: Palgrave Macmillan, 2004)

2.6 Post-colonial tragedy

Plays and translations

Achebe, Chinua, *Things Fall Apart* (London: Heinemann, 1958)

Fugard, Athol, *The Township Plays* (Oxford: Oxford University Press, 1993)

Kurosawa, Akira (director), *Throne of Blood* (1957)
Mizoguchi, Kenji (director), *Ugetsu* (1953)
Osofisan, Femi, *Morountodun and Other Plays* [includes *No More the Wasted Breed*] (Ikeja: Longman Nigeria, 1982)
    Another Raft (Lagos: Malthouse Press, 1988)
    Recent Outings: Two Plays Comprising Tegonni, an African Antigone and Many Colours Make the Thunder-King (Lagos: Opon Ifa Readers, 1999)
    Major Plays Books 1 and 2 (Lagos: Opon Ifa Readers, 2005–6)
Rotimi, Ola, *The Gods Are Not To Blame* (London: Oxford University Press, 1971)
Soyinka, Wole, *Collected Plays*, 2 vols. (Oxford: Oxford University Press, 1973)
    Death and the King's Horseman, ed. Simon Gikandi (New York: Norton, 2003)
20 Plays of the No Theatre, ed. Donald Keene (New York: Columbia University Press, 1970)

Secondary sources

Agbaur, Ehema, 'Africanising Macbeth', *Research in African Literatures*, 27 (Spring 1996), pp. 102–9
Awodiya, Muyiwa, *The Drama of Femi Osofisan: A Critical Perspective* (Ibadan, Nigeria: Kraft Books, 1995)
    Femi Osofisan: Interpretative Essays (Lagos: Centre for Black and African Arts and Civilisation, 1996)
Balme, Christopher B., *Decolonizing the Stage: Theatrical Syncretism and Post-Colonial Drama* (Oxford: Clarendon Press, 1999)
Banham Martin, Errol Hill and George Woodyard (eds.), *The Cambridge Guide to African and Caribbean Theatre* (Cambridge: Cambridge University Press, 1994)
Bhabha, Homi, 'Of Man and Mimicry: The Ambivalence of Colonial Discourse', in *The Location of Culture* (London: Routledge, 1994), pp. 85–92
Breitinger, E. (ed.), *Theatre and Performance in Africa: Intercultural Perspectives* (Bayreuth: Bayreuth University, 1994)
Crow, Brian, *An Introduction to Post-Colonial Theatre* (Cambridge: Cambridge University Press, 1996)
Dunton, C., *Make Man Talk True: Nigerian Drama in English since 1970* (London: Hans Zell Publishers, 1992)
Gainor, J. Ellen (ed.), *Imperialism and Theatre: Essays on World Theatre, Drama and Performance* (London: Routledge, 1995)
Gibbs, J. (ed.), *Critical Perspectives on Soyinka* (London: Heinemann, 1981)
Gilbert, Helen, and Joanne Tompkins, *Post-Colonial Drama: Theory, Practice, Politics* (London: Routledge, 1996)
Gilbert, Helen (ed.), *Post-Colonial Stages: Critical and Creative Views on Drama, Theatre and Performance* (Hebden Bridge: Dangaroo, 1999)
Jeyifo, Biofran, *Wole Soyinka: Politics, Poetics and Postcolonialism* (Cambridge: Cambridge University Press, 2004)

Jeyifo, Biofran (ed.), *Modern African Drama* (New York: Norton, 2002)
Katrak, K. H., *Wole Soyinka and Modern Tragedy: A Study of Dramatic Theory and Practice* (Oxford: Greenwood, 1986)
Ogunba, O. (ed.), *Soyinka: A Collection of Critical Essays* (Ibadan, Nigeria: Syndicated Communications, 1994)
Olaniyan, T., *Scars of Conquest/Masks of Resistance: Inventions of Cultural Identities in African, African-American and Caribbean Drama* (Oxford: Oxford University Press, 1995)
Omotoso, K., *Achebe or Soyinka? A Study in Contrasts* (London: Hans Zell Publishers, 1995)
Soyinka, Wole, *Myth, Literature and the African World* (Cambridge: Cambridge University Press, 1976)
    Art, Dialogue and Outrage: Essays on Literature and Culture (1988; rev. and expanded edn, Methuen, 1993)
Terasaki, Etsuko, *Figures of Desire: Wordplay, Spirit Possession, Fantasy, Madness and Mourning in Japanese Noh Plays* (Ann Arbor: University of Michigan Press, 2002)
Walder, Dennis, *Athol Fugard* (Basingstoke: Macmillan, 1984)
Wertheim, Albert, *The Dramatic Art of Athol Fugard* (Bloomington: Indiana University Press, 2000)
Wetmore, K., *The Athenian Sun in an African Sky: Modern African Adaptations of Classical Greek Tragedy* (London: McFarland, 2002)
Yeats, W. B., 'Certain Noble Plays of Japan', in *Essays and Introductions* (London: Macmillan, 1961)

2.7 Beckett

Beckett, Samuel, *The Complete Dramatic Works* (London: Faber and Faber, 1986)
Adorno, Theodor, 'Trying to Understand *Endgame*', in *Notes to Literature*, trans. Shierry Weber Nicholsen (New York: Columbia University Press, 1991)
Bergson, Henri, *Laughter: An Essay on the Meaning of the Comic*, trans. Cloudesley Brereton (London: Macmillan, 1911)
Berlin, Normand, 'Boundary Situation: King Lear and Waiting for Godot', in *The Secret Cause: A Discussion of Tragedy* (Amherst: University of Massachussetts Press, 1981), pp. 113–28
Birkett, Jennifer, and Kate Ince (eds.), *Samuel Beckett* (London: Longman, 2000)
Brater, Enoch (ed.), *Beckett at 80 / Beckett in Context* (Oxford: Oxford University Press, 1986)
Burkman, Katherine H. (ed.), *Myth and Ritual in the Plays of Samuel Beckett* (London: Associated University Presses, 1987)
Cavell, Stanley, *Must We Mean What We Say?* (New York: Scribner, 1969; updated edn, Cambridge: Cambridge University Press, 2002)
Critchley, Simon, *Very Little. . . . Almost Nothing: Death, Philosophy, Literature* (London: Routledge, 1997; 2nd edn, 2004)

Mcdonald, Ronan, *Tragedy and Irish Literature: Synge, O'Casey, Beckett* (Basingstoke: Palgrave Macmillan, 2001)

O'Brien, Eoin, *The Beckett Country: Samuel Beckett's Ireland* (Monkstown: Black Cat and Faber, 1986)

Palmer, D. J. (ed.) *Comedy: Developments in Criticism* (London: Macmillan, 1984)

Pilling, John (ed.), *The Cambridge Companion to Beckett* (Cambridge: Cambridge University Press, 1994)

Rosen, Stephen, *Samuel Beckett and the Pessimistic Tradition* (New Brunswick: Rutgers University Press, 1976)

Case studies: Physical violence and dismemberment, and language

Artaud, Antonin, *The Theatre and its Double*, trans. Victor Corti (London: Calder, 1970)

Barker, Howard, *Arguments for a Theatre* (1989; 3rd edn, Manchester: Manchester University Press, 1997)

Bate, Jonathan (ed.), *Titus Andronicus*, The Arden Shakespeare (London: Routledge, 1995)

Bond, Edward, *Saved* (London: Methuen, 1965)

Brown, John Russell, *Theatre Language: A Study of Arden, Osborne, Pinter and Wesker* (London: Allen Lane, 1972)

Dessen, Alan, *Titus Andronicus*, Shakespeare in Performance series (Manchester: Manchester University Press, 1989)

Esslin, Martin, *Pinter: The Playwright*, (1967; 4th edn, London: Methuen, 1982)

Howard, Jean E., *Shakespeare's Art of Orchestration: Stage Technique and Audience Response* (Urbana and Chicago: University of Illinois Press, 1984)

Kane, Sarah, *Complete Plays* (London: Methuen, 2001)

Kennedy, Andrew, *Six Dramatists in Search of a Language: Studies in Dramatic Language* (Cambridge: Cambridge University Press, 1975)

Knowles, Ronald, '*The Caretaker* and the "Point" of Laughter', in M. Scott (ed.), *Harold Pinter: The Birthday Party, The Caretaker, The Homecoming* (London: Macmillan, 1986), pp. 146–61

McGuire, Philip, *Speechless Dialect: Shakespeare's Open Silences* (Berkeley: University of California Press, 1985)

McLuskie, Kathleen, and Jennifer Uglow (eds.), *The Duchess of Malfi*, Plays in Performance (Bristol: Bristol Classical, 1989)

Pinter, Harold, *Harold Pinter: Plays One, Two, and Three* (London: Faber and Faber, 1996)

Raby, Peter (ed.), *The Cambridge Companion to Pinter* (Cambridge: Cambridge University Press, 2001)

Rebellato, Dan, 'Sarah Kane: An Appreciation', *New Theatre Quarterly*, 59 (1999), pp. 280–81

Rovine, Harvey, *Silence in Shakespeare: Drama, Power and Gender* (Ann Arbor: University of Michigan Press, 1987)

Saunders, Graham, *'Love Me or Kill Me': Sarah Kane and the Theatre of Extremes* (Manchester: Manchester University Press, 2002)

Scarry, Elaine, *The Body in Pain: The Making and Unmaking of the World* (Oxford: Oxford University Press, 1985)

Sierz, Aleks, *In-Yer-Face Theatre: British Drama Today* (London: Faber, 2001)

Warren, Roger, *Cymbeline*, Shakespeare in Performance series (Manchester: Manchester University Press, 1989)

White, Martin, *Renaissance Drama in Action: An Introduction to Aspects of Theatre Practice and Performance* (London and New York: Routledge, 1998)

3 Tragic theorists

Aristotle, *Poetics*, trans. W. H. Fyfe, Loeb Classical Library (London: Heinemann, 1927)

Poetics, trans. Stephen Halliwell, Loeb Classical Library (Cambridge, MA: Harvard University Press, 1995)

Poetics, trans. Malcolm Heath (Harmondsworth: Penguin, 1996)

Battersby, Christine, *The Phenomenal Woman: Feminist Metaphysics and Patterns of Identity* (Oxford: Polity, 1998)

Booth, Stephen, *King Lear, Macbeth, Indefinition and Tragedy* (New Haven: Yale University Press, 1983)

Camus, Albert, *The Myth of Sisyphus*, trans. Justin O'Brien (Harmondsworth: Penguin, 1975)

The Outsider, trans. Joseph Laredo (Harmondsworth: Penguin, 1983)

Derrida, Jacques, 'Plato's Pharmacy', in *Dissemination*, trans. Barbara Johnson (1981), pp. 63–171

The Gift of Death, trans. David Wills (Chicago and London: University of Chicago Press, 1995)

Draper, R. P. (ed.), *Tragedy: Developments in Criticism* (London: Macmillan, 1980)

Girard, René, *Violence and the Sacred*, trans. Patrick Gregory (Baltimore: Johns Hopkins University Press, 1977)

Halliwell, Stephen, *Aristotle's Poetics* (London: Duckworth, 1986)

Golden, Leon, *Aristotle on Tragic and Comic Mimesis* (Atlanta: Scholars Press, 1992)

Gordon, Paul, *Tragedy After Nietzsche: Rapturous Superabundance* (Urbana: University of Illinois Press, 2001)

Hegel, G. W. F., *Aesthetics: Lectures on Fine Arts*, trans. T. M. Knox, 2 vols (Oxford: Clarendon Press, 1975)

House, Humphrey, *Aristotle's Poetics* (London: Hart-Davis, 1956)

Jones, H. J. F., *On Aristotle and Greek Tragedy* (London: Chatto and Windus, 1962)

Kant, Immanuel, *Religion within the Limits of Reason Alone*, trans. T. M. Greene and H. H. Hudson (New York: Harper and Brothers, 1960)

Kaufmann, Walter (ed.), *Existentialism from Dostoevsky to Sartre* (1956; expanded edn, New York and London: New American Library, 1975)

Hegel: Reinterpretation, Texts and Commentary (Garden City, NY: Anchor Books, 1965)

Tragedy and Philosophy (New York: Doubleday, 1968; Princeton: Princeton University Press, 1992)

Kierkegaard, S., *The Concept of Anxiety*, trans. Reidar Thomte (Princeton: Princeton University Press, 1980)

Fear and Trembling, trans. Alastair Hannay (Harmondsworth: Penguin, 1985)

Either/Or: A Fragment of Life, trans. Alastair Hannay (Harmondsworth: Penguin, 1992)

Lear, Jonathan, 'Katharsis', *Phronesis*, 33 (1988), pp. 297–326

Macintyre, Alasdair, *After Virtue: A Study in Moral Theory* (London: Duckworth, 1981)

May, Keith M., *Nietzsche and the Spirit of Tragedy* (Basingstoke: Macmillan, 1990)

Nietzsche, Friedrich, *The Birth of Tragedy*, trans. S. Whiteside (Harmondsworth: Penguin, 1993)

Beyond Good and Evil, trans. R. J. Hollingdale (Harmondsworth: Penguin, 1973; rev. edn, 1990)

On the Genealogy of Morals, trans. Francis Golffing (New York: Doubleday, 1956)

The Gay Science, trans. Josefine Nauckhoff and ed. Bernard Williams (Cambridge: Cambridge University Press, 2001)

Penelhum, Terence, *God and Skepticism: A Study in Skepticism and Fideism* (Dordrecht and Lancaster: Reidel, 1983)

Plato, *The Republic*, trans. F. M. Cornford (Oxford: Clarendon Press, 1941)

Sartre, Jean-Paul, *Existentialism and Humanism*, trans. Philip Mairet (London; Methuen, 1948; new edn, 1973)

Huis Clos, trans. Stuart Gilbert, *Huis Clos and Other Plays* (Harmondsworth: Penguin, 2000)

Nausea, trans. Robert Baldick (Harmondworth: Penguin, 1963)

Schopenhauer, Arthur, *The World As Will And Representation*, trans. E. F. J. Payne (New York: Dover Publications, 1969)

Silk, M., and J. P. Stern, *Nietzsche on Tragedy* (Cambridge: Cambridge University Press, 1981)

Stinton, T. C. W., 'Hamartia in Aristotle and Greek Tragedy', *Classical Quarterly*, 25 (1975), pp. 221–54

Case studies: fate, politics and gender

Aeschylus, *The Seven Against Thebes*, trans. Christopher M. Dawson (Englewood Cliffs, NJ: Prentice-Hall, 1970)

Alexiou, Margaret, *The Ritual Lament in Greek Tradition* (London: Cambridge University Press, 1974)

Aristotle, *Nicomachean Ethics*, trans. Christopher Rowe (Oxford: Oxford University Press, 2002)

Bahti, Timothy, 'Theories of Knowledge: Fate and Forgetting in the Early Works of Walter Benjamin', in Rainer Nagele (ed.), *Benjamin's Ground: New*

Readings of Walter Benjamin (Detroit: Wayne State University Press, 1988), pp. 61–82

Bamber, Linda, *Comic Women, Tragic Men: A Study of Gender and Genre in Shakespeare* (Stanford CA: Stanford University Press, 1982)

Basterra, Gabriela, *Seductions of Fate: Tragic Subjectivity, Ethics, Politics* (Basingstoke: Palgrave Macmillan, 2004)

Belsey, Catherine, *The Subject of Tragedy: Identity and Difference in Renaissance Drama* (London: Methuen, 1985)

Benjamin, Andrew, 'Shoah, Remembrance and the Abeyance of Fate: Walter Benjamin's "Fate and Character"', in Laura Marcus and Lynda Nead (eds.), *The Actuality of Walter Benjamin* (London: Lawrence and Wishart, 1998), pp. 135–55

Benjamin, Walter, 'Fate and Character', in *One-Way Street and Other Writings*, trans. Edmund Jephcott and Kingsley Shorter (London: NLB, 1979)

Bentham, Jeremy, *The Panopticon Writings*, ed. Miran Božovič (London: Verso, 1995)

Berry, Philippa, *Shakespeare's Feminine Endings: Disfiguring Death in the Tragedies* (London: Routledge, 1999)

Brereton, Geoffrey, *Principles of Tragedy: A Rational Examination of the Tragic Concept in Life and Literature* (London: Routledge, 1968)

Boal, Augusto, *Theater of the Oppressed*, trans. C. A. and M.-O. McBride (1979; new edn, London: Pluto, 2000)

Butler, Judith, *Antigone's Claim: Kinship Between Life and Death* (New York: Columbia University Press, 2000)

Büchner, Georg, *Complete Plays*, trans. John Reddich (Harmondsworth: Penguin, 1993)

Callaghan, Dympna, *Woman and Gender in Renaissance Tragedy: A Study of King Lear, Othello, The Duchess of Malfi, and The White Devil* (London: Harvester Wheatsheaf, 1989)

Shakespeare Without Women: Representing Gender and Race on the Renaissance Stage (London: Routledge, 2000)

Callaghan, Dympna (ed.), *A Feminist Companion to Shakespeare* (Oxford: Blackwell, 2000)

Eliot, George, *Mill on the Floss*, ed. Gordon S. Haight, World's Classics (Oxford: Oxford University Press, 1980)

Figes, Eva, *Tragedy and Social Evolution* (London: Calder, 1976)

Foley, Helene, *Female Acts in Greek Tragedy* (Princeton: Princeton University Press, 2001)

Foucault, Michel, *Discipline and Punish: The Birth of the Prison*, trans. Alan Sheridan (Harmondsworth: Penguin, 1979)

Power/Knowledge: Selected Interviews and Other Writings, trans. Colin Gordon (Brighton: Harvester Press, 1980)

Hall, Edith, 'Tony Harrison's *Prometheus*: A View from the Left', *Arion*, 10.1 (2002), pp. 129–40

Hardy, Thomas, *Mayor of Casterbridge*, ed. Dale Kramer, World's Classics (Oxford: Oxford University Press, 1987)

Harrison, Tony, *Prometheus* (London: Faber and Faber, 1998)

Havard, Robert, *Lorca: Poet and Playwright* (Cardiff: University of Wales Press, 1992)

Hayward, Susan, *Cinema Studies: The Key Concepts* (London and New York: Routledge, 1996; 3rd edn, 2006)

Hegel, G. W. F., *The Phenomenology of Spirit*, trans. A. V. Miller (Oxford: Oxford University Press, 1977)

Holst-Warhaft, Gail, *Dangerous Voices: Women's Laments and Greek Literature* (London and New York: Routledge, 1992)

Irigaray, Luce, *Speculum of the Other Woman*, trans. Gillian Gill (Ithaca: Cornell University Press, 1985)

Kirkham, P., and J. Thumin (eds.), *Me Jane: Masculinity, Movies and Women* (London: Lawrence and Wishart, 1995)

Lacan, Jacques, *The Ethics of Psychoanalysis 1959–60: The Seminar of Jacques Lacan*, trans. Dennis Porter (London: Tavistock/Routledge, 1992)

Lorca, Fedenio Garija, *Three Plays*, trans. Michael Dewell and Carmen Zapata (London: Penguin, 1992)

Loraux, Nicole, *Mothers in Mourning: With the Essay of Amnesty and Its Opposite*, trans. Corinne Pache (Ithaca: Cornell University Press, 1998)

Nussbaum, Martha, *The Fragility of Goodness: Luck and Ethics in Greek Tragedy and Philosophy* (Cambridge: Cambridge University Press, 1986)

Thomson, George, *Aeschylus and Athens* (1941; 3rd edn, London: Lawrence and Wishart, 1966)

Thomson, Peter, and Glendyr Sacks (eds.), *The Cambridge Companion to Brecht* (Cambridge: Cambridge University Press, 1993)

Willett, John (ed.), *Brecht on Theatre* (London: Methuen, 1964; 2nd edn, 1973)

Wohl, Victoria, *Intimate Commerce: Exchange, Gender and Subjectivity in Greek Tragedy* (Austin, TX: University of Texas Press, 1998)

Wood, Michael, *The Road to Delphi: The Life and After-Life of Oracles* (New York: Farrar, Straus and Giroux, 2003)

Yeats, W. B., 'The Tragic Theatre', in *Essays and Introductions* (London: Macmillan, 1961)

Zeitlin, Froma, *Under the Sign of the Shield: Semiotics and Aeschylus's 'Seven Against Thebes'* (Rome: Edizioni dell' Ateneo, 1982)

Žižek, Slavoj, *The Žižek Reader*, ed. Elizabeth Wright and Edmond Wright (Oxford: Blackwell, 1999)

4.1 Visual culture

Bolla, Peter de, *Art Matters* (Cambridge, MA: Harvard University Press, 2001)

Dyer, Geoff, Nestor Garcia Canclini and Gabriel Kuri, *Enrique Metinides* (London: Ridinghouse, 2003)

Golding, Martin, 'Photography, Memory and Survival', *Literature and Theology*, 14.1 (March 2000), pp. 52–68

Kelly, Greg, and Eric Foss (directors), *Beyond Words: Photographers of War*, Canadian Broadcasting Company (2006)

Laqueur, Thomas W., 'The Sound of Voices Intoning Names' [review of Serge Klarfeld, *French Children of the Holocaust: A Memorial*], *London Review of Books* (5 June 1997), pp. 3–6

Lessing, G. E., *Laocoon: An Essay on the Limits of Painting and Poetry*, trans. Edward Allen McCormick (1962; 2nd edn, Baltimore: Johns Hopkins University Press, 1984)

McCullin, Don, *Unreasonable Behaviour* (London: Jonathan Cape, 1990)

Marinovich, Greg, and Joao Silva, *The Bang Bang Club* (London: Heinemann, 2000)

Sontag, Susan, *On Photography* (New York: Farrar, Straus and Giroux, 1977)

Spivey, Nigel, *Enduring Creation: Art, Pain and Fortitude* (Berkeley: University of California Press, 2001)

Taylor, John, *Body Horror: Photojournalism, Catastrophe and War* (Manchester: Manchester University Press, 1998)

4.2 Novels

Bakhtin, M., *The Dialogic Imagination: Four Essays*, trans. C. Emerson and M. Holquist (Austin, TX: University of Texas Press, 1981)

Carver, Raymond, *Where I'm Calling From: Selected Stories* (New York: Harvill, 1993)

Draper, R. P. (ed.), *Hardy: The Tragic Novels*, Macmillan casebook (London: Macmillan, 1975; 2nd edn, 1991)

Eliot, George, *Middlemarch* (1871–2), ed. W. J. Harvey (Harmondsworth: Penguin, 1965)

Flaubert, G., *Madame Bovary* (1857), trans. Gerard Hopkins, World's Classics (Oxford: Oxford University Press, 1981)

Hardy, Thomas, *Tess of the D'Urbervilles*, ed. David Skilton (Harmondsworth: Penguin, 1978)

The Return of the Native, ed. George Woodcock (Harmondworth: Penguin, 1979)

King, Jeanette, *Tragedy in the Victorian Novel: Theory and Practice in the Novels of George Eliot, Thomas Hardy and Henry James* (Cambridge: Cambridge University Press, 1978)

Kramer, D. (ed.), *Thomas Hardy: The Forms of Tragedy* (London: Macmillan, 1975)

Stendhal, *The Red and the Black*, trans. Catherine Slater, World's Classics (Oxford: Oxford University Press, 1991)

Tanner, Tony, *Adultery in the Novel: Contract and Transgression* (Baltimore and London: Johns Hopkins University Press, 1979)

Tolstoy, Leo, *Anna Karenin* (1878), trans. Rosemary Edmonds (Harmondsworth: Penguin, 1954; rev. 1978)

Williams, Raymond, 'Social and Personal Tragedy: Tolstoy and Lawrence', in *Modern Tragedy* (1966; republished, London: Hogarth Press, 1992)

Wright, T. R., *George Eliot's Middlemarch* (London: Harvester Wheatsheaf, 1991)

The Religion of Humanity: The Impact of Comtean Positivism on Victorian Britain (Cambridge: Cambridge University Press, 1986)

4.3 Film

Appel, Alfred, *Nabokov's Dark Cinema* (New York: Oxford University Press, 1974)

Bronfen, Elizabeth, 'Femme Fatale: Negotiations of Tragic Desire', *New Literary History*, 35.1 (Winter 2004), pp. 103–16

Coursen, H. R., *Shakespeare Translated: Recent Derivatives on Film and TV* (New York and Oxford: Peter Lang, 2005)

Bruce Crowther, *Film Noir: Reflections in a Dark Mirror* (London: Columbus, 1988)

Jackson, Russell (ed.), *The Cambridge Companion to Shakespeare on Film* (Cambridge: Cambridge University Press, 2000)

MacKinnon, Kenneth, *Greek Tragedy Into Film* (London: Croom Helm, 1986)

Mulvey, Laura, 'Visual Pleasure and Narrative Cinema', in *Narrative, Apparatus, Ideology: A Film Theory Reader*, ed. Philip Rosen (New York: Columbia University Press, 1986), pp. 198–209

Naremore, James, *More Than Night: Film Noir in its Contexts* (Berkeley: University of California Press, 1998)

Polan, Dana, *In a Lonely Place* (London: BFI Publishing, 1993)

Schickel, Richard, *Double Indemnity* (London: British Film Institute, 1996)

Silver, Alain, and James Ursini (eds.), *Film Noir Reader* (New York: Limelight editions, 1996)

Warshow, Robert, 'The Gangster as Tragic Hero', *Partisan Review*, 15.2 (February 1948), pp. 240–4

Žižek, Slavoj, *The Fright of Real Tears: Krzysztof Kiéslowski between Theory and Post-Theory* (London: BFI Publishing, 2001)

'Death and the Maiden', in *The Žižek Reader*, ed. by E. Wright (1999)

4.4 Psychoanalysis

Freud, Sigmund, *The Standard Edition of the Complete Psychological Works of Sigmund Freud*, trans. under the general editorship of James Strachey, in collaboration with Anna Freud, 24 vols. (London: The Hogarth Press, 1953–74) [abbreviated as *SE*]

Armstrong, Philip, *Shakespeare's Visual Regime: Tragedy, Psychoanalysis and the Gaze* (Basingstoke: Palgrave Macmillan, 2000)

Benjamin, Walter, *The Origin of German Tragic Drama*, trans. J. Osborne (London: NLB, 1977)

Cathy Caruth, *Unclaimed Experience: Trauma, Narrative and History* (Baltimore and London: Johns Hopkins University Press, 1996)

Kuhns, Richard, *Tragedy: Contradiction and Repression* (Chicago and London: University of Chicago Press, 1991)

Lacan, Jacques, 'Tuche and Automaton', in *The Four Fundamental Concepts of Psychoanalysis*, trans. Alan Sheridan (New York: Norton, 1973)

Morrell, Roy, 'The Psychology of Tragic Pleasure', *Essays in Criticism*, 6 (1956), pp. 22–37

Morrison, Toni, *Beloved* (1987; London: Picador, 1988)

Nuttall, Tony, *Why Does Tragedy Give Pleasure?* (Oxford: Clarendon Press, 1996)

Ramadanovic, Peter, *Forgetting Futures: On Memory, Trauma and Identity* (Lanham, MD, and Oxford: Lexington Books, 2001)

Simon, Bennett, *Tragic Drama and the Family: Psychoanalytic Studies from Aeschylus to Beckett* (New Haven and London: Yale University Press, 1988)

4.5 Theology

Delaney, Carol, *Abraham on Trial: The Social Legacy of Biblical Myth* (Princeton: Princeton University Press, 1998)

Gardner, Helen, *Religion and Literature* (Oxford: Oxford University Press, 1971)

Jaspers, Karl, *Tragedy is Not Enough*, trans. H. Reiche, H. T. Moore and K. W. Deutsch (London: Victor Gollancz, 1953)

Lash, Nicholas, 'Friday, Saturday, Sunday', *New Blackfriars*, 71 (1990), pp. 109–19

Mackinnon, Donald, *Borderlands of Theology, and Other Essays*, ed. G. W. Roberts and D. E. Smucker (London: Lutterworth Press, 1968)

Explorations in Theology (London: SCM Press, 1979)

'Theology and Tragedy', *Religious Studies*, 2.2 (1967), pp. 163–9

Moltmann, Jurgen, *The Crucified God: The Cross of Christ as the Foundation and Criticism of Christian Theology*, trans. R. A. Wilson and John Bowden (London: SCM Press, 1974)

Quash, Ben, *Theology and the Drama of History* (Cambridge: Cambridge University Press, 2005)

Raphael, Daiches, 'Tragedy and Religion', in *The Paradox of Tragedy* (London: Allen and Unwin, 1960)

Richards, I. A., *Principles of Literary Criticism* (London: Kegan Paul, 1924)

Simon, Ulrich, *Pity and Terror: Christianity and Tragedy* (Basingstoke: Macmillan, 1989)

Steiner, George, *Real Presences: Is There Anything In What We Say?* (London: Faber, 1989)

Surin, Kenneth (ed.), *Christ, Ethics and Tragedy* (Cambridge: Cambridge University Press, 1989)

Ticciati, Susannah, 'Does Job Fear God for Nought?' *Modern Theology*, 21.3 (2005), pp. 353–66

Ward, Graham, 'Suffering and Incarnation', in G. Ward (ed.), *The Blackwell Companion to Postmodern Theology* (Oxford: Blackwell, 2001), pp. 192–208

5   Tragic sites

Blanchot, Maurice, *The Writing of Disaster*, trans. Ann Smock (Lincoln, NB: University of Nebraska Press, 1986)

Cohen, Josh, *Interrupting Auschwitz: Art, Religion, Philosophy* (New York and London: Continuum, 2005)

Dorfman, Ariel, *Widows*, trans. Stephen Kessler (London: Abacus, 1983)

Gillis, John R. (ed.), *Commemorations: The Politics of National Identity* (Princeton: Princeton University Press, 1994)

Holst-Warhaft, Gail, *The Cue for Passion: Grief and its Political Uses* (Cambridge, MA: Harvard University Press, 2000)

Levi, Primo, *If This Is A Man*, and *The Truce*, trans. Stuart Woolf (1960; new edn, London: Abacus, 1987)

Ondaatje, Michael, *Anil's Ghost* (London: Bloomsbury, 2000)

Sturken, Marita, *Tangled Memories: The Vietnam War, the AIDS epidemic and the Politics of Remembering* (Berkeley: University of California Press, 1997)

Wallace, Jennifer, ' "We Can't Make More Dirt": Tragedy and the Excavated Body', *Cambridge Quarterly*, 32.2 (2003), pp. 103–11

  Digging the Dirt: The Archaeological Imagination (London: Duckworth, 2004)

Index